The FITTING BOOK

Make SEWING PATTERN ALTERATIONS & Achieve THE PERFECT FIT YOU DESIRE

GINA RENEE DUNHAM

Author: Gina Renee Dunham
Chief Editors: Dianne Vogt and Wayne Vogt
Copy Editor: Sharon Rubel
Illustrator: Gina Renee Dunham
Assistant Illustrator: Sarah Marsh
Photographer: Timothy Dunham
Interior Format Designer: Ahmet Samsa
Book Cover Designer: Danica Glodjovic

Zugerstrasse 94
6415 Arth
Switzerland

www.GinaReneeDesigns.com
Email: comments@GinaReneeDesigns.com

The Fitting Book
Make Sewing Pattern Alterations & Achieve the Perfect Fit You Desire

Disclaimer:
This book is not to be interpreted as a promise or guarantee of any outcome. The author and publisher do not guarantee your success nor are they responsible for your results.

This Book Is Dedicated to...

My parents, who have always supported me in my decisions. They have given me the strongest foundation in which to live my life to the fullest - one of faith and love. They have taught me to have a strong work ethic, challenged me to succeed, and helped me achieve my dreams.

They allowed me to express myself with my own style growing up, a style which was very different from the norm. They were willing to let their youngest child move from Colorado to New York City alone, as a 19-year-old, to pursue a career in fashion, and they supported my decision every step of the way.

They have never held me back and always wish the best for me. I love you, Dad and Mom. I am thankful for you every day.

Supporting Fitting Videos & Bonus All-Access Page

Use the QR Codes in This Book!

Every fitting correction in this book has a corresponding fitting video. These fitting videos are what started me on the journey of creating this book. They are short, 1-minute long videos, due to the previous Instagram® time limit. The short length of the videos is enough to grasp the concept.

You will notice a QR code in the lower corner of every fitting correction. To go to the associated video, scan the QR code with the camera on your smartphone. Most phones do not require a special app for this, but the camera settings must be turned on to scan QR codes. Check the camera settings first. Open the camera, tap the screen to focus on the QR code, and click on the link that pops up. This will bring you directly to the corresponding fitting video on your smartphone.

I created these videos before I decided to make this book, and even though many of the images have been slightly adjusted, the concepts are the same. In the future, I hope to recreate the videos, making them longer and more detailed.

Try out your camera by scanning this code. It will bring you to the "Bonus All-Access" webpage.

What's on the Bonus All-Access Webpage?

✂ For a limited time only, send me your receipt of the printed book and receive the ebook free. The ebook contains direct links to all the fitting videos, so they are just one click away on your tablet or computer. The contents of the ebook are easily searchable, so you can find the topic you need more quickly.

✂ Sign up for my FREE mini-course about patternmaking topics. This runs only once or twice per year, and you do not want to miss it.

✂ Join the waitlist to learn The GRD Method™ of patternmaking. Achieve the customized fit you desire by creating a solid foundation to design the clothes you dream of.

✂ Download your free guide to my favorite patternmaking tools. You will use these tools for years to come!

If you do not have a smartphone to scan the QR codes, that's more reason to email me the receipt of your printed book to receive your free ebook. This offer is only valid for new book purchases, not used books. To email me our receipt, go to:

https://www.ginareneedesigns.com/fitting-book/

Try out your camera and go to the Bonus All-Access webpage now!

Table of Contents

Table of Contents

Table of Contents

I
Enjoy *Creativity.*

Realize how *Talented* I am.

Value My *Unique* Creations.

Am *Proud* of my Sewing Skills.

Can Pass on Sewing *Knowledge* to others.

Can Keep *Hand-Crafted* items for Generations.

Gina Renee Designs

Promotes the Art of Sewing to Create a More Sustainable and Creative World.

Connect with Me on Instagram® @GinaReneeDesigns
or on Facebook® & Pinterest®
by Searching for "Gina Renee Designs."

Make Clothes You Love That Fit.

Introduction

Y ou deserve to have clothes that fit well and make you feel great.

Commercial sewing patterns target a mass customer base, using an average of people's measurements. If you're like me, your measurements may not fall within the average range. Even if I had average measurements, it does not mean the shapes of the patterns are correct for my body.

The best part of sewing is that, with practice, we can learn how to make clothes that fit well and make us feel great.

There is nothing better than wearing a garment and being proud that you made it, happy that it is your style, and pleased with the fit.

It can take years to master fit. Still, with fabrics and silhouettes constantly changing, we are also constantly learning. It is a challenge that will continue to be there for as long as fashion matters to us.

I have created this book to help tackle the most common mistakes I have come across from fitting thousands of garments while working in the clothing industry since 2003. This is the book I wish I would have had during my studies and throughout my many years of learning how to fit.

This fitting book can be used for men's, women's, and even children's clothing. However, not all corrections are needed for menswear or childrenswear, such as the bust/skirt/dress adjustments, but many corrections apply to all genders and ages. Many of the corrections can be implemented on both knit and woven styles.

This is a fitting book, not a pattern drafting book. It shows you how to assess the fit of your garments. You will learn how to fit garments using pinning, cutting, or taping methods. Finally, it shows how to adjust the sewing pattern step by step.

I hope you find this fitting book helpful. I'm excited to join you on your patternmaking journey!

Abbreviations, Terminology, & Tools Needed

Sewing and patternmaking have their own vocabulary and tools.

Patternmaking terminology can be different for each patternmaker or company. For example, a sloper, which is a pattern with added wearing ease for movement, can also be called many other names. Some examples:

- Block
- Basic/base pattern
- Master pattern
- Working pattern

They are all the same thing, but different patternmakers call them different names. Every clothing company I have worked for uses their own terminology, especially for the example given above.

The following pages share abbreviations and terminology which are frequently used, followed by the tools and supplies which will be required for fitting and altering sewing patterns.

Abbreviations & Terminology List

Body (in Relation to Fabric) = The way a fabric hangs. A fabric with more body is fuller and has more structure. The fabric will stand farther away from the person's body.

Commercial Pattern = A sewing pattern purchased from a larger, more established company. These are also referred to as "style" patterns or "home" sewing patterns.

Draglines = A "line" of fabric that drapes in an unwanted area. Often a negative term in fitting garments. It can also be called a wrinkle or a deep crease in the fabric.

Drape (in Relation to Fabric) = The way a fabric hangs. A fabric with more drape is more slinky and hangs closer to the body (e.g. chiffon fabric).

Draping = The process of pinning and hanging fabric directly on a dress form or person. This can be a more artistic way of creating patterns. You design as you handle the fabric.

Ease over Body = The amount of room you add to the pattern beyond your body measurements. It can also be referred to as "ease" or "wearing ease."

Fitting Sample = A garment you make as a test run of your actual garment. It can also be referred to as a muslin or a toile.

Flat Pattern = Drafting (drawing) patterns directly onto paper based off body measurements. Flat pattern techniques also include pattern manipulation, Slash & Spread, and Slash & Close.

"Go to Zero" = Where you are finishing a correction on a pattern piece, this is where the correction stops. The correction line finishes at the original pattern line.

Grading = The amount added to or subtracted from a base pattern size to create other garment sizes.

Grainline = The direction of the fabric running lengthwise, parallel to the selvages.

Indie Pattern = This is the abbreviated term for an independently-designed pattern. It is a style pattern made by a pattern designer and often purchased online.

Industry Standards = Standard measurements or patternmaking practices that have been devised over the years in the clothing industry. They are not customized to your body but rather based on mass-customer measurement data.

In Total = This is a phrase in which patternmakers refer to correction amounts that are the total amount. For example, if we open up the garment ½" (1.6 cm) across the entire shoulder area, we would say to give ½" (1.6 cm) in total.

Knit Fabric = A cloth created by yarns that are looped together in a sequence. The loops allow the material to stretch. The yarn thickness varies from fine to thick, creating different weights of fabric.

Abbreviations & Terminology List

Moulage = A bodice pattern and garment based on your body measurements. It is form-fitting and should be very tight. The moulage can be used as a base for corsets, bras, and strapless dresses.

Muslin = A plain, natural cotton fabric that is used to make a fitting sample. (The UK refers to this as calico, but in the USA, a calico is a quilting fabric and is not the same!)

On the Half = This is a phrase in which patternmakers refer to correction amounts that are only half of the garment. We work on only half of the garment for symmetrical patterns. For example, if we open up across the shoulders on the garment ½" (1.6 cm), we would say to give ¼" (0.8 cm) on the half because we only work on half of the garment pattern.

Ready-to-Wear = Clothes you can buy in stores that are made for a mass-customer base. The term is abbreviated as RTW.

Seam Allowance = Often abbreviated to "S.A." This is the distance to sew from the edge of the fabric.

Seam Line = This is the actual sewing line where the stitches will be. It can also be referred to as the sew line.

Selvages = The finished edges running lengthwise on a piece of fabric ("selvedge" in British English). There are often holes or stiffer edges in the selvages from the weaving or knitting loom.

Sloper = A pattern that has ease added to it for movement. It is used as a base for creating style patterns. It can also be called a block, basic/base pattern, master pattern, or working pattern.

Style Pattern = These are patterns with added styling and design lines that are created from a sloper pattern. They are also referred to as "sewing" or "design" patterns. Commercial or indie patterns are examples of style patterns.

True = Making the seam lines smooth and continuous in pattern drafting. The common phrase used is "true the lines." Use curved rulers to draw the seam lines continuously when the pattern pieces are joined together.

Wearing Ease = Extra space between the body and the garment to allow for movement while wearing the garment. It can also be called "ease" or "ease over body."

Woven Fabric = A cloth created by yarns that are intertwined. The yarns are not looped, and therefore, the material does not stretch unless elastane is in the composition. A woven fabric may have a natural stretch, which is called a mechanical stretch, due to yarns that are crimped.

Abbreviations & Terminology - Body

On the Body

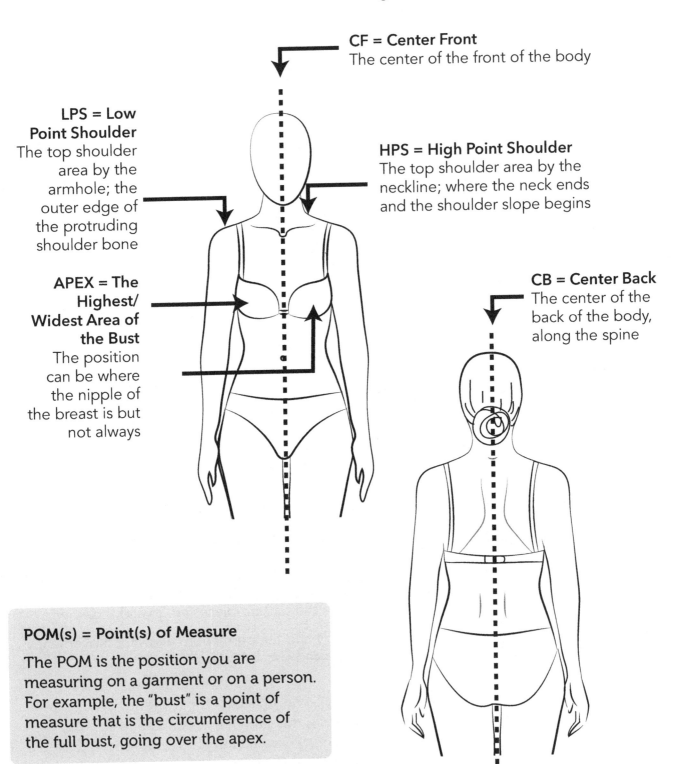

CF = Center Front
The center of the front of the body

LPS = Low Point Shoulder
The top shoulder area by the armhole; the outer edge of the protruding shoulder bone

HPS = High Point Shoulder
The top shoulder area by the neckline; where the neck ends and the shoulder slope begins

APEX = The Highest/ Widest Area of the Bust
The position can be where the nipple of the breast is but not always

CB = Center Back
The center of the back of the body, along the spine

POM(s) = Point(s) of Measure

The POM is the position you are measuring on a garment or on a person. For example, the "bust" is a point of measure that is the circumference of the full bust, going over the apex.

Abbreviations & Terminology - Pattern

On Front and Back Top Pattern Pieces

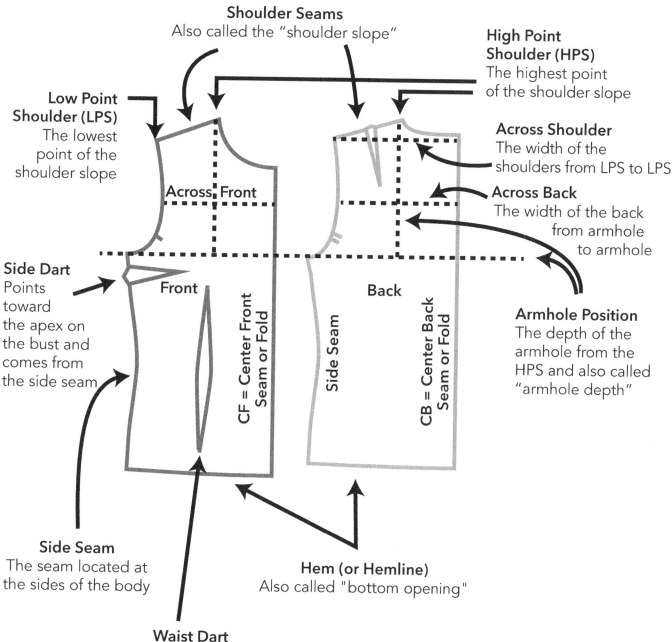

Shoulder Seams
Also called the "shoulder slope"

High Point Shoulder (HPS)
The highest point of the shoulder slope

Low Point Shoulder (LPS)
The lowest point of the shoulder slope

Across Shoulder
The width of the shoulders from LPS to LPS

Across Front

Across Back
The width of the back from armhole to armhole

Side Dart
Points toward the apex on the bust and comes from the side seam

Front

CF = Center Front Seam or Fold

Side Seam

Back

CB = Center Back Seam or Fold

Armhole Position
The depth of the armhole from the HPS and also called "armhole depth"

Side Seam
The seam located at the sides of the body

Hem (or Hemline)
Also called "bottom opening"

Waist Dart
This allows for shaping and is often a fish-eye shape. There can be a waist dart on the back body panel, too.

On a Sleeve Pattern

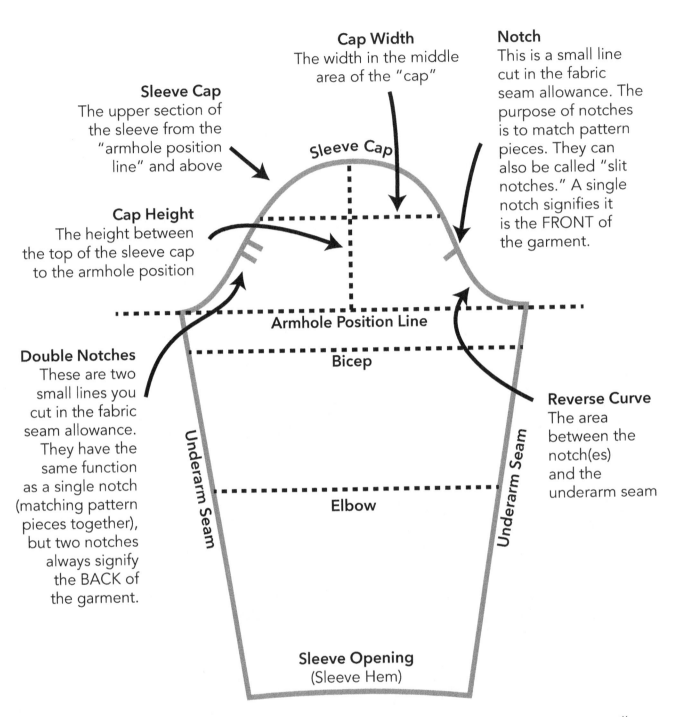

Cap Width
The width in the middle area of the "cap"

Notch
This is a small line cut in the fabric seam allowance. The purpose of notches is to match pattern pieces. They can also be called "slit notches." A single notch signifies it is the FRONT of the garment.

Sleeve Cap
The upper section of the sleeve from the "armhole position line" and above

Cap Height
The height between the top of the sleeve cap to the armhole position

Sleeve Cap

Double Notches
These are two small lines you cut in the fabric seam allowance. They have the same function as a single notch (matching pattern pieces together), but two notches always signify the BACK of the garment.

Armhole Position Line

Bicep

Underarm Seam

Underarm Seam

Reverse Curve
The area between the notch(es) and the underarm seam

Elbow

Sleeve Opening
(Sleeve Hem)

Commercial and indie sewing patterns can call for different notch shapes. The patterns will often have triangular notches because they are easier to see. Since it takes longer to cut triangle notches, I always cut slit notches. Slit notches are also used in production sewing lines to match the pattern pieces together.

Abbreviations & Terminology - Pattern

On Skirt and Pants Pattern Pieces

Waistline
The seam located at the waist area on the body

Waistline

Back Waist Dart
The dart which allows shaping for the backside

Hip Position Line

Side Seam
The seam located at the sides of the body

Front

CF = Center Front Fold

Side Seam

Back

CB = Center Back Seam or Fold

Hem
This indicates the length of the skirt. It can also be referred to as the bottom opening or hemline.

Waistline
This is the seam located at the waist area on the body. In styles that have a waistband, the top of the waistband is the waistline. On slopers/base patterns, there is no waistband since it is considered a style detail. The waistband is then created from the sloper/base pattern.

Front Rise

Hip Position Line

Waistline

Back Rise
This is the curved seam along the center back of the body. The back rise and front rise together are referred to as the total rise.

Inseam

Knee

Knee

Side Seam

Crotch Point
The position where the rise ends and inseam begins

Side Seam
The seam located at the sides of the body

Inseam
The seam along the inner leg

Hem
This indicates the length of the pants. It can also be referred to as the bottom leg opening or hemline.

Draglines Versus Bubbles

A dragline can also be called a wrinkle. Draglines are generally unwanted in our garments, and they are often a sign of poor fit.

However, not all draglines can be avoided, especially when it comes to sleeves. Some excess fabric offers more movement allowing you to lift your arms. This causes some unavoidable draglines in the undersleeve.

It is acceptable to have some draglines on the garment because they allow the body to move. Every person has a different shape and posture, and these differences can cause draglines. To the right are some examples of what draglines look like. These draglines are a sign of poor fit, and they should be eliminated to improve the appearance of the garment.

While assessing the fit for draglines, the wearer must stand straight with the shoulders and arms relaxed. As soon as the wearer moves, there will be draglines, and that is acceptable. The draglines to target are those that occur when the wearer is standing still. After correcting draglines in a fitting, move and sit while wearing the garment to see if the correction restricts the body movement. If it does, adjust the correction. Accept that some draglines appear due to ease required for the body to move.

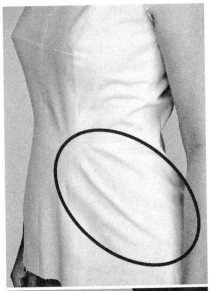
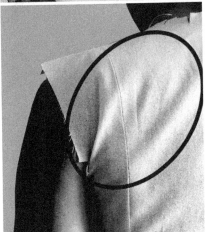

What's Not a Dragline? Bubbles...

To the right, you will see what I call "bubbles." They are not defined "lines" like wrinkles, but are more like bubbles of extra fabric. To reduce the bubbles, pin the garment in the affected areas. After correcting bubbles in a fitting, move and sit while wearing the garment to see if the correction restricts the body movement. Alternatively, open up tight areas. Unwanted bubbles are a sign that the pattern shape is incorrect. The photos on the right are of a moulage sample. To fix the bubbles in the first photo, I have pinned the garment along the princess seam and waist seam as shown in the second photo.

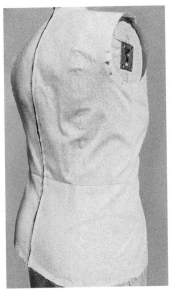
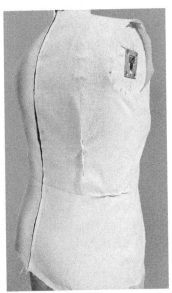

Terminology: Slash & Spread vs. Slash & Close

Main Patternmaking Techniques

There are two main terms for altering patterns: 1) Slash & Spread
2) Slash & Close

Slash & Spread (Cut & Open)

Slashing and spreading is when you cut the pattern and open it up. Pivot the pattern at one point to open the other end of the pattern. You are altering the shape by opening up the pattern in specific areas. Whenever you Slash & Spread the pattern pieces, tape a piece of paper underneath the gap, filling in the area you opened. Slash & Spread corrections are indicated in this book by grey images with white gaps.

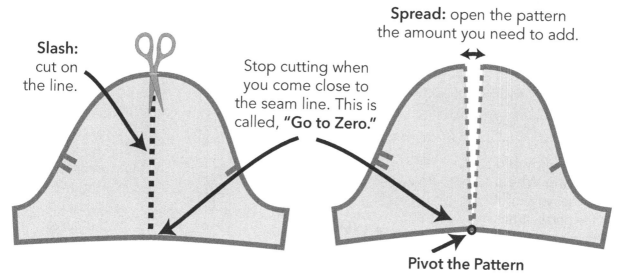

Slash: cut on the line.

Stop cutting when you come close to the seam line. This is called, **"Go to Zero."**

Spread: open the pattern the amount you need to add.

Pivot the Pattern

Slash & Close (or Fold Closed)

Slashing and closing is done by cutting and overlapping the area you want to remove. It can also be done by folding the pattern closed. You are altering the shape by closing (removing) the pattern in specific areas. Slash & Close corrections are indicated in this book by white images with grey-filled overlap areas.

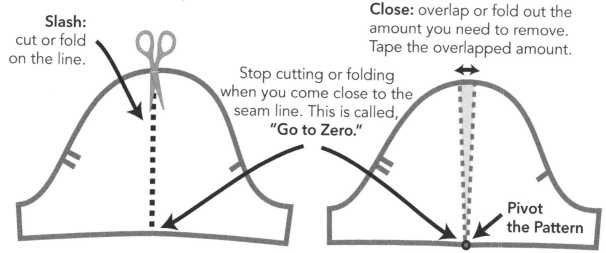

Slash: cut or fold on the line.

Stop cutting or folding when you come close to the seam line. This is called, **"Go to Zero."**

Close: overlap or fold out the amount you need to remove. Tape the overlapped amount.

Pivot the Pattern

Tools & Supplies

Essentials for Patternmaking

Matte Finish Clear Adhesive Tape
Use a matte finish tape because it allows you to write on it with a pencil. Shiny tape does not allow pencil writing.

For a list of my favorite patternmaking tools, scan the QR code:

French Curve
You can also use other curved rulers, but this is my favorite for armholes and necklines.

Tape Measure
A double-sided tape measure is preferable if you can source one. Use either inches (imperial) or centimeters (metric).

Hip Curve
You can also use other curved rulers, but this is my favorite for the shape. The units of measure do not matter since it is used only for the curves, not for measuring.

Pointed Tracing Wheel
This is really helpful for darts. It has sharp, pointed tips which go through paper layers.

Awl
An awl is a pointed tool to poke holes in the paper pattern. If you do not have one, use the point of sharp scissors.

Notcher
This is a tool that creates a small cut/slit in the paper pattern. If you do not have one, cut a little triangle with scissors.

Clear Grid Ruler
A clear ruler makes it easy to add seam allowances to pattern pieces. The suggested dimensions are 18" x 2" (45 cm x 5 cm).

Tip: Before making fitting samples which are used in fitting only, do NOT wash or dry muslin fabric. The fabric grain can become more skewed when washing. Iron the fabric before cutting it.

Other tools needed:

- Pencil
- Eraser
- Pencil Sharpener
- Paper Scissors
- Fabric Scissors
- Pins
- Muslin Fabric or Broadcloth
- Patternmaking or Craft Paper

The Customization Process in Patternmaking

How does the entire customization process look in patternmaking and sewing? There are many different levels in this process and many methods in achieving each step.

The goal of customization in patternmaking and sewing is to achieve a specific desired style and fit. Whether you want to design clothes from a customized sloper or sew clothes that fit using commercial sewing patterns, you can learn how in a step-by-step process.

I lay out the process in 10 steps with a visual scale for you to reference. We will go through each step with detailed explanations.

You may have a specific design you want to create, or you may want to sew clothes that fit well. Whatever your goals are during the customization process, you can achieve your desired results.

Regardless of which step you begin with, the goal is to create a garment you love that fits. This fitting book will help you achieve that.

What Does the Patternmaking Process Look Like?

This is a visual reference of a customization scale in patternmaking. The more you accomplish on this scale, the more customized your fit and designs will be. The more steps that are skipped, the harder it can be to achieve the customized fit and unique designs you desire.

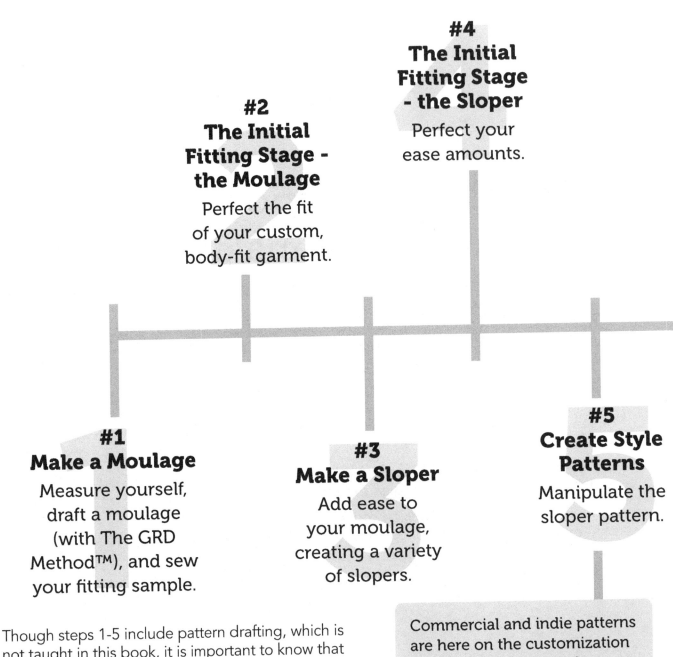

#2
The Initial Fitting Stage - the Moulage

Perfect the fit of your custom, body-fit garment.

#4
The Initial Fitting Stage - the Sloper

Perfect your ease amounts.

#1
Make a Moulage

Measure yourself, draft a moulage (with The GRD Method™), and sew your fitting sample.

#3
Make a Sloper

Add ease to your moulage, creating a variety of slopers.

#5
Create Style Patterns

Manipulate the sloper pattern.

Though steps 1-5 include pattern drafting, which is not taught in this book, it is important to know that there are many options in achieving a customized fit. Pattern drafting is a complete topic in itself and is beyond the scope of this 278-page book. Furthermore, many people will find it sufficient to modify existing patterns to achieve a customized fit, which is taught in this book.

Commercial and indie patterns are here on the customization scale. However, since they use industry standard sizing, starting only with slopers and no moulage, you may need to make more fitting adjustments.

The Customization Scale in Patternmaking

When I started my sewing journey, I didn't know where to begin to achieve a well-fitted garment. I struggled for years to learn about fitting. My goal is to help you so your journey is easier than mine was. I find this customization scale a great way to visualize the different levels that exist in patternmaking. You may begin at several steps on the customization scale. It is not required to start at #1. This book begins on step #6 of the scale. Wherever you begin on this scale, the goal is the same: to make clothes you love that fit.

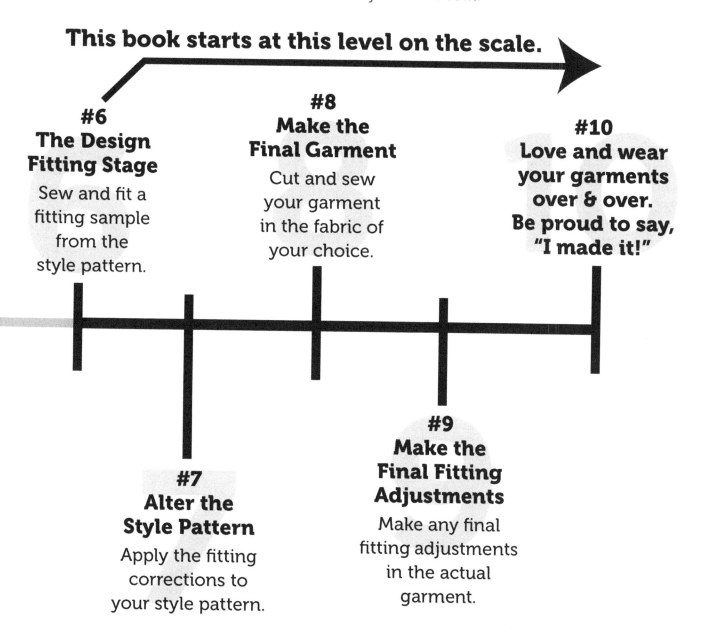

This book starts at this level on the scale.

#6
The Design Fitting Stage
Sew and fit a fitting sample from the style pattern.

#8
Make the Final Garment
Cut and sew your garment in the fabric of your choice.

#10
Love and wear your garments over & over. Be proud to say, "I made it!"

#7
Alter the Style Pattern
Apply the fitting corrections to your style pattern.

#9
Make the Final Fitting Adjustments
Make any final fitting adjustments in the actual garment.

Fitting stages may need to be repeated. If you are using commercial sewing patterns (which always use industry standards), you will likely need to repeat the fitting process at this later design fitting stage to achieve the customized fit you want.

Make a Moulage

#1 on the Customization Scale

The word moulage is French, meaning "casting" or "mold." A moulage is based directly on your body measurements and has no ease added to it. It is extremely tight-fitting. If you have heard the phrase, "It fits like a glove," that's the goal of the moulage.

A moulage is created by draping it directly on a person or with the flat pattern technique. The draping technique is when you place muslin fabric directly on a person, then mark, cut and pin the fabric in place to create a pattern. The flat pattern technique is when you draft your pattern shapes on paper based on your specific body measurements. The flat pattern technique is precise.

Over the years I have created my own patternmaking method using the flat pattern technique. It is called, "The GRD Method™." My method does not use industry standards for the dart depths and shoulder slopes. It is the only method in creating a moulage which will give you accurate dart depths and shoulder slopes based on your own body measurements.

Creating a moulage with the flat pattern technique is the best way to create slopers that fit accurately. Since the moulage is an extremely form-fitting garment, it will show draglines very easily. By seeing the draglines tightly against the body, you can fix the problems from the start. Be careful in using patternmaking methods that use industry standards because this will make the fitting process much more challenging. There are multiple patternmaking methods. The more methods you try, the more knowledge you will gain. If you have tried one method, and you did not achieve your desired results, try a different method.

The moulage has 5 darts in the front bodice and 2 in the back bodice allowing for a variety of ways to manipulate the pattern. This offers the freedom of design with optimized fit. With the correct dart depths in the correct locations, the moulage provides a solid foundation for patternmaking.

Here is what a moulage pattern looks like:

The moulage is a garment that fits close to your body. It includes the hip portion of your body, whereas many bodice slopers will stop at the waistline.

The Initial Fitting Stage - the Moulage

#2 on the Customization Scale

When fitting garments in the moulage or sloper stages, I use the term "initial fitting stage." It is the step before creating the style patterns prior to the "design fitting stage."

Since the moulage is drafted directly from your body measurements, it is extremely form-fitting. This helps you see the draglines much more easily for the initial fitting stage and allows you to fix main fitting issues from the start.

The initial fitting stage looks at the primary topics: if it is too tight, too loose, and whether it has bubbles or draglines. The goal is to make a replica of your body which you can use as a base for corsets, bras, or strapless dresses. It can also be used to create a customized dress form.

It is so important to achieve a well-fitted moulage for a solid foundation in patternmaking. If you do not fix the issues at this stage, the following stages will also have fitting issues. It can also take multiple fitting samples in order to achieve the customized fit you want.

You can reference this fitting book to help you during any of the fitting stages, but you should never have to do major corrections like a Full/Small Bust Adjustment when you began with a custom patternmaking process from your accurate body measurements. Though this book will help at all the fitting stages, it focuses on corrections at the design fitting stage.

There is something about customized clothing that feels amazing. It takes effort and time, but it is well worth the investment for a solid foundation!

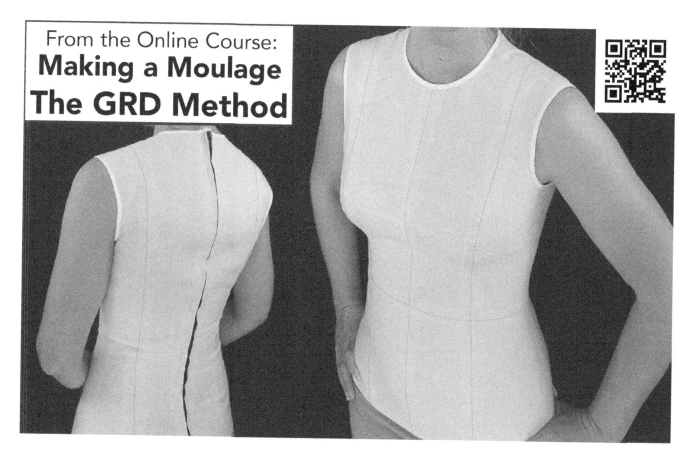

From the Online Course:
**Making a Moulage
The GRD Method**

Make a Sloper

#3 on the Customization Scale

A sloper is the same thing as a basic/base pattern, block, working pattern, or master pattern. In this book, I refer to it as a "sloper."

There are two ways slopers are created:

1) Customized from your moulage or body measurements (customized sloper), or

2) Standardized from averages of body measurements (standard sloper).

How do you achieve your customized sloper? Once your moulage fits well, you will add ease to it, which becomes the customized sloper. Starting from the moulage is the most accurate way to create a sloper that fits you. The GRD Method™ is the only moulage method that does not use industry-standard dart depths and shoulder slopes. In the online course, you will add ease to your moulage to create your first customized sloper.

Many people start with creating a sloper because the moulage method is not as commonly known. If you begin with a sloper or a moulage with industry standards for dart depths and shoulder slopes, you will likely need more fitting amendments to achieve the customized fit you desire.

Where are standard slopers used? All the sewing patterns you buy are made from standard slopers. They are not customized slopers. The standard measurements are derived from extensive body measurement data.

You will make different slopers for woven tops, dresses, blazers, jackets, and coats. Grade down for base patterns made with knit fabrics. With The GRD Method™ the opportunities are endless once you achieve your perfect fit.

The 5-dart sloper looks like the moulage but with added ease for movement.

The number of darts in slopers can vary. I always suggest keeping one sloper with all 5 darts (derived from your moulage) because it will provide the most options for a specialized fit.

However, to simplify the process, you may adjust your sloper into a 2-dart or single-dart sloper. Knit slopers will be modified to have no darts.

The Initial Fitting Stage - the Sloper

#4 on the Customization Scale

The Customization Process in Patternmaking

Different slopers are needed for tops, dresses, blouses, blazers, jackets, and coats. There are different amounts of ease added to each pattern that allow the garments to be layered and worn together seamlessly. The ease also accommodates the differences in fabric characteristics and achieves the desired silhouette. The amount of ease plus the body measurements is what is called "ease over body."

During the initial fitting stage of a customized sloper, the primary purpose is to check that you are happy with the amount of ease added. It is common to make some additional fitting adjustments in this stage. If your moulage fits well, the sloper should fit with minor adjustments.

Knit tops may have "negative ease" taken because knit fabrics stretch. This results in below-body measurements. Knit tops have no darts in them because the stretch of the fabric acts as the fitting of the darts.

Woven tops, blouses, and dresses will have darts for womenswear. The ease amount for the circumferences of the bust and waist is generally between 1-2" (2.5 cm-5 cm). The ease amount for the hip circumference should be 2"+ (5 cm+) to accommodate the seated position.

Blazers, jackets, and coats will have the most ease over body with 2+" (5 cm+) added to the main circumference measurements of the bust, waist, and hips.

Ease is subjective to each person. There are no set rules you have to use. As fashion changes, ease preferences and silhouettes change.

Knit Tops Sloper Woven Tops/Blouse Sloper Jackets/Coats Sloper

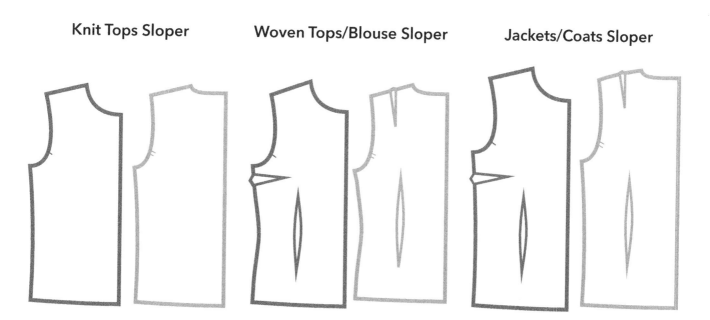

The number and locations of darts can vary per sloper.

Create Style Patterns

#5 on the Customization Scale

And the fun begins! At this stage, you have two options:

1) Design your dream clothes using your customized sloper, or

2) Find the styles you love from existing commercial or indie style patterns.

Both options are referred to as "design" or "style" patterns.

For the first option, you finally get to design clothes from your customized sloper. This modification of a sloper is called pattern manipulation. You manipulate the sloper in the correct ways to optimize the fit based on the dart depth locations. This will result in a beautiful design that fits well.

Every patternmaker has different ways of manipulating patterns. I have seen some very creative ways over the years - some with which I agree and others which I would not recommend. Pattern manipulation is an integral part of the fitting process. If it is not done correctly, it can lead to a garment that fits poorly.

For the second option, commercial and indie sewing patterns have already done the work for you! If you have a customized sloper, you can manipulate your sloper with the design lines and styling details they've already laid out. This will save you a huge amount of time in the design fitting stage because you have already done the hard work in the initial fitting stage. You will also bypass many of the fitting corrections in this book because your sloper fits.

When you are purchasing a sewing pattern, the design and silhouette is defined. This is a great option for sewists who find styles they like in sewing pattern collections, and it can also help save time in the design stages. It is so easy to fall in love with a style you see that has already been created! If you do not have a sloper, you will begin sewing a fitting sample right away.

Option 1

Option 2

The Design Fitting Stage

#6 on the Customization Scale

This fitting book specializes in the design fitting stage - which is stage 6 on the customization scale. Of course, you can certainly use this book while you are making a moulage and sloper in stages 1-4. However, some of the major corrections in this book like the Full/Small Bust Adjustments would not be needed in earlier fitting stages because you have made your sloper from your measurements. These corrections are specifically for people who are using commercial and indie patterns and are not starting from a customized sloper. In other words, you may need to work harder at this stage to achieve your desired fit when you start from commercial and indie patterns since they use industry standard slopers. This book will help you achieve your customized fit!

To begin customizing your fit, first sew a fitting sample (also called a muslin or toile). Even if you have made a style pattern from your customized sloper, still do this step to check style lines, fabrics, and the final fit.

During this design fitting stage, reference this book to:

A) Identify the Fitting Issues; and

B) Pin, Cut, and Tape the Fitting Sample.

Improve the fit as much as you can during this design fitting stage before cutting the garment in the final fabric. After pinning, cutting, and taping the fitting sample, transfer these updates to the paper pattern to improve the shapes of the pattern pieces.

In some cases another fitting sample may be needed to check the fit again. Repeat the process until you are completely satisfied with the fit. Adjusting fitting issues requires patience. When you make one correction, sometimes other issues can pop up. This is why multiple fitting samples may be needed to confirm that no other fitting issues have arisen.

There are many possibilities to achieve a customized fit and many methods. One of the biggest insights I have gained over the years is that every pattern maker has a different method. There is not just one way to achieve a nice fit. This is one reason why I included so many fitting options in this book.

A) Identifying the Issue

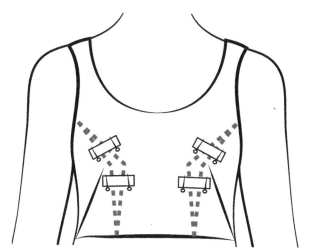

B) Cutting, Taping, and Pinning the Fitting Sample

Alter the Style Pattern

#7 on the Customization Scale

At this stage, you are ready to fix the sewing pattern. The adjustments will customize the pattern according to your fitting corrections. Follow this book which shows you how to update your style pattern according to how you pinned, cut, and taped your fitting sample.

The step in this book is:

C) Correcting the Pattern.

It is important to always reference your fitting sample during this stage. You will measure your sample to find the amounts and locations where you pinned, cut, or taped. Then, transfer the same amounts to your pattern. Notice that this book does not give you measurements, and that is because each person's corrections will be different.

When measuring the location of the fitting corrections on your sample, use the edge of your garment as a reference for the location of your pins or taped positions. For example, if you have cut your garment at the apex and stopped cutting at the armhole (shown below and on the previous page), measure the exact position of the apex from the armhole and from the high point shoulder.

My dad always taught me the carpentry rule, "Measure twice, cut once." I think it is also a great rule for patternmaking and sewing!

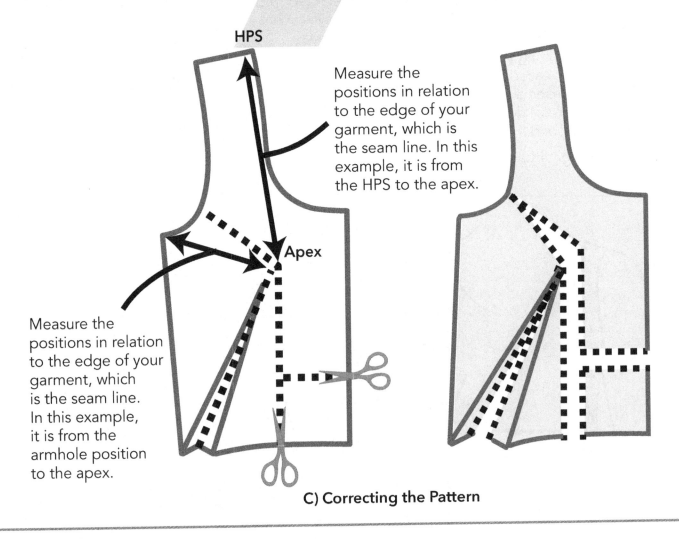

HPS

Measure the positions in relation to the edge of your garment, which is the seam line. In this example, it is from the HPS to the apex.

Apex

Measure the positions in relation to the edge of your garment, which is the seam line. In this example, it is from the armhole position to the apex.

C) Correcting the Pattern

Make the Final Garment

#8 on the Customization Scale

Yay! It is the moment you have been waiting for: sewing your final garment.

You have made it so far with this customization process, and it is time to sew the garment you will love for years to come. Now that you have altered your sewing pattern, you are ready to cut the final fabric and sew it all together!

The sewing process is so therapeutic. There is something about the "hummmm" of the sewing machine that makes me excited every time I hear it. Something about sewing keeps us coming back for more. Whether it is the huge sense of accomplishment or the happiness you feel when you LOVE an item you made, something draws you back to the process of sewing.

However, when sewing, frustrating moments can often pop up. When you work through the issues that arise, you learn more. Sometimes you may even improve the item in ways you didn't expect! It pushes creativity and patience to new levels. The more you sew, the more confidence you gain.

After overcoming those problems, it is so exciting to try on your garment for the first time. It is nothing short of pure joy.

Think of the many reasons you love to sew, and write them down!

How do you feel when the items you have envisioned come to life?

When you love your clothes, isn't it worth all the effort in the fitting stages? I know my favorite clothes in my wardrobe were well worth the effort because they fit.

Enjoy the fun of sewing!

Make the Final Fitting Adjustments

#9 on the Customization Scale

Sometimes, when you wear your garments for the first time, you may notice there could be a few minor adjustments to perfect the fit. It could be due to the previous fitting correction made, which leads to another issue, or it could be due to the physical characteristics of the fabric.

At this stage, you have the choice to either make minor adjustments or to leave your garment the way it is. If you choose to adjust it, you will often find that there's enough room in the seam allowances for your modifications. If the garment cannot be fixed, it can still be a great process to fit the garment (without cutting it) to learn from the experience.

If you make fitting adjustments, you may want to transfer those changes to your final pattern pieces. However, if you think the changes are only related to your fabric choice, and you may use a different fabric in the future, you can leave the pattern as is.

Every fabric has different physical properties which can greatly affect the fit and appearance of the garment. The properties include the stretch levels, thickness, drape, weight, and texture. This is why we usually try to use a similar fabric in the fitting sample stage to mimic the final fabric as closely as possible.

The differences in fabrics are part of the challenge we face in patternmaking and sewing. As long as new fabrics are created and fashion pushes innovation to new levels, we will learn and change along with them.

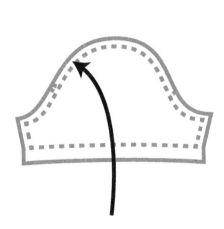

You may be able to use the seam allowances in final fitting adjustments.

Fitting problems could develop if the fabric of the fitting sample is markedly different from the fabric you will use in your finished garment. Try a drape test before making the fitting sample, as described on page 39, to see the physical characteristics of your garment fabric. Then, try to find a muslin or fabric for the fitting sample that has a similar drape to your final fabric.

Love & Wear Your Garments

#10 on the Customization Scale

It is time to say with excitement, "Wow, I made this, and it is so me!" There is nothing better than wearing something that fits and is 100% your style.

No matter where you began on this scale, I hope your result is a perfectly-fitting garment that you love. You have worked so hard, and it is well worth it when you are pleased with the results.

I hope the garments you make become favorites in your wardrobe! I hope you wear them over and over again and never want to give them up.

It's that sense of pride you feel when someone compliments you, and you reply, "Thanks, I made it!"

It is time to stop wasting time and money by sewing clothes that do not fit. Now, with the knowledge and skills you have gained, you will be able to tackle the fitting issues and make the clothes you dream of.

It is so exciting to imagine all the possibilities now open to you. You are so amazing and talented, and you are capable of making one-of-a-kind, unique items for yourself that fit.

It's time to show off that you are a smokin' hot TEN on the customization scale!

Love & Wear the Custom Clothes You've Made!

Factors in Fitting

There are several different factors in fitting, and we will dive into the main topics in this section, including:

- Why Body Size Charts Vary

- Sizing, Ease, and Fabric

- The Importance of a Fitting Sample

- Woven Fabric Selection for Your Fitting Sample

- Knit Fabric Selection for Your Fitting Sample

- Darts Explained

The goal is to achieve #10 on the customization scale by making the garment fit well and feel great. Making a fitting sample in the correct fabric will help you achieve this goal. As you work through every important step in the process, you will progress along the customization scale.

Why Body Size Charts Vary

Standard Sizing

Many home sewists and seamstresses struggle with the standard sizing in commercial sewing patterns which often leads to fitting issues.

Commercial sewing patterns and ready-to-wear garments that you buy in stores are all based on industry standard measurements. These "averages" are derived from thousands of different body types.

Why do size charts vary so much between sewing pattern and clothing companies? Each company receives their data based on many different factors. For example, age and geographical regions play a huge role in determining size charts. They are based on many different body shapes that exist in the world.

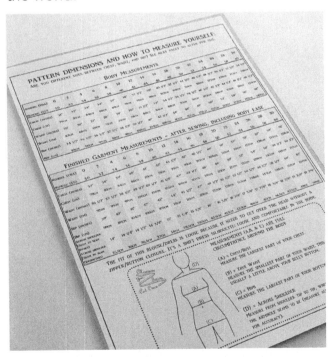

Many of the larger clothing companies have paid to receive data from private companies that specialize in body measurements. These measurement companies have done extensive research by body scanning and measuring thousands of people. Clothing companies determine who their target customer is based on age, gender, and culture/location. Then, body measurement companies provide data to the clothing companies based on their ideal customer. Clothing companies also use this data when they grade their patterns for different sizes.

The measurement services can also determine the average postures and shoulder slope standards, which is an even more detailed body type analysis. Some clothing companies receive data from national or international organizations specializing in body size surveys. These organizations take averages from a pool of thousands of participants. The modern way of measuring the body is through 3D body scanning, which gives precise results.

Though many people complain that sizes vary from company to company, this can often be a good thing, as there is a greater chance that one company will have products specifically for your body type. While it is not consistent, the wider range of options allows a greater chance for each person to find a brand that works.

How do indie pattern designers come up with their body charts? Simply put, there is not a set system of coming up with body measurements or grading. Indie patternmakers could use the same data that clothing companies do, though it is expensive. They could also have their own system based on years of patternmaking experience. The number of indie pattern designers has increased dramatically over the past several years, leading to a variety in sizing and grading among sewing patterns. This leads to a greater chance of finding a company which creates patterns to suit your body type the best.

Sizing, Ease, and Fabric

Main Factors in Fitting

Garments from each clothing and pattern company will fit your body type differently. Even if your bust, waist, and hip measurements correspond to the company's size chart, that does not always mean the garment will fit. Factors like shoulder slopes, dart depths, posture, and arm measurements can affect fit in major ways.

Even if a company has a set standard for measurements, it can change over the years. An example of this is when a new target customer with different measurements is identified. That new data changes the average, which can then affect each graded size to be bigger or smaller.

Another reason fit can change within a company is that the patternmaking staff can change, meaning there are now different people handling the product. Each patternmaker uses different methods which can lead to different fits.

The biggest difference among patternmakers is how the sloper is manipulated. There are some ways to manipulate a sloper that do not afford the best outcome. This can lead to the sloper becoming unbalanced. If the slopers are not balanced, the style patterns will reflect those same issues.

Another variable is fabric, which changes with time and affects the fit. Innovative new fabrics can give different drape levels and change how the fabric stretches. For example, many clothes in the past did not have elastane, which allows fabrics to stretch. When elastane was initially added to knit and woven fabrics, this drastically changed patternmaking and fit.

Another factor in commercial patterns is the amount of ease added. There are two types of ease. The first is wearing ease, which is added so the body can move easily in the garment. Wearing ease is usually added in the sloper stage. The amount of ease added is called "ease over body" which is the amount added to the body measurements. Ease over body not only gives room for movement but also helps define the silhouette of a style. This brings us to the second type of ease which is design ease. The design ease defines our silhouettes like loose, fitted, flared, straight, A-line, bubble, mermaid, etc. Since silhouettes fluctuate over time between loose and fitted, the patterns also fluctuate. New design silhouettes can also be driven by design teams.

Here is an example of design ease: When a silhouette is loose-fitting, the goal is to have a more relaxed appearance and not too tight. Some people may not prefer the amount of design ease added to the garment, and they may say it does not fit. However, the garment may fit as intended, but the wearer's preference is not consistent with the designer's vision. Design ease is very subjective.

Often, sewing pattern companies will give extra ease which makes the garment bigger than is needed. This is to allow for extra fabric during the final fitting stage to accommodate the different body shapes. However, it can also cause frustration when you make an entire garment that is much bigger than the intended silhouette.

Because of all the previously mentioned factors, commercial patterns often need to be corrected to fit your body type and measurements. This book walks you through the most common adjustments used for correcting store-bought patterns.

The Importance of a Fitting Sample

Do I Have To Make a Fitting Sample?

Many people do not take the time to make a fitting sample and only plan to make fitting adjustments on the final garment. While many alterations can be done on the actual garment level in the final fitting stage, especially when extra seam allowance is given, this is not always possible. Some examples of this are the "Slash & Spread" and "Slash & Close" methods (found on page 19), which can drastically change a pattern's shape.

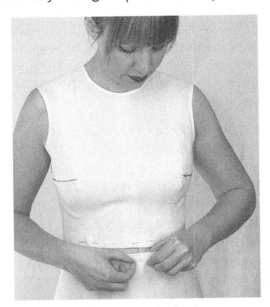

The exception to making fitting samples are knit styles. If you do not have a similar stretch and weight of fabric, the fitting sample will not be an accurate fit. When working with knit fabrics, I will often go straight to making the actual garment but add additional seam allowance width for alterations. I usually pre-sew a garment with a loose basting stitch to easily remove it later. The basting stitch allows me to fit the garment as a fitting sample.

Once I'm pleased with the fit, I will remove the loose basting stitches and sew with the correct stitch for stretchable knits (zig zag, overlock, or knit stitch). Take caution, though. It can be risky to remove even basting stitches from knits, as it can create holes in the fabric.

If you can find a similar knit fabric or have extra fabric you want to use for your final garment, make a fitting sample. There is always a higher risk that the garment will not fit as nicely if you do not make the sample.

I have been working in the garment industry since 2003. My primary career has been to make clothes fit. I have fitted thousands and thousands of garments over the years. New fabrics, new design lines, and new silhouettes play important roles in this fitting process. We often have to go through three to four prototypes before a garment is approved for production. This is the standard process in the garment industry to achieve a nicely-fitting garment with new design lines.

Another fitting method is called tissue fitting. This method uses store-bought tissue patterns which are connected with pins or tape and are then used for fitting. This method is a great option for those learning the shapes of the pattern pieces, and it is possible to catch many fitting issues. The difficulty with tissue fitting comes while checking the wearing ease because the tissue can tear easily when the body moves. If the pattern was made for a stretch or knit fabric, which can have negative wearing ease, tissue fitting will not be an option since it will not stretch, and therefore, will not fit the body.

I highly suggest making a fitting sample before sewing the finished garment in your final fabric. If you need to have one or two fittings prior to making garments that fit, it is worth the effort. You will be happy with the result and be able to wear it for years. Learning the new skill of how to make your clothes fit is an investment in yourself. As you improve your skills, you will make fewer fitting samples. Enjoy the process of fitting! It is so rewarding to wear clothes you love that fit.

Woven Fabric Selection

For Your Fitting Sample

Choosing the right fabric for your fitting sample is critical in achieving the correct fit. As a starting point, I suggest making the sample in a muslin fabric for woven styles. Muslin is a cotton fabric that is a plain weave material (as shown in the photo on the right). It is usually not dyed, is unbleached, and has a natural color. Try to find a muslin with a similar weight to your final fabric.

Alternatively, you could also use a fabric that drapes (hangs) similarly and is a similar weight (thickness) as the final fabric you will use for your garment. In order to visualize the drape of your fabric, make a fist with your hand, keeping your knuckles and the tops of your fingers parallel to the floor. Then lay a corner of the fabric over your fist. This will show you the body or drape of the fabric.

The farther away it hangs from your hand, the more body it has. There is more structure, fullness, or stiffness to it.

The closer it hangs to your hand means it has more drape. The fabric will be more slinky and possibly flow more. Do a drape test to compare your final fabric to your muslin fabric to see if they are similar.

Using a fabric that is similar in drape and weight to your final fabric will give you better judgment in the fitting stages.

Fabric with more body:
has more stiffness, fullness, or structure.

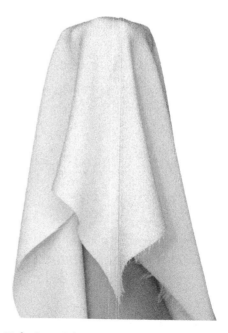

Fabric with more drape:
lies softer, closer to the hand, and is more slinky.

Knit Fabric Selection or Wovens with Stretch

For Your Fitting Sample

If you are making a garment out of a knit or stretchable fabric, use a similar stretching fabric for a fitting sample. The most important characteristics in a sample knit are that it stretches the same amount and has a similar weight and thickness as your final fabric. Do the drape test with your knit fabric to see the amount of body or drape the fabric has. This helps you envision the final garment better. (Refer to the previous page.)

To find the stretch of a fabric, take the cut edge of the fabric on the cross-grain edge (not the selvage edge), and measure 10" (20 cm) with a ruler flat on the table. Allow a little space between the selvage and the end of the ruler, placing a pin at "zero" and another pin at 10" (20 cm). This is the original amount unstretched and is shown in photo (1) below.

Stretch the 10" (20 cm) with your entire hand to its maximum. Grasp as much of the fabric as you can with your thumb and hand.

For this example, the maximum amount when stretched is 15" (30 cm). This is shown in photo (2) below.

The calculation of stretch percentage is as follows:

Maximum amount when stretched 15" (30 cm)

(-) Minus the **original amount unstretched** 10" (20 cm)

(=) Equals 5" (10 cm) the **stretched amount**

Now, take the **stretched amount** (5" or 10 cm) and divide it by the **original amount unstretched** (10" or 20 cm).

Inches: 5"/(divided by) 10" = 0.50   **Centimeters:** 10 cm/(divided by) 20 cm = 0.50

Take that divided amount (0.50) and multiply it by 100 to find the percentage. 0.50 x 100 = 50. This means that the stretch amount is 50% for this fabric.

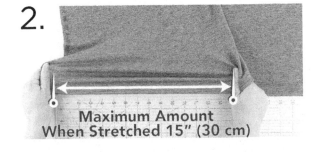

1. Unstretched Amount 10" (20 cm)

2. Maximum Amount When Stretched 15" (30 cm)

If the fabric stretches in length, cut off the selvage and repeat these steps to the length. Fabric that also stretches in length is called a 4-way stretch.

Many people do this incorrectly and only hold it with the ends of their fingers to stretch it, which results in an inaccurate measurement. →

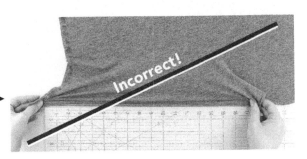

Incorrect!

Darts Explained

The Dart Protrusion Rule

Darts have an important task: to give shape to areas that protrude or need movement. I call this the "dart protrusion rule." A dart points to a curve on the body that protrudes (sticks out), or a dart allows more room for movement.

The deepest part of the dart removes fabric where you do not need it. The point of the dart allows more room for the area it is pointing to. Darts are generally only used in woven fabrics. Knit fabrics generally stretch over the curves of the body, and therefore, darts are not needed.

You can eliminate darts in the pattern manipulation stage by replacing them with design lines, yokes, gathering, or pleats. However, you must have darts in the sloper stage to achieve a proper fit.

Let's go through some of the most important dart positions in fitting: the first is the bust dart. A bust dart can come from any direction of the front bodice, but it must point toward the apex. The dart points to the protruding breast area and allows for fullness, giving a nice shape to the bust.

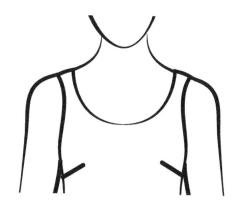

To make style patterns from a sloper, move the point of the bust dart away from the apex. This gives a nice appearance by not having the dart point directly on the apex. Use the following amount according to your bust cup size:

3/4" (2 cm) = A cup

1" (2.5 cm) = B cup

1 1/4" (3 cm) = C cup

1 1/2" (3.5 cm) = D cup

1 3/4" (4.5 cm) = E cup

2" (5 cm) = + E cup

The next important dart in tops is the raglan sleeve dart along the shoulder slope. Many designers try to eliminate this dart. However, this dart allows a much better fit to the high and low point shoulder areas. The point of the shoulder dart goes to the low point shoulder tip that protrudes. Without a dart in a raglan sleeve, there will be excess fabric along the armhole seams, and it likely will not rest against the body at the high point shoulder.

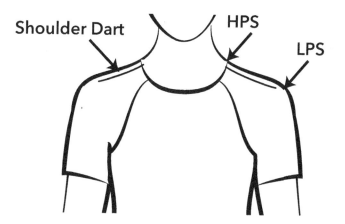

Shoulder Dart **HPS** **LPS**

Other darts can achieve silhouette differences, rather than only perfecting fit. Waist darts on a bodice, for instance, tailor the garment at the waist and offer a slimmer cut.

Darts at the knees of pants or at the elbows offer shaping for joints. This follows the same dart protrusion rule as before: the dart gives shape to areas that protrude, like the roundness of the elbow and knee.

(continued on next page)

The Dart Protrusion Rule (continued)

Though they offer more ergonomic shapes, knee and elbow darts are optional. Knee darts can be found in activewear, like hiking or ski pants. Elbow darts can be found in tailored blazers (often slashed out in the undersleeve panel), as well as in ski or motorcycle jackets.

Darts that are NOT optional are: back waist darts in pants and skirt slopers. The back waist darts point toward the backside, which protrudes from the body. Without these darts, you can never achieve a comfortable fit, especially while sitting. Remember: you can always close the darts during pattern manipulation by adding yokes or design lines, but these darts MUST be in the sloper to achieve a nice fit.

Many patternmakers do not slash and close out these darts properly in the dart manipulation process. This is the number one fitting issue I have seen throughout my years in patternmaking. If darts are not slashed and closed, or are not deep enough in style patterns, the result will be a gaping waistline.

The front waist darts on a skirt or pair of pants are optional. Here are two reasons why you may want to include front waist darts on bottoms:

1) If your stomach curves outward, you may want a dart to account for the protruding tummy curve, especially on high-waisted garments (seen in image (1) below).

2) Place a straight ruler from your stomach to your legs. If there is a large gap between your pelvis and the ruler (as seen in image (2) below), you may want to add darts. This will allow fullness for your hips to move.

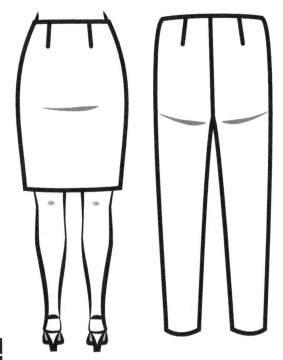

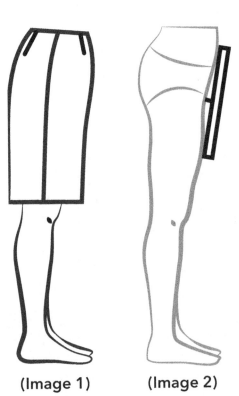

(Image 1)   (Image 2)

Tips for Getting Started

In this section, we will discuss important information before you begin your fittings and corrections.

The topics include:

- Seam Allowances
- Measuring Seam Lines
- Sleeve Ease Amounts
- The Tape & Pin Method in Fitting

The best practice for correcting patterns begins with marking seam allowances. It is critical to account for seam allowances both before and after making pattern corrections since all the pieces need to fit together along the seam line.

When it comes to sleeve corrections, begin and end with the same ease amount in the sleeve cap for the sleeve to fit properly into the armhole. This chapter will show you the best practices for measuring curved seams on paper patterns.

Finally, at the end of this chapter, I will share my favorite method in fitting which I learned while working in high fashion - the Tape & Pin method.

Seam Allowances

Mark Seam Lines on the Pattern

All the corrections in this book show the pattern pieces without the seam allowances marked. Always do the corrections per this book to the seam line. If the pattern piece does not have seam allowances marked, mark them on the pattern. Most patterns include seam allowances, but the seam lines are not marked on the patterns, meaning you must mark the seam line inside the pattern.

Read the pattern for the seam allowance width. If the pattern does not mark the seam lines, mark them prior to making the pattern correction. Always correct from the seam line.

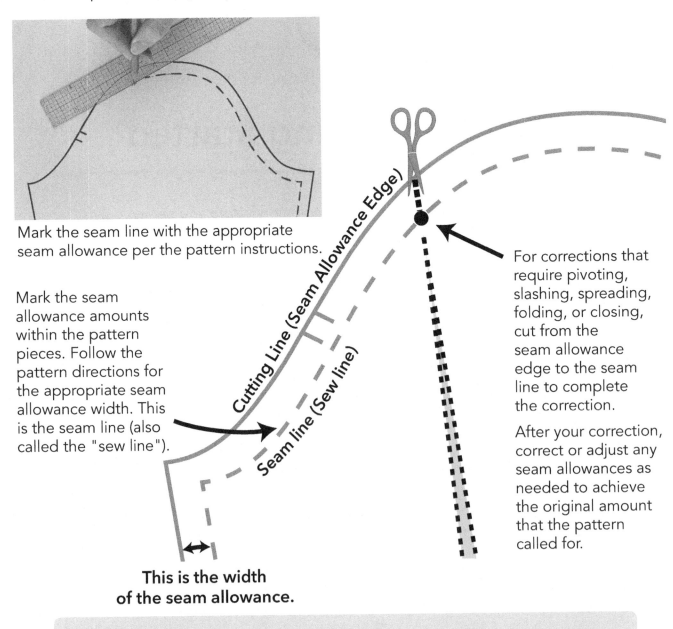

Mark the seam line with the appropriate seam allowance per the pattern instructions.

Mark the seam allowance amounts within the pattern pieces. Follow the pattern directions for the appropriate seam allowance width. This is the seam line (also called the "sew line").

Cutting Line (Seam Allowance Edge)

Seam line (Sew line)

For corrections that require pivoting, slashing, spreading, folding, or closing, cut from the seam allowance edge to the seam line to complete the correction.

After your correction, correct or adjust any seam allowances as needed to achieve the original amount that the pattern called for.

This is the width of the seam allowance.

REMEMBER: All the corrections in this book show the pattern pieces without the seam allowances marked. Always do the correction to the seam line.

Measuring Seam Lines

How To Measure Curved Seams

Always measure each pattern piece after the correction to be sure it fits with corresponding pattern pieces around it. When you measure a pattern piece, measure the seam line. Do not measure the seam allowance edge (cutting line). When measuring internal seam lines, start and stop measuring at the adjacent seam lines, not to or from the seam allowance edge (cutting line).

Think of the entire pattern in terms of a puzzle. If you make an adjustment on one piece, it may no longer fit into the other piece. You always need to measure the seams that were adjusted and make the corresponding adjustments to adjacent seams, ensuring they will fit back together in the sewing process.

If you made pattern corrections in areas with facings or if the garment has a lining, apply the same pattern corrections to the corresponding pieces. Often necklines, sleeveless armholes, and hemlines have facings.

The best way to measure a curved seam on a paper pattern is with a flexible tape measure. Pivot the tape measure with your finger along the curve of the seam line, allowing the tape measure to walk along the line.

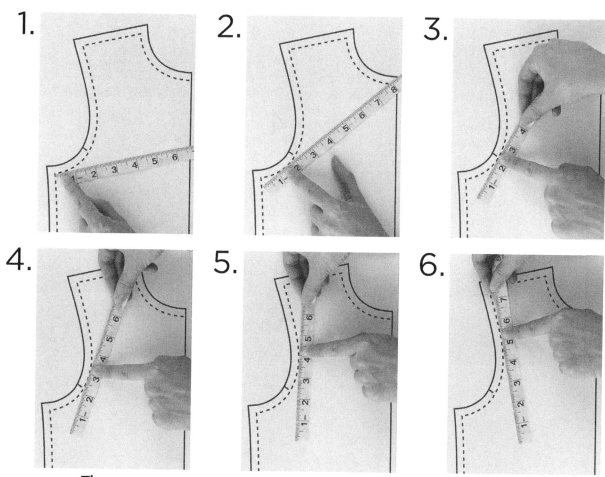

The tape measure is always on the inside of the pattern piece.

(continued on next page)

How To Measure Curved Seams (continued)

Always place the tape measure inside the pattern piece when measuring curved seams on patterns. Never place the tape measure on the outer edge of the seam line in the seam allowance area.

It is a good idea to measure curves multiple times because it is easy to measure incorrectly. By measuring multiple times you will be able to cross-check your work to be certain that everything will match.

The sleeve will always be bigger than the armhole on woven styles due to the ease amount (see the following page for determining the ease amount). The images below show how to measure the sleeve correctly, pivoting the tape measure with your finger along the curve as you move along the sleeve cap.

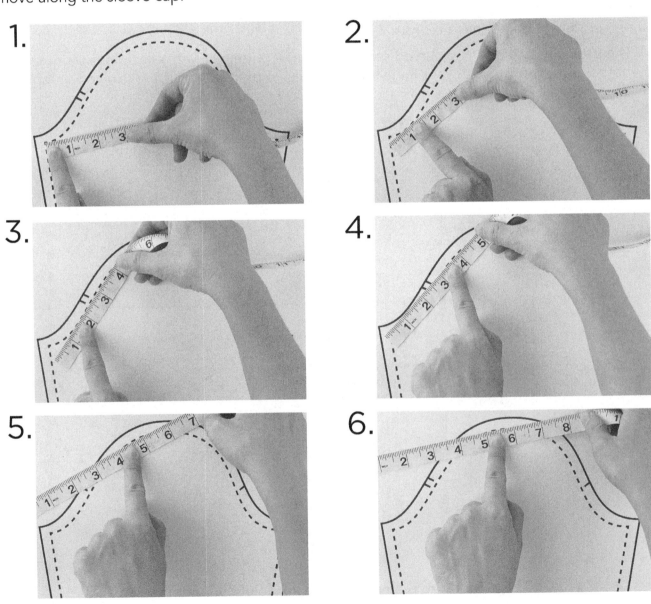

The tape measure is always on the inside of the pattern piece.

Sleeve Ease Amounts

Armhole Versus Sleeve Measurements

Before you make any adjustments to the sleeve or armhole seam, check the ease amount in the sleeve pattern in comparison to the armhole measurement. The same amount of ease must be considered while making pattern corrections. Determine the ease by the "difference method" as follows:

Example:

Measure the pattern pieces before making any corrections.

The sleeve armhole seam measures 19 1/2" (49.5 cm).

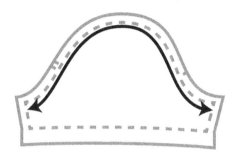

The armhole seam line of the front and back pieces combined = 19" (48.2 cm).

Front armhole + Back armhole

To find the amount of ease in the sleeve:

Sleeve measurement 19 1/2" (49.5 cm)
(Subtract) (-) Armhole seam measurement 19" (48.2 cm)

(Equals) (=) 1/2" (1.3 cm) of ease on the sleeve.

This is the "difference method." The corrected sleeve pattern should be 1/2" (1.3 cm) bigger than the front and back armholes when added together.

There is also a "percentage method," but this is rarely used since the result is very similar to the "difference method."

Ensure the notches on the sleeve and armhole align after any sleeve or armhole corrections, as shown on page 140 in Step 5. Move the notches as needed for them to align.

How To Measure Yourself

The Importance of Accurate Measurements

We all want to achieve the perfect fit, and it starts with taking proper body measurements.

By taking correct measurements of yourself, you will be able to cross check your existing patterns against your measurements and also use them in drafting patterns like a moulage or a sloper.

When measuring yourself, wear the same bra and panties you would wear on a regular basis. Do not wear shoes or additional clothes when taking your initial body measurements. Although, if you are measuring for a gown or something specific, wear the shoes/heels of your choice.

The most important point to remember when measuring yourself is to keep your stance consistent. Stand like a dress form, straight up, with your arms and elbows down and relaxed.

It is critical to stand still while taking your measurements. Take a deep breath in, breathe out, then take your measurement in a relaxed stance.

Bust/Chest: Measure the largest circumference of the bust going over the apex area. This should be parallel to the floor. (The term bust is used for womenswear. The term chest is used for menswear. These points of measure are in the same position, and the terms are interchangeable.)

Waist: Measure the smallest part of the waist, usually slightly higher than the belly button. This should be parallel to the floor.

If you are unsure where your waistline is, lean to the side; your waist is where your torso bends.

Hips: Measure the largest part of the bottom area. This should be parallel to the floor.

It is helpful to measure the distances between the bust, waist, and hips at the CF, so you have a position reference for your patterns. To measure your across shoulder, see the instructions on page 87. To measure your sleeve cap height/width, see pages 144-146. To measure your above bust, bust, and bust positions, see pages 158-159.

It is common that when you measure multiple times, you may end up with a different measurement each time. The variance in measurements can be due to the skin, muscles, and soft tissue. Slight differences in how you place the tape measure can also affect the results.

If you obtain a different measurement each time and are unsure which one to use, take an average of the measurements.

Use the "ribbon" method as shown on page 87 to assist in taking your measurements. You can leave the ribbon on at all times, creating a designated self-measuring tape.

I reveal my Top 10 Tips showing how to measure yourself accurately in a free mini-course series. If you haven't seen this free series, sign up by scanning the QR code below.

Thousands of people have watched the series, which is offered twice per year for a limited time only. Even sewists with 30-40 years of experience have raved about how much they have learned from this mini-course.

I highly suggest watching the series to learn more about measuring yourself accurately. It also covers fitting tips and helps you determine how to create a solid foundation for your sewing pattern journey.

Sign up to be notified when the next free mini-course is open.

The Tape & Pin Method in Fitting

How To Open Seams in Fitting

I learned this fitting method of taping and pinning samples at my first job in the New York City fashion industry in 2003. This was the method we used in nearly every fitting, and I still use this method today. It will greatly improve the accuracy of your fittings.

Cut a seam or an area you would like to slash open. Use two pieces of tape: one on the inside of the garment and one on the outside. Use LONG pieces of tape.

The method is as follows:

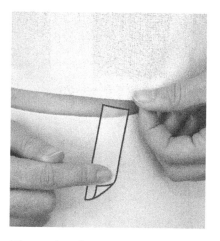

Place the first piece of tape with the non-sticky side against your body. Slide it underneath one side of the fabric. It should stick to the fabric.

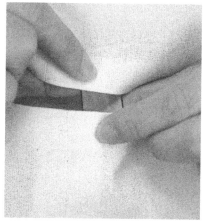

Slide the other end underneath the other side of the fabric. Both ends should be sticking to the fabric with the distance you want to open.

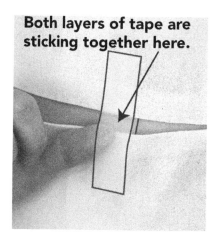

Both layers of tape are sticking together here.

Place the second piece on the top side of the fabric, so the center parts of the tape stick together.

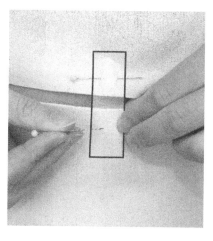

Pin through each end of the tape layers. The pins help keep the tape in place.

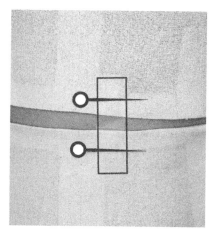

The pins go through **BOTH** layers of tape.

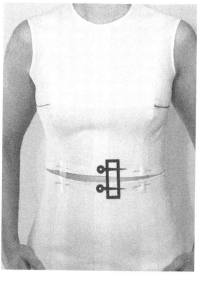

Movement can still break the tape, so take care, and watch out for the sharp pins.

Using Patternmaking Rulers

The following pages show how to place curved and straight patternmaking rulers on the pattern pieces. It takes practice using the curved rulers. Many times, you will need to flip the ruler around for the curve to be in the correct location.

In general, position the curvier part of the ruler toward the direction where there is the most shaping. So, the waist and bust area would have the curvier parts of the ruler toward these curvier parts of the body.

I rarely use the measurements on the curved rulers. The main use of the ruler is to draw a nice line.

In my opinion, not all curved rulers are created equal. Each brand has its own curved shapes. If you are interested in the rulers I recommend, you can find a list of my favorite tools on the Bonus All-Access webpage for the book. Scan the QR Code below.

There are three main rulers you will need in patternmaking:

1) Straight Clear Grid Ruler

2) French Curve

3) Hip Curve

How To Use the Pattern Rulers

Specific Ruler Placement for Pants Patterns

Follow this as a reference for flipping the curved rulers to achieve beautiful curved lines. With time, you will be able to look at a pattern and instantly know if it is a nice shape.

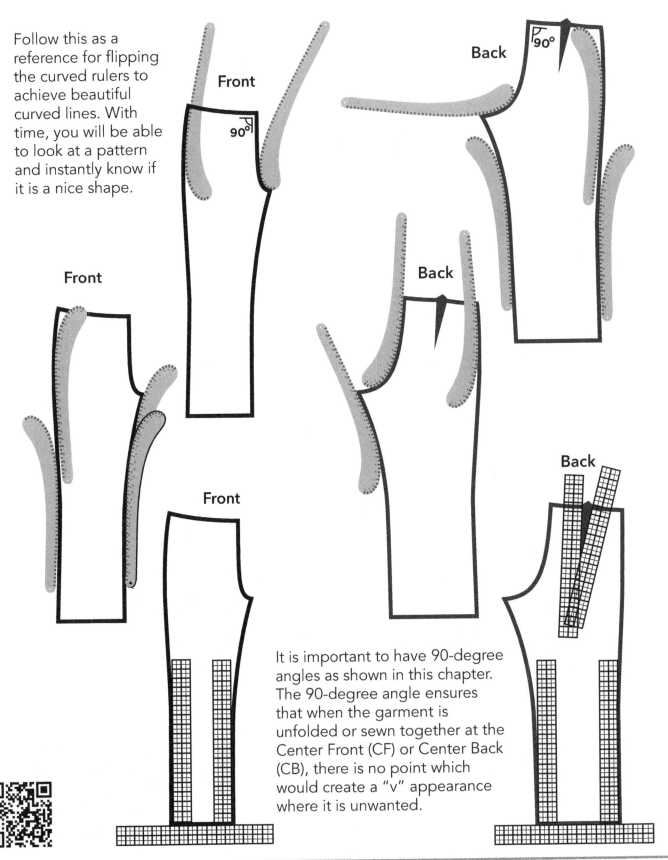

It is important to have 90-degree angles as shown in this chapter. The 90-degree angle ensures that when the garment is unfolded or sewn together at the Center Front (CF) or Center Back (CB), there is no point which would create a "v" appearance where it is unwanted.

True the Seams

Make the Seams Smooth and Continuous on Pants

Always align the pattern pieces together after you make any corrections to ensure the front and back pieces are smooth and continuous. This is called "truing" the pattern. The phrase "true the seams" can also be used after a pattern correction is finished. It means to make the new seam line smooth.

Align the side seams at the waistline, then true the waistline, making it smooth and continuous. There should not be any points. There should be a 90-degree angle at the CF and CB waistline.

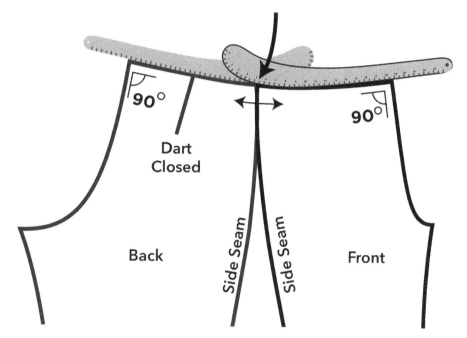

When you align the inseams at the rise (crotch point), the rise seams should be continuous. There should not be any points, and the rise should be smooth.

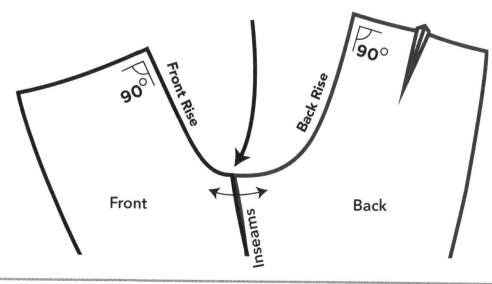

How To Use the Pattern Rulers

Specific Ruler Placement for Tops - Front Panel

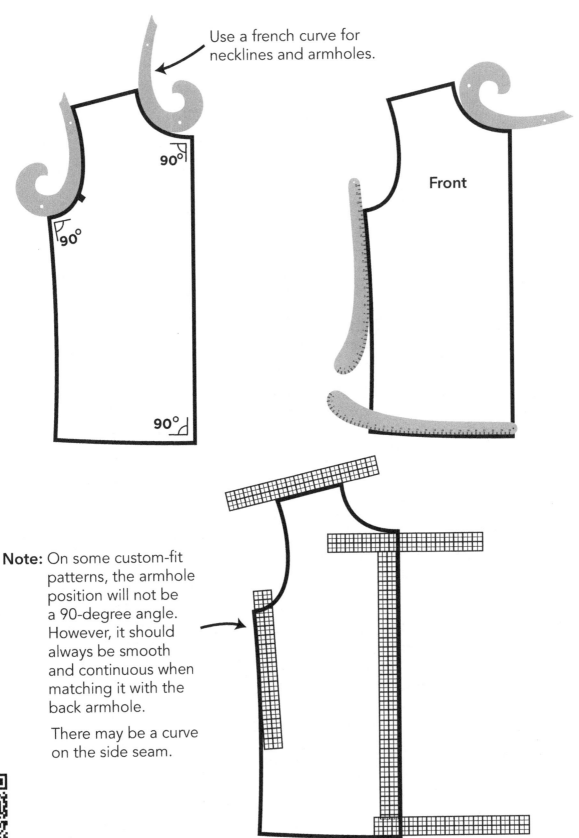

Use a french curve for necklines and armholes.

90°

90°

90°

Front

Note: On some custom-fit patterns, the armhole position will not be a 90-degree angle. However, it should always be smooth and continuous when matching it with the back armhole.

There may be a curve on the side seam.

How To Use the Pattern Rulers

Specific Ruler Placement for Tops - Back Panel

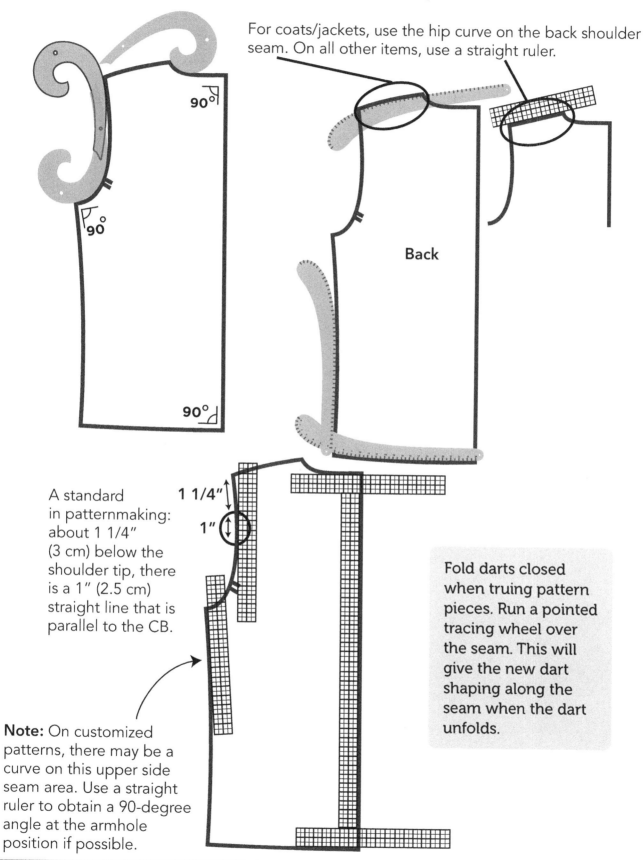

For coats/jackets, use the hip curve on the back shoulder seam. On all other items, use a straight ruler.

90°

90°

90°

90°

Back

A standard in patternmaking: about 1 1/4" (3 cm) below the shoulder tip, there is a 1" (2.5 cm) straight line that is parallel to the CB.

1 1/4"

1"

Fold darts closed when truing pattern pieces. Run a pointed tracing wheel over the seam. This will give the new dart shaping along the seam when the dart unfolds.

Note: On customized patterns, there may be a curve on this upper side seam area. Use a straight ruler to obtain a 90-degree angle at the armhole position if possible.

True the Seams

Make the Seams Smooth and Continuous on Tops

True the pattern by aligning the front and back panels along the shoulder seams and side seams.

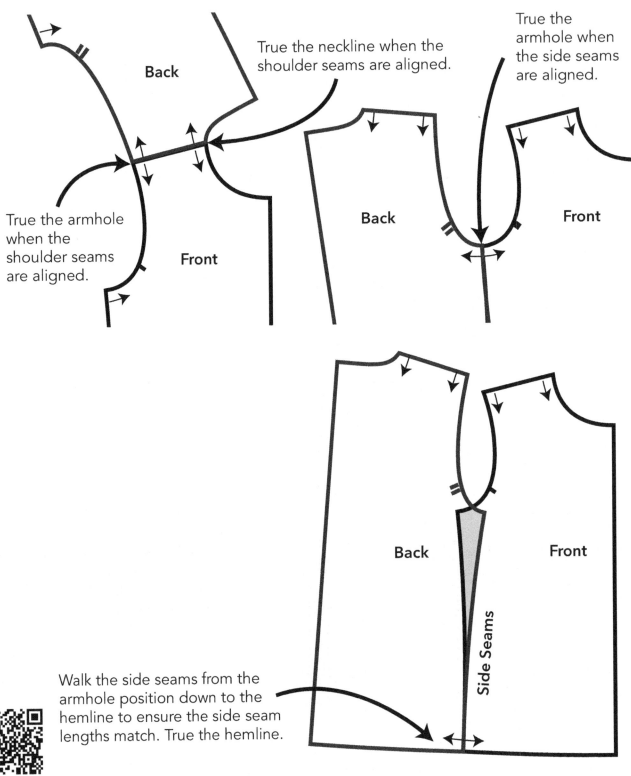

True the neckline when the shoulder seams are aligned.

True the armhole when the side seams are aligned.

Back

Front

True the armhole when the shoulder seams are aligned.

Back

Front

Back

Front

Back

Front

Side Seams

Walk the side seams from the armhole position down to the hemline to ensure the side seam lengths match. True the hemline.

How To Use the Pattern Rulers

Specific Ruler Placement for Sleeves

For the curvature of the sleeve cap, flip and turn the french curve in multiple ways to achieve a nice shape. Get used to flipping the rulers and trying different parts of the curves!

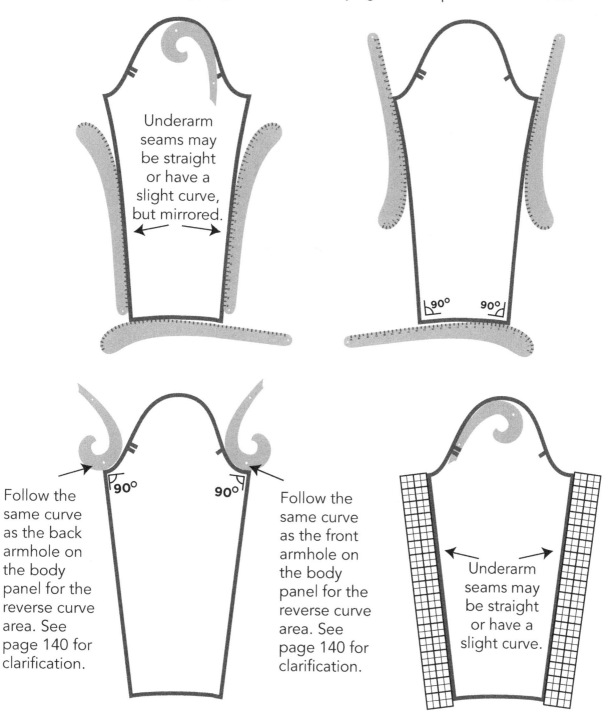

Underarm seams may be straight or have a slight curve, but mirrored.

90° 90°

Follow the same curve as the back armhole on the body panel for the reverse curve area. See page 140 for clarification.

90° 90°

Follow the same curve as the front armhole on the body panel for the reverse curve area. See page 140 for clarification.

Underarm seams may be straight or have a slight curve.

Make the Seams Smooth and Continuous on Sleeves

Align the underarm seams to ensure the armhole seam and the sleeve hemline have smooth and continuous lines, "truing the lines."

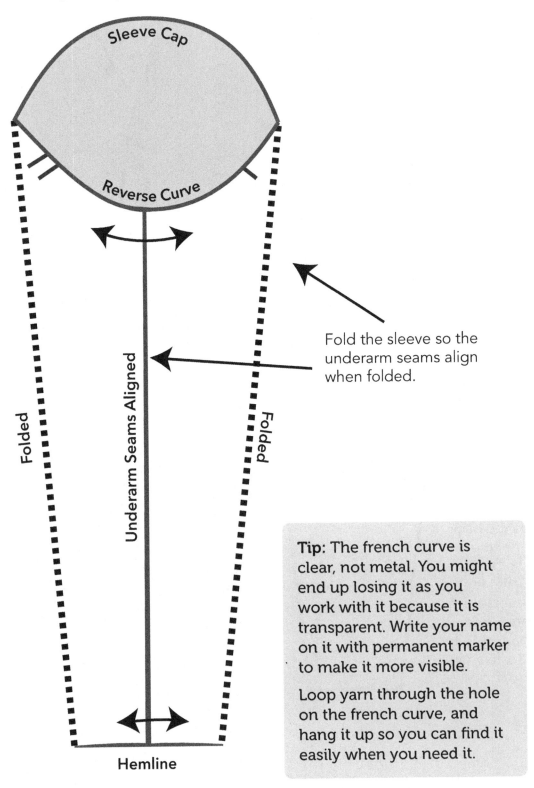

Fold the sleeve so the underarm seams align when folded.

Tip: The french curve is clear, not metal. You might end up losing it as you work with it because it is transparent. Write your name on it with permanent marker to make it more visible.

Loop yarn through the hole on the french curve, and hang it up so you can find it easily when you need it.

FITTING TOPS

Checking the Balance of Top or Bodice Patterns

Making sure the pattern is balanced is a critical step in patternmaking. When a pattern is unbalanced, there will often be fitting issues associated with it.

Sewing patterns you purchase should always be balanced, but many times they are not. This is why you should always check the balance before proceeding with fitting corrections.

On customized patterns like a moulage or sloper, many of the balance rules are broken on purpose. This is due to the customization process because the patterns were made specifically for your body. If you start from a moulage or sloper that was based totally on your body measurements and not from industry standards, the balance of the pattern will not follow the rules in this section. This is to be expected since it is customized. Skip the balancing steps if you have a custom-fit sloper.

However, when you start with a sewing pattern built from industry standards, always start with a balanced pattern. As the pattern becomes customized through the fitting process, this may change the balance and break the balance rules. However, when possible, try to keep the rules as explained on the following pages.

We start with balanced patterns, but sometimes we do not end with balanced patterns because our bodies may require adjustments to the standard rules.

A Balanced Jacket or Coat Pattern

Checking If the Pattern Is Balanced

Before making any fitting corrections, make sure the pattern is 100% balanced. A balanced pattern produces a garment that hangs well without twisting or having excessive draglines. Start with a balanced pattern to achieve a well-fitted garment. Do this exercise to see if the pattern pieces are balanced. First explained are jacket and coat patterns for woven fabrics.

1. If the style has design lines with multiple pattern pieces, join the pattern pieces to create a front panel and back panel.

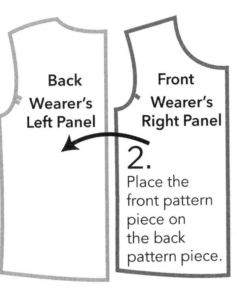

Back Wearer's Left Panel

Front Wearer's Right Panel

2. Place the front pattern piece on the back pattern piece.

3. Match the underarm positions. Jackets and coats have a height difference in the shoulder seams. The back shoulder seam will be up to 1/2" (1.3 cm) higher than the front shoulder seam. The difference will vary from pattern to pattern.

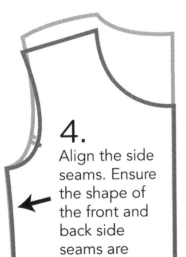

4. Align the side seams. Ensure the shape of the front and back side seams are mirrored. They should both have the same shape. If they do not align, follow page 186 to balance the side seams.

Tip: If there are any side darts on the front pattern piece, account for the dart depths. "Jump" over the dart or fold the dart closed when checking the side seam alignment.

Why do I show a wearer's right front and a wearer's left back panel throughout this book?

It is the easiest method to check the balance as you work on patterns. You can quickly lay the front on top of the back to check all the balancing points and lines.

A Balanced Jacket or Coat Pattern

Checking If the Pattern Is Balanced (continued)

This is a continuation for balancing jacket and coat patterns for woven fabrics.

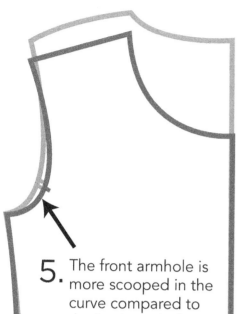

6. Here is another way to view the height difference from the back to the front. Align the shoulder seams at the HPS. The back armhole position (depth) can be up to 1/2" (1.3 cm) lower in the back armhole depth. This allows for the movement of the shoulder blade and garments worn underneath. The front shoulder slope may be more drastic than the back. If the front or back armhole needs to be raised or lowered, follow pages 131 or 134.

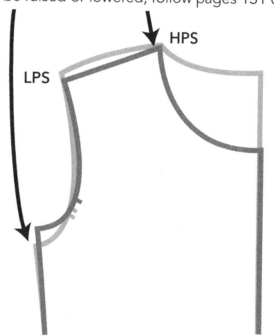

LPS

HPS

5. The front armhole is more scooped in the curve compared to the back armhole.

The front armhole is always indicated by a single notch. The back armhole is indicated by double notches. Use these notches to match to the sleeve pattern as shown on page 140.

7. You can add a slight curve at the back shoulder to allow for more movement of the shoulder blade.

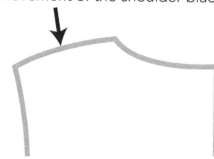

8. By having the back armhole lower than the front, the shoulder blade has more movement. There is also more space for garments worn underneath.

When the shoulder seams and side seams are sewn together, you can see how the armhole has more room in the back. Watch the fitting video through the QR code for a demonstration.

A Balanced Knit Top Pattern

Checking If the Pattern Is Balanced

Knit top patterns can include dress bodices or tee-shirts which are made for stretchable knit fabrics.

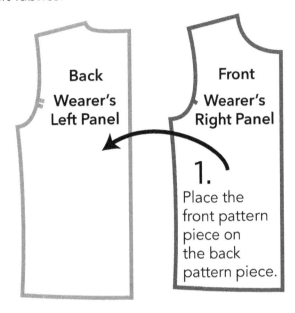

Back
Wearer's
Left Panel

Front
Wearer's
Right Panel

1.
Place the front pattern piece on the back pattern piece.

Why do I show a wearer's right front and a wearer's left back panel throughout this book?

It is the easiest method to check the balance as you work on patterns. You can quickly lay the front on top of the back to check all the balancing points and lines.

2. Draw a horizontal guideline perpendicular to the CF, going through the armhole position. The armhole position should hit the guideline in the front and the back when the HPS is aligned. The front armhole is always indicated by a single notch. The back armhole is indicated by double notches. Use these notches to match to the sleeve pattern as shown on page 140.

If the armhole position does not align, take the middle point between the two. Re-draw both the front and back armhole positions to that point.

3. Align the side seams, and ensure the shape of the front and back side seams are mirrored. They should both have the same shape. If they do not align, follow page 186 to balance the side seams.

LPS

HPS

4.
The shoulder seams will always be straight on a knit top. There will be no curve on the shoulder seams for woven tops, either.

During the customization process, there will be a different slope from the front to back, meaning the angle is different. This can vary from person to person based on your shoulder slope.

Good News: Gina Renee Designs' patterns are always balanced! If you are using a Gina Renee pattern, you can skip these steps.

A Balanced Woven Top Pattern

Checking If the Pattern Is Balanced

Woven top patterns can include dress bodices or blouses, which were made for a woven fabric. These are usually garments worn next to your body and not outer-layer garments.

If the garment pulls toward the back when it is worn, the pattern is likely not balanced. If the wearer often lifts the garment at the shoulder seams to pull the garment toward the front while wearing the garment, the back armhole is likely too low. Additional fitting issues when a pattern is unbalanced are explained in step 4 on the next page.

1. If the style has design lines with multiple pattern pieces, join the pattern pieces to create a front panel and back panel.

   Lay the front pattern piece on the back pattern piece, aligning the HPS.

   The same rules apply for styles without darts. This example shows the darts as a reference.

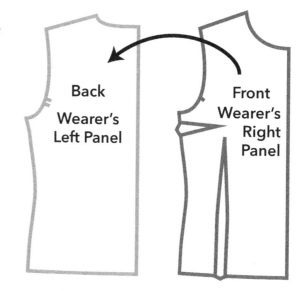

Back
Wearer's Left Panel

Front
Wearer's Right Panel

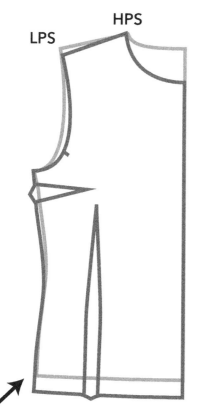

LPS   HPS

3. Align the side seams, and ensure the shape of the front and back side seams are mirrored. They should both have the same shape. When there is a side dart, walk the pattern pieces up to the dart, jump over the dart as if it was closed. Alternatively, you may fold the dart closed.

   If the side seams do not align, follow page 186 to balance them.

2. Whenever there is a side dart, there is a difference in the side seam lengths. The front appears longer because the dart is included. When the dart is closed, the side seam lengths should be the same.

(continued on next page)

Checking the Balance of Top or Bodice Patterns

Checking If the Pattern Is Balanced (*continued*)

5. If the armhole position does not align, find the middle point between the two. Re-draw both the front and back armhole positions to that point.

The front armhole is always indicated by a single notch. The back armhole is indicated by double notches. Use these notches to match to the sleeve pattern as shown on page 140.

4. Draw a horizontal guideline perpendicular to the CF, going through the armhole position. The armhole position should hit the guideline in the front and the back when the HPS is aligned.

In some cases, the back pattern piece may have a lower armhole, but this can restrict the movement when the arms reach forward, and it can also increase the draglines in the back body panel. When I learned patternmaking, I was taught to have a lower back armhole position. Over the years, I have found the lower back armhole causes more draglines in the back body panel and prohibits arm movement, specifically when reaching forward. Therefore, I now start with the same armhole positions on woven blouses and men's/women's tops.

Good News: Gina Renee Designs' patterns are always balanced! If you are using a Gina Renee pattern, you can skip these steps.

The back shoulder slope is often less angled than the front. This allows the shoulder blade to move more freely.

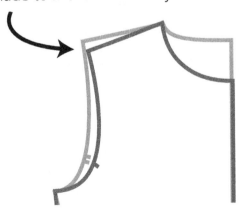

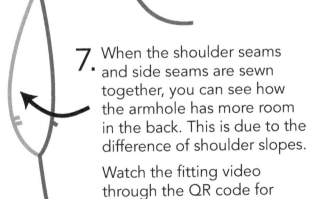

7. When the shoulder seams and side seams are sewn together, you can see how the armhole has more room in the back. This is due to the difference of shoulder slopes.

Watch the fitting video through the QR code for a demonstration.

First Steps in Assessing the Fit

Many times, people ask me, "Where do I start when I'm fitting?" Many people start at the top of the garment and work their way down, so the entire garment is thoroughly reviewed.

There is not a set order in fitting. It is usually best to work on the most prominent fitting issue first, then continue with other fitting issues. The goal in fitting is to do as many corrections as possible to each fitting sample, in order to achieve the best overall fit.

The chapters in this book are in the order I recommend to fit, except for the "Diagonal Draglines Demystified" chapter. That chapter is at the end because of the complex topic, and it refers to previous corrections within the book. If you see a prominent fitting issue, such as apparent draglines, correct it first. Then go from the top of the garment down as shown in the order of this book.

Sometimes after one fitting issue is corrected, other issues show up in subsequent fitting samples. Many times, it can take more than one fitting sample to achieve perfection. Try your best to enjoy this process. Fitting can require patience, but the amount you learn and grow from it is worth the effort involved. Other times, when there are only minor corrections, there is no need to make additional fitting samples.

A helpful tip as you fit: have someone take front, side, and back photos of you while wearing the fitting sample (or set a timer on your camera and do it yourself straight-on). Stand straight and relaxed, do not hold the camera yourself, and face a window with direct daylight. Overhead lighting will make the appearance of draglines worse than they are. Use these photos as you assess the fit. Sometimes having these photos allows you to see the garment in another way.

Let's take a look at the first steps in assessing your fitting sample!

Checking the Seam and Circumference Positions

Assess the Front of the Fitting Sample

First, check the overall fit for these points on the front bodice. If there are diagonal draglines or other fitting issues, they will be addressed later. The image below shows a moulage fitting sample from the online course, "Making a Moulage - The GRD Method™." Even though your style may not look like this image, use the guideline as a reference to check seam placements and other details.

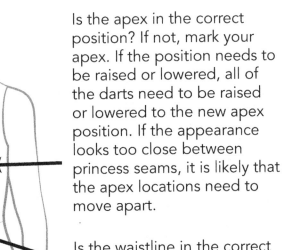

Check the neckline, making sure it is not too high or too low. It should not feel too tight. Raise or lower it as needed.

Are the bust, waist, or hips too tight or loose? If it is too tight, open the side seam as needed. If it is too loose, pin it to become tighter. If you pin the hip area, sit down to ensure it is still comfortable.

For style patterns there is already ease built in, and the design ease given is subjective. It is up to you if you are pleased with the level of tightness/looseness.

Is the apex in the correct position? If not, mark your apex. If the position needs to be raised or lowered, all of the darts need to be raised or lowered to the new apex position. If the appearance looks too close between princess seams, it is likely that the apex locations need to move apart.

Is the waistline in the correct position? Is it too high or too low? If so, mark the new placement after correcting any dragline fitting issues. If you need to move the waistline, move the line as needed. It is common to have a curved line for your waist on the pattern.

If you notice the bustline in the wrong position, mark the fitting sample, and move all the darts/apex points as needed. In the initial fitting stage of a moulage and sloper, I do not recommend a Slash & Spread or Slash & Close method for moving the waistline or bustline because this often leads to further fitting issues. However, if you are a petite person and need to shorten commercial/indie sewing patterns, you may use the Slash & Close method. Pin the fitting sample horizontally above the waistline on the front and back panels, and mark the pattern in the same position to Slash & Close. Alternatively, if you are a very tall person and need to lengthen a commercial/indie sewing pattern, you may use the Slash & Spread method. Cut the fitting sample horizontally above the waistline, and tape the position on the front and back panels. Both corrections for a petite or taller person will shift the waist and hip areas according to the amount you pinned or cut the sample.

When you move shoulder seams, princess seams or side seams, you are giving to one panel and taking from the other panel. Mark where the new lines should be on the fitting sample. Refer to the new lines marked on the fitting sample to adjust the pattern.

Checking the Seam and Circumference Positions

Assess the Back of the Fitting Sample

Next, check the overall fit for the following points on the back bodice. If there are diagonal draglines or other fitting issues, they will be addressed later. To do this, it is easiest to take photos of your garment and assess the photos. Reference the fitting sample in a mirror, and hold a secondary mirror in your hand to see it better.

Back View

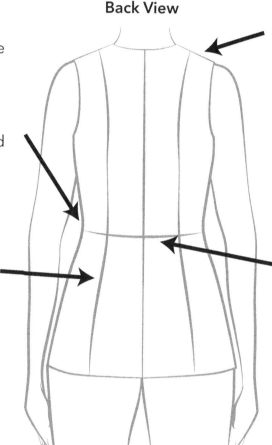

Check that the side seams are in the correct position and not twisting toward the front or back. If the seam needs to be moved, mark it on the fitting sample. To correct it on the pattern, measure where you marked on the fitting sample and give to one panel, while taking from the other panel to move the seam as needed.

If there are princess seams, check the placement and see if you are pleased with the visual distance from each other. Often if the princess seams are too wide apart, it can make the person look bigger.

Look at the shoulder seams; are they angled or turning? Mark if the seams need to be adjusted. When looking straight-on into the mirror, you should be able to see the shoulder seam ever so slightly the entire way. This is also easily viewed in the front photo.

Is the back waistline in the correct position? Is it too high or too low? If so, mark the new placement after correcting any dragline fit issues. If you need to move the waistline, move the line as needed. It is common to have a curved line for your waist on the pattern.

Note: Vertical draglines are a sign that the circumference of the garment is too big. In a moulage there should be no vertical draglines because it is a replicate of your body with no wearing ease.

In a sloper or style pattern, too much wearing ease can cause vertical draglines. If you would like the garment to be tighter, pin the vertical seams closest to the vertical draglines. After you pin, ensure the body movement is sufficient. The desired looseness of your garment is subjective. When there is more fabric than is required to move, it means there is additional design ease.

Horizontal draglines are often a sign that the garment is too tight or too long. See the next page for this topic.

Look for Horizontal Draglines

Actionable Steps To Improve the Fit

Horizontal draglines can occur in a garment for two reasons:

The most common reason horizontal draglines appear is because the garment is too tight, though it may not be tight in the same location as the draglines. If any area below the draglines is too tight, this could cause the garment to "hike" or "ride" up which creates the horizontal draglines.

If the garment is not too tight below the draglines, it may be too tight in the area where the draglines are located. This could include the entire circumference in that area, or only that specific area.

The first thing to do when the garment is too tight is to open the side seams and allow the garment to relax. Using the seam allowance, pin the side seams to make it looser.

If you are still having issues with horizontal draglines after increasing the circumference at the side seams, the issue is likely the secondary reason for draglines: the pattern is too long. In this case, pin horizontally above the draglines to remove the extra length.

The protocol for fitting horizontal draglines is as follows:

1) Open the circumference of the garment by opening it at the side seams.
   The location you open can either be below the draglines or at the draglines.
   If this does not automatically eliminate the draglines, continue to the next step.

2) Pin the garment horizontally above the draglines, reducing the length of the garment and sometimes adjusting the shape. Slash & Close the pattern as you have pinned it.

Since this fitting issue can come up anywhere on the garment, I do not give specific pattern correction visuals. Follow the above protocol.

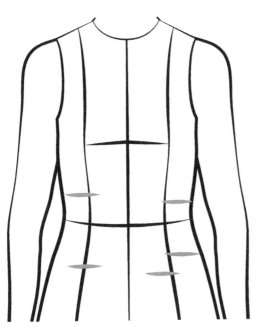
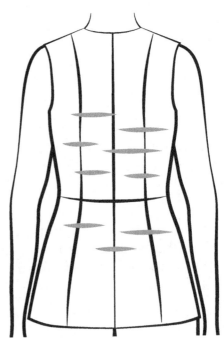

Neckline Corrections

We will continue with the upper portion of the garment by looking at neckline fitting corrections. Then we will work our way down the garment in subsequent chapters.

When reviewing neckline fitting issues, often the problem is not in the neckline shape but instead comes from the neck width differences, shoulder slope area, or the across front area. When the issue is related to the across front area, it is due to incorrect dart depths for your body shapes, which were in the original sloper used to create the style pattern.

This book contains multiple options to fix fitting issues. The options shown in the book are not in the order of which to try first. It is totally up to you which option you would like to try based on the type of garment you have or the fitting issues you see. Even though these options are numbered, the numbers have no importance unless stated otherwise.

If you are not sure which option to choose, start with the one that is the closest to your garment type and fitting issue. Do not let the many options stop you from moving forward with your pattern corrections. Choose one and go with it. If you get to Step (B) of pinning/cutting your sample and it does not improve, try the next option. You can always tape together any cut samples, and try other options to find the best correction for your fitting issue. Fitting can pretty much be renamed "troubleshooting." It is a great approach to learn as you go!

Often, there are even more methods or ways of correcting the pattern. This book gives you the most commonly used corrections. Let's assess the upper portion of your garment!

Front Neck Gaping

No Princess Seams

A) Identifying the Issue - There is excess fabric along the front neckline.

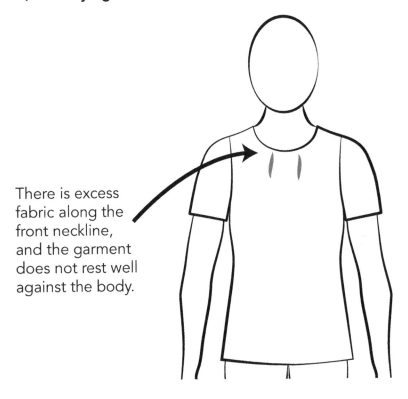

There is excess fabric along the front neckline, and the garment does not rest well against the body.

If there are additional draglines elsewhere on the garment which are pointing toward the bust, this is a sign that you may need a Full Bust Adjustment. See the bust corrections chapter to properly identify that fitting issue.

B) Pinning the Problem - Pin the excess fabric at the neckline, and measure the amount you pinned.

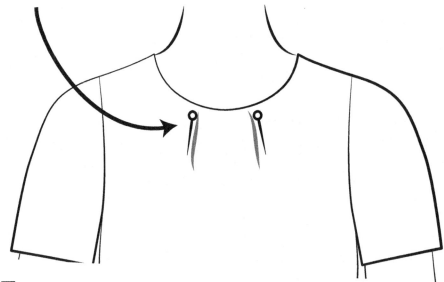

Remember: Adjust corresponding pattern pieces, like facings and linings, with the same pattern corrections.

Front Neck Gaping

No Princess Seams *(continued)*

Pattern Check! Compare the neck width of the front and back pattern pieces by aligning them at the HPS. If the front neck is wider than the back, reduce it so it is the same or smaller than the back. Mark the seam allowances. The images in this book show the pattern pieces to the seam line without seam allowances.

The back neck width is smaller than the front.

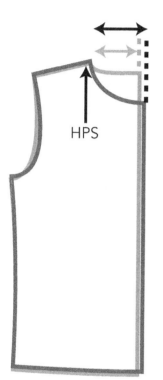

HPS

The back neck width is the same as the front.

The back neck width is the same as the front, considering CF or CB zipper width.

The back neck width is wider than the front neck width.

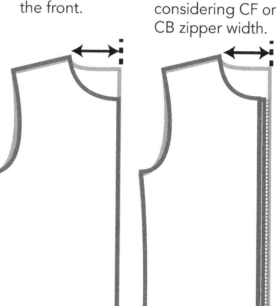

This option can be applied when you have considered the zipper or button placket width.

This is an incorrect pattern! The back neck width is smaller than the front. In rare cases, it is acceptable to have the back neck width smaller than the front, but this only comes after you customize the pattern. Always start with the three options to the right.

These are all correct patterns! The back neck width is the same as or wider than the front. If there is a zipper or button placket at the center front or back, account for half of the zipper/placket width in the neck width. A sewn-in zipper can add about 3/16" (0.5 cm) to each side for a total of 3/8" (1 cm). Many people forget to consider this, and then gaping occurs. If there is an invisible zipper, do not account for this since the fabric kisses, and there is no gap.

I prefer to go with the example on the right, making the front neck width smaller than the back neck width by 1/8" (0.3 cm) on the half.

It is "on the half" since we only work on one half of the front or back pattern.

If there is back neck gaping in addition to front neck gaping, the preferred correction would be the first of these three: keeping the back neck width the same as the front.

No Princess Seams (continued)

C) Correcting the Pattern - To balance the neck widths, there are several options. You may add to the neck at the center back, making the entire back panel wider. Alternatively, you can remove the amount away from the center front. If you remove the amount from the center front, consider that this will reduce the bust, waist, and hip measurements. An alternative option is shown below which does not affect the circumference measurements.

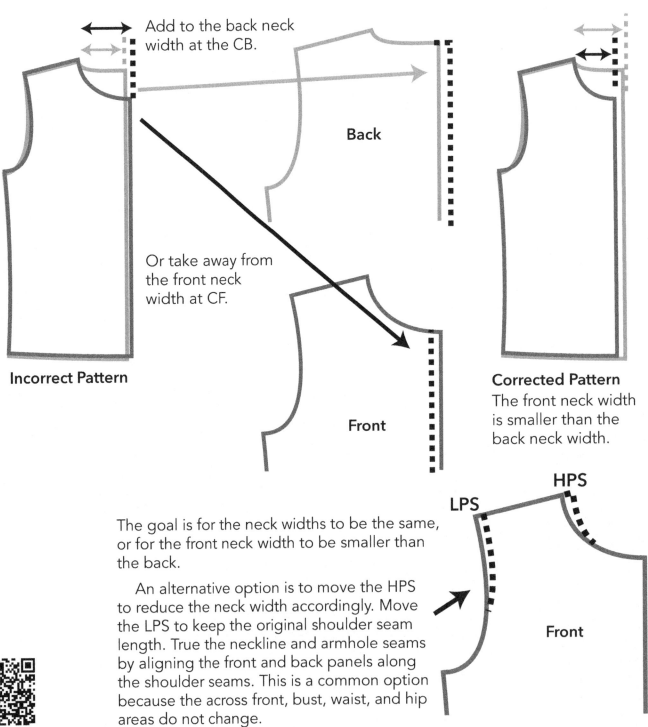

Add to the back neck width at the CB.

Back

Or take away from the front neck width at CF.

Front

Incorrect Pattern

Corrected Pattern
The front neck width is smaller than the back neck width.

The goal is for the neck widths to be the same, or for the front neck width to be smaller than the back.

An alternative option is to move the HPS to reduce the neck width accordingly. Move the LPS to keep the original shoulder seam length. True the neckline and armhole seams by aligning the front and back panels along the shoulder seams. This is a common option because the across front, bust, waist, and hip areas do not change.

HPS

LPS

Front

Front Neck Gaping - Option 1

With Princess Seams from the Armhole

This correction may also be used for back neck gaping on styles with princess seams. If the gaping issue is in the back instead of the front, follow the same correction, but apply it to the back panels.

A) Identifying the Issue - There is excess fabric along the front neckline. If there are additional draglines elsewhere on the garment which are pointing toward the bust, this is a sign that you may need a Full Bust Adjustment. See the bust corrections chapter to properly identify that fitting issue.

There is excess fabric along the front neckline, and the garment does not rest well against the body.

The neckline or princess seam shapes can vary per style, but the correction is the same concept. If there is a princess seam coming from the shoulder seam, follow Option 2 in the following correction.

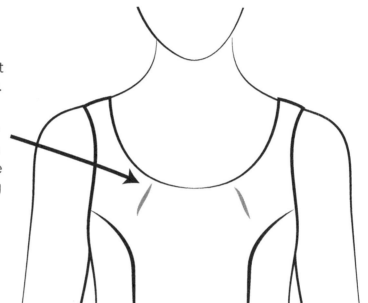

B) Pinning the Problem - Pin the excess fabric at the neckline, and measure the amount you pinned.

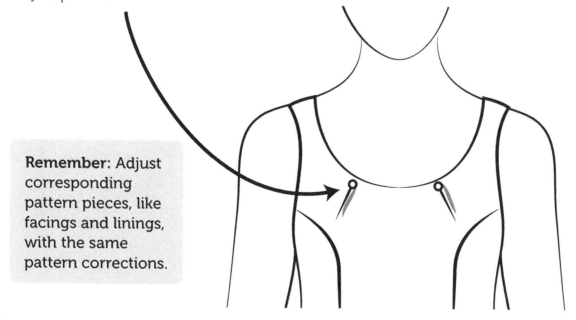

Remember: Adjust corresponding pattern pieces, like facings and linings, with the same pattern corrections.

With Princess Seams from the Armhole *(continued)*

C) Correcting the Pattern - First, compare the neck widths of the front and back pattern pieces. If the front neck is wider than the back, reduce it so it is the same or smaller than the back. See this correction on pages 73-74.

 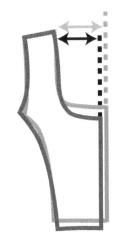

1.

Correct Examples:

The front neck width should be the same or smaller than the back width. Consider half of the zipper/placket width as explained on page 73. The light grey lines show the back panel, and the dark grey lines show the front panel.

This may already solve the fitting issue. Re-cut the panel you updated and fit it again. If the gaping still occurs, move to the next steps.

Skip Step 1 on this page if you are correcting a gaping neckline in the **back** of the garment.

Continue with a Slash & Close Correction:

Mark the exact area where you pinned the sample with the same amount you measured. Go to zero at the princess seam.

Slash & Close the amount you marked. The dotted line shows the new shape after you close the gap.

True the neckline and princess line as needed to obtain a continuous curve.

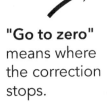

2.

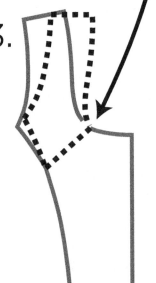

3.

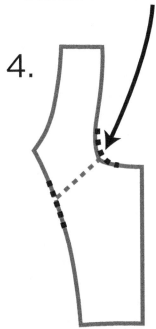

4.

"Go to zero" means where the correction stops.

If the gaping issue is in the back instead of the front, follow the same correction, but apply it to the back panels.

Front Neck Gaping - Option 2

With Princess Seams from the Shoulder

A) Identifying the Issue - There is excess fabric along the front neckline. If there are additional draglines elsewhere on the garment which are pointing toward the bust, this is a sign that you may need a Full Bust Adjustment. See the bust corrections chapter to properly identify that fitting issue.

There is excess fabric along the front neckline, and the garment does not rest well against the body.

The neckline or princess seam shapes can vary per style, but the correction is the same. If the princess seam comes from the armhole, follow Option 1 in the previous correction.

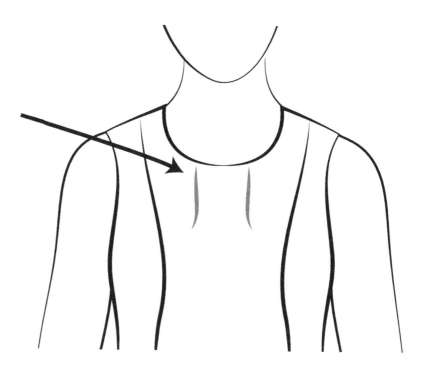

B) Pinning the Sample - Pin the fabric together along the front princess seams until the excess at the neckline is removed.

You may pin on the front panel, side panel, or both. Pin on both right and left sides of the garment for the correct amounts. Measure the amount you pinned.

You may need to continue pinning all the way up to the shoulder seam.

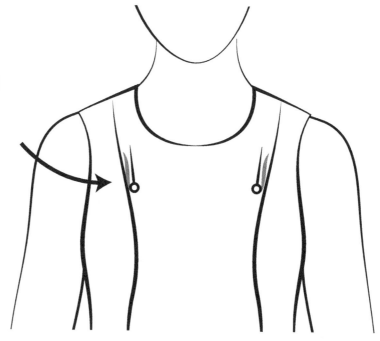

With Princess Seams from the Shoulder *(continued)*

C) Correcting the Pattern - First, compare the neck widths of the front and back pattern pieces. If the front neck is wider than the back, reduce it so it is the same or smaller than the back. See this correction on pages 73-74.

1.

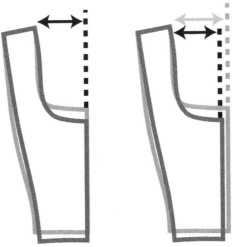

Correct Examples:

The front neck width should be the same or smaller than the back width. Consider half of the zipper/placket width as explained on page 73. The light grey lines show the back panel, and the dark grey lines show the front panel.

This may already solve the fitting issue. Re-cut the panel you updated and fit it again. If the gaping still occurs, move to the next steps.

Mark the exact area where you pinned the sample with the same amount that you measured. Go to zero at the apex and shoulder seam, or where you stopped pinning.

If you pinned both the front and side panel on the fitting sample, you will mark both panels.

If you pinned only one panel, you will mark only the side you pinned.

If you pinned at the shoulder seam too, mark the amount there. You would then need to adjust the back shoulder seam to match the new shoulder length.

2.

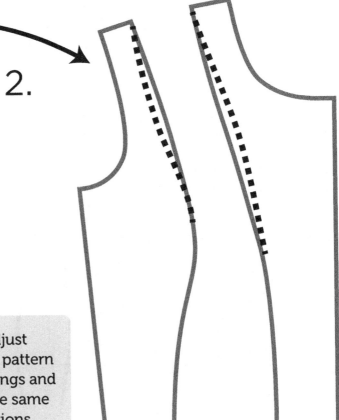

Remember: Adjust corresponding pattern pieces, like facings and linings, with the same pattern corrections.

Horizontal Draglines at the Neck

Shoulder Slope Correction

A) Identifying the Issue - There are horizontal draglines on the front or back pattern near the neck. This is an indication that the shoulder slope of the pattern does not match the shoulder slope of your body.

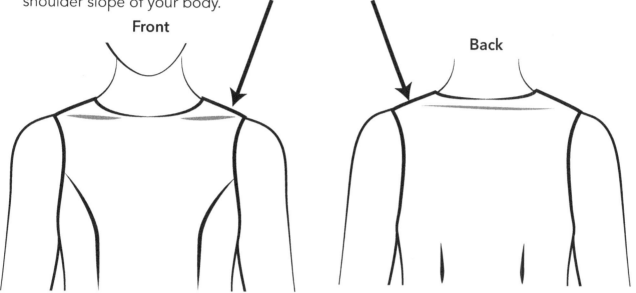

Front

Back

B) Cutting and Pinning the Sample - Cut along the shoulder seam, stopping before you come to the high point shoulder area. Allow the shoulder seam to open at the low point shoulder until the draglines disappear. Tape and pin it open. Measure the amount you opened.

Stop cutting at the high point shoulder (HPS).

Allow the low point shoulder (LPS) area to open up.

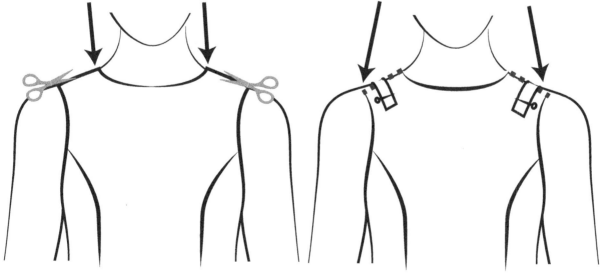

If the armhole feels too low, note the amount to raise it.

Horizontal Draglines at the Neck

Shoulder Slope Correction (*continued*)

C) Correcting the Pattern - Add to the shoulder slope at the LPS, reducing the angle. You may add to the front, back, or both, depending on how it looked when you opened the shoulder seam. If the seam falls more to the front, give more to the front and vice versa. In total, raise the shoulder seam at the LPS the amount you measured on the sample. True the armhole seams by aligning the front and back panels along the shoulder seams.

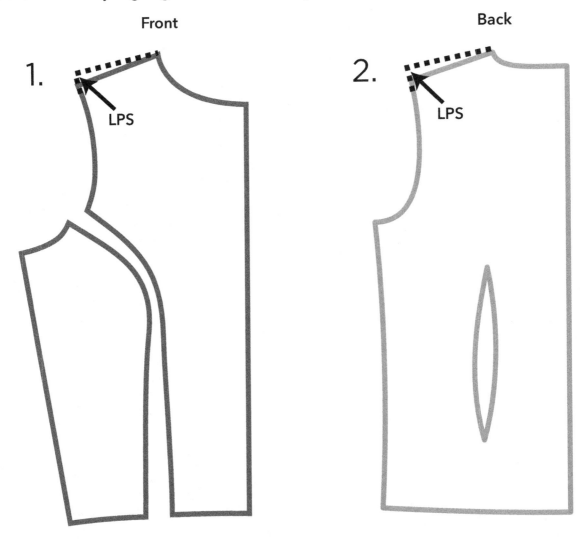

Front

Back

If there is a sleeve or if the armhole position felt too low on the fitting sample, follow the continued correction on the next page.

Horizontal Draglines at the Neck

Shoulder Slope Correction (continued)

C) Correcting the Pattern (continued) - After adding to the shoulder, the armhole became bigger. There are two options to make the sleeve fit into the new armhole. In Option 1 below, Slash & Spread the sleeve pattern to become bigger. Alternatively, in Option 2 below, raise the armhole to fit the previous sleeve. Choose the option you prefer based on the instructions below.

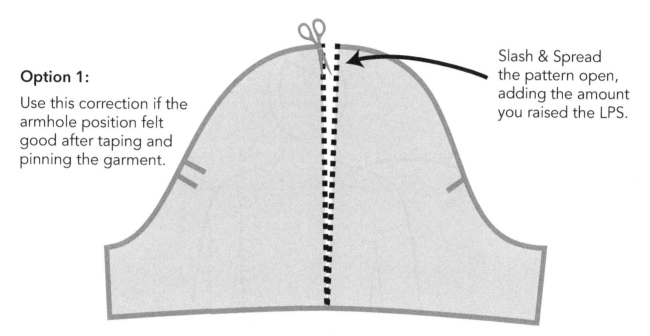

Option 1:

Use this correction if the armhole position felt good after taping and pinning the garment.

Slash & Spread the pattern open, adding the amount you raised the LPS.

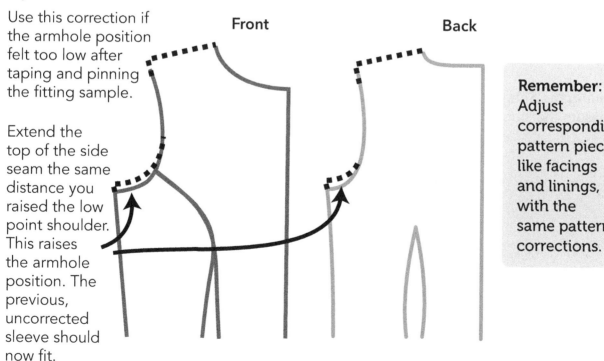

Option 2:

Use this correction if the armhole position felt too low after taping and pinning the fitting sample.

Extend the top of the side seam the same distance you raised the low point shoulder. This raises the armhole position. The previous, uncorrected sleeve should now fit.

Front

Back

Remember: Adjust corresponding pattern pieces, like facings and linings, with the same pattern corrections.

Back Neck Gaping

Start with Option 1 - Neck Width Update

There are two options for correcting back neck gaping. I suggest starting with Option 1 to correct the neck width first. Then, move on to Option 2 only if the fitting issue is still there after Option 1 is completed. If the garment has princess seams, follow the **"Front Neck Gaping"** correction found on pages 75-76 but apply the correction to the back pieces.

A) Identifying the Issue - There is excess fabric along the back neck area, causing gaping.

There is excess fabric at the back neck, and the garment does not rest close to the body.

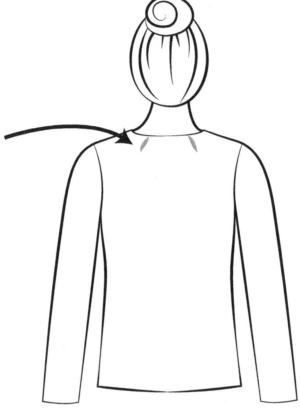

B) Pinning the Sample - Option 1 - Pin the back neckline where it is gaping. Measure the amount you pinned.

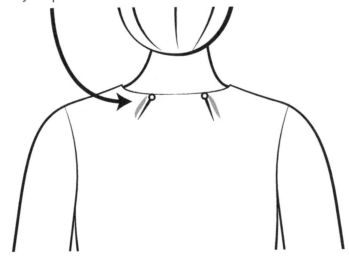

Back Neck Gaping

Option 1 - Neck Width Update *(continued)*

C) Correcting the Pattern - Option 1 - Compare the front and back neck widths. Consider half of the zipper or button placket width when comparing the front and back neck widths. When there is back neck gaping, make sure the back neck width is the **same** as the front neck width.

Align the high point shoulder on the front and back panels.

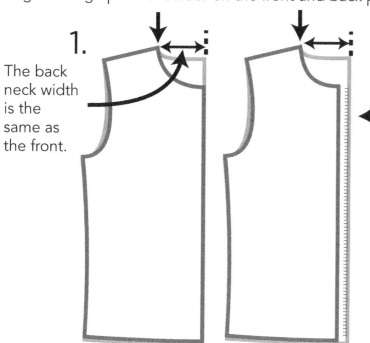

1.

The back neck width is the same as the front.

If there is a zipper or button placket at the front or center back, account for half of the zipper/placket width in the neck width. A sewn-in zipper can add about 3/16" (0.5 cm) to each side for a total of 3/8" (1 cm). Many people forget to consider this, and then gaping occurs. If there is an invisible zipper, do not account for this since the fabric kisses, and there is no gap.

If the back neck is wider than the front, reduce the back neck width and armhole along the shoulder seam. The back shoulder seam length should match the front shoulder seam length after the correction. If the amount you pinned was more than the amount you move the back neck width and armhole in, continue to Option 2.

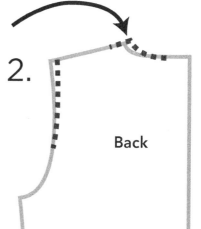

2.

Back

Important to Remember: Since you are working on half of the pattern, only account for half of the amount that you pinned in total.

Occasionally, you may make a back neck width smaller than the front neck width when customizing the pattern. However, this is less commonly done.

Neckline Corrections

Option 2 - Creating or Deepening a Dart (*continued after Option 1*)

If there is excess fabric in the back neck area after correcting the neck width, or if you pinned more than the amount you moved in the neck width in Option 1, continue with this correction. Add a dart at the back neck or shoulder area to achieve a nicer fitting neckline. If you already have a dart on the back neckline or shoulder seam, deepen it. This dart can always be shifted into design lines like yokes or princess seams.

B) Pinning the Sample - Option 2 - Choose a dart location. Pin where you want your dart to be, either at the neckline **or** at the shoulder seam.

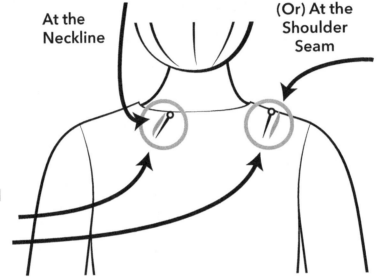

At the Neckline

(Or) At the Shoulder Seam

If you want the dart at the shoulder, you will likely need to open up the shoulder seam to pin the back area properly. If you do not open the shoulder seam, the front will pull, which is normal when the shoulder seam is still closed.

Notice the area where the gaping stops and sits well against the skin. This will be the length of the dart.

C) Correcting the Pattern - Option 2

Mark the corresponding area. Base the dart depth on how much you pinned.

For a shoulder dart location, add to the back shoulder seam length so the front and back shoulder seams still match after the dart has been closed. From the new LPS, draw a line the length of the dart that blends to the armhole seam.

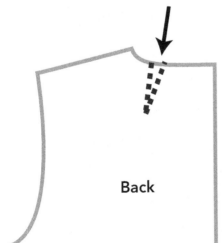

Back

Fold the dart closed, and use a pointed tracing wheel along the folded neckline or shoulder seam.

The dart may be integrated into design lines, such as a yoke, or kept as a dart.

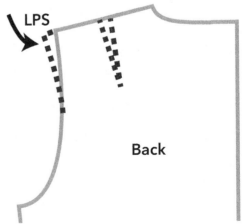

LPS

Back

Across Shoulder Corrections

Obtaining the correct shoulder width is critical in achieving a well-fitted garment. The first step is to locate your low point shoulder (LPS). The next step is to measure your across shoulder width from one LPS to the other LPS. Then, check your pattern width in comparison to your body measurement.

Each layer of clothing will have a different measurement for the across shoulder width to account for the different levels of ease for each layer worn underneath. The layers underneath will have smaller measurements, while the layers worn on top will have larger measurements.

Fashion trends can also drive the across shoulder width. If you think back to the 1980s, the trend was to have broad shoulders with shoulder pads to level out the shoulder slope. This gave a look of power to women in office settings as more and more women rose through the ranks in the workplace. The clothes we wear can contribute to our sense of confidence and affect the way others perceive us.

Other times when the shoulder width is oversized in fashion, it is called a dropped shoulder seam. This appearance gives a more comfortable look and feel. Sweatshirts and midlayers often have an overly dropped shoulder for the style, often in combination with a dolman or kimono sleeve.

As puff-capped sleeves come in and out of fashion, they can appear nicer with smaller shoulder widths, so the emphasis of the puff is not too big. As fashion silhouettes change, so will the shoulder width!

How To Find the Perfect Across Shoulder Width

Finding Your Low Point Shoulder (LPS)

How do you find your perfect across shoulder width? Many people overestimate this measurement and make it too long. The across shoulder measurement goes from one LPS to the other LPS. A shoulder width measurement goes from the HPS to the LPS, and it is also referred to as the shoulder seam length. The terminology can be frequently interchanged.

When you have the correct shoulder width for your body, you reduce draglines, increase comfort, and improve the range of movement for the arm.

Here's how to find your perfect width:

1. Feel your low point shoulder (LPS) by feeling your protruding shoulder tip bone. You may need to dig a little to find it. If you are having trouble locating the bone, follow your front collar bone all the way to the edge of your LPS. The shoulder tip (LPS) is at the end of the collar bone, and it protrudes up slightly. Another method is to bend your elbow, and place your hand on your hip. Some people can feel the bone more easily when the arm is in this position.

2. When you think you have found the low point shoulder, place your finger on the tip of the bone, and look in the mirror. Leaving your finger on the LPS, raise your arm 30-degrees. If the finger resting on the shoulder bone does not rise or lower as you move, you have found your low point shoulder. If your finger rises with the arm, you are too far.

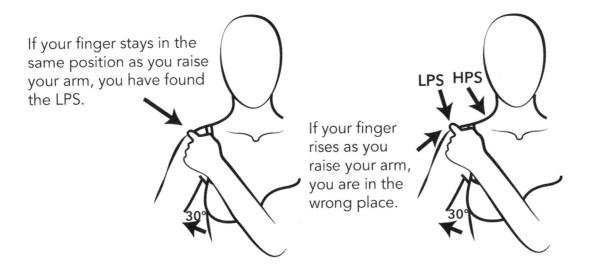

If your finger stays in the same position as you raise your arm, you have found the LPS.

If your finger rises as you raise your arm, you are in the wrong place.

LPS HPS

30°   30°

3. Mark the outer edge of the shoulder bone with a washable marker in the exact location on the left and right sides. Alternatively, use stickers or tape, and mark on that instead.

How To Measure Yourself

Finding Your Across Shoulder Width

1. If your measuring tape has a hole in the metal tip, loop about 3 yards/meters of ribbon through that hole. If your tape measure has no hole, make a very small hole with the point of a pair of scissors. Loop ribbon through the hole, as shown in the photo on the right.

2. Stand in front of a mirror. Whenever self-measuring or self-fitting, this is something I always suggest.

3. Mark your shoulder tips as shown on the previous page.

4. Place a piece of adhesive tape on the end of your measuring tape, and adhere it to one side of your low point shoulder (LPS) where you marked.

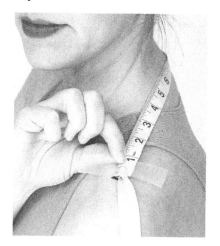 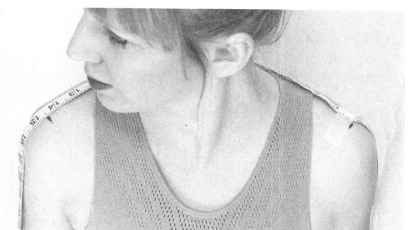

5. Place the measuring tape along your back shoulders until it comes to the other marked side. Hold the ribbon with one hand and the tape measure with the other hand down by your side.

6. Take a breath in and out and relax your shoulders.

7. Very carefully and without moving your shoulders, look down at your measurement. If you cannot see it, look in the mirror to see the measurement. Do not twist your spine too much when checking the measurement since this will change the result.

8. This is a good starting point for the across shoulder width on knit shirts. Add 1/4" (0.6 cm) of ease to this measurement for woven shirts. Use this measurement to compare to the pattern's measurements. For each additional layer of clothing like sweaters, jackets, and coats, add ease to account for the fullness of the garments worn underneath.

This point of measure (POM) is called the **"Across Shoulder"** because it is the total width of your shoulders across the whole body. When comparing this measurement to a pattern that is only half of the garment, take half of the measurement. See page 15 for the location to measure on the pattern.

Shoulders Too Wide

Making the Shoulders Smaller on the Garment - Options 1 & 2

There are two pattern correction options to reduce wide shoulders on your garment. Steps (A) and (B) are the same for both options. Both options of correcting the pattern are shown on the following pages.

A) Identifying the Issue - The armhole seam hangs too far past the low point shoulder tip (LPS). It may feel like the shoulders are too wide, or it may look like they are too wide.

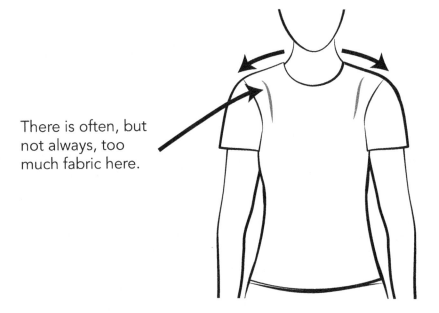

There is often, but not always, too much fabric here.

B) Pinning the Sample - Pin the across shoulder area at the LPS until you are happy with the location of the armhole seam. Pin the back armhole the same way to make the adjustment on both the front and the back panels.

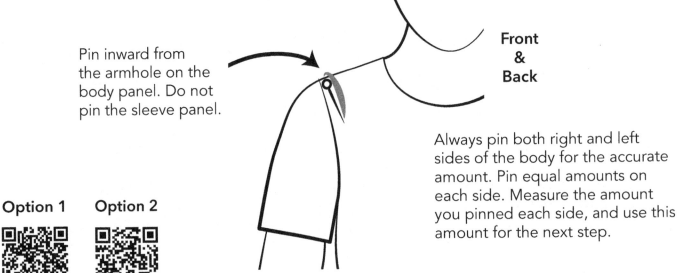

Pin inward from the armhole on the body panel. Do not pin the sleeve panel.

Front & Back

Always pin both right and left sides of the body for the accurate amount. Pin equal amounts on each side. Measure the amount you pinned each side, and use this amount for the next step.

Option 1   Option 2

Shoulders Too Wide

Making the Shoulders Smaller on the Garment - Option 1 *(continued)*

This correction is great if you do not want to alter the armhole and sleeve. However, the downside is that the shoulder slope is slightly modified for the angle. Reducing more than 3/8" (1 cm) on each side could create new fitting issues due to the change of the shoulder slope. Consider doing Option 2 if you need to reduce more than 3/8" (1 cm).

C) Correcting the Pattern - Option 1 - To properly take in the shoulder, cut the pattern as shown.

1. The same correction must be done on both the front and the back panels. Mark the pattern with a straight line starting about 1/3 of the way from the LPS along the shoulder seam. This longer line goes to the across front and back areas at the curve of the armhole.

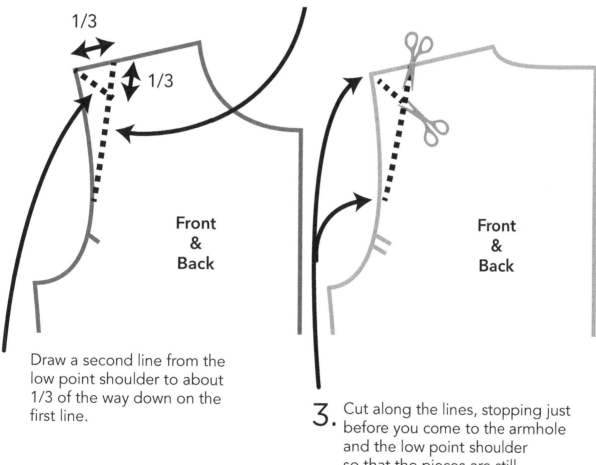

Draw a second line from the low point shoulder to about 1/3 of the way down on the first line.

3. Cut along the lines, stopping just before you come to the armhole and the low point shoulder so that the pieces are still connected. This is the beginning of the Slash & Close correction.

(continued on next page)

Shoulders Too Wide

Making the Shoulders Smaller on the Garment - Option 1 *(continued)*

C) Correcting the Pattern - Option 1 *(continued)* - Continue the Slash & Close correction on both the front and back pattern pieces.

4. Overlap the pattern along the longer cut line the same amount you pinned the fitting sample. This is closing the pattern and reducing the wide shoulder width.

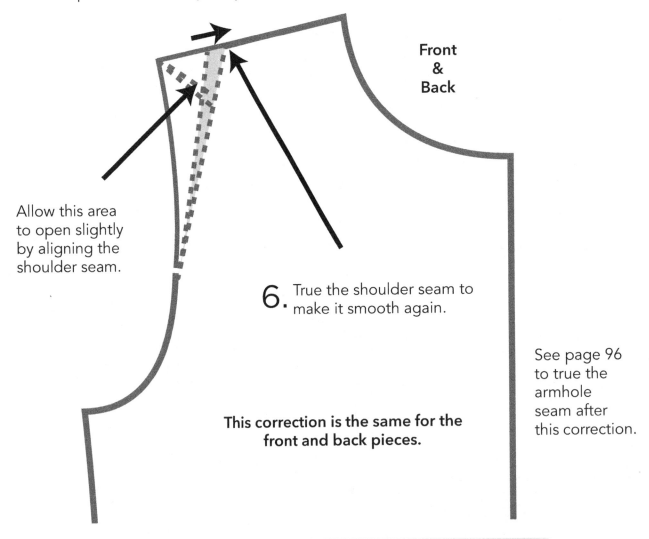

Front
&
Back

Allow this area to open slightly by aligning the shoulder seam.

6. True the shoulder seam to make it smooth again.

See page 96 to true the armhole seam after this correction.

This correction is the same for the front and back pieces.

For this correction, a sleeve correction is not required since the armhole measurement remains the same.

Shoulders Too Wide

Making the Shoulders Smaller on the Garment
Option 2 *(continued from page 88)*

This correction is used if you do not want to alter the angle of the shoulder slope. However, the downside is that the sleeve requires a minor correction because the armhole is slightly increased. This is my preferred method.

C) Correcting the Pattern - Option 2 - Draw a new armhole position to reflect the new across shoulder measurement. This is the same amount you pinned the fitting sample.

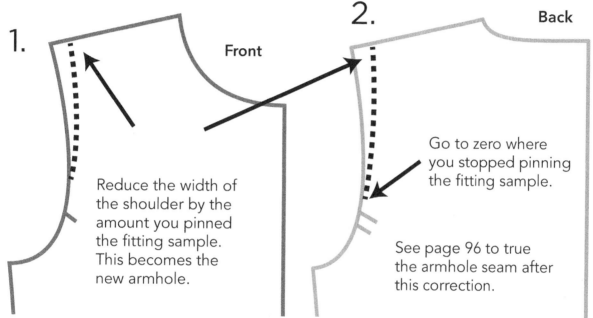

1.

Front

2.

Back

Reduce the width of the shoulder by the amount you pinned the fitting sample. This becomes the new armhole.

Go to zero where you stopped pinning the fitting sample.

See page 96 to true the armhole seam after this correction.

Across Shoulder Corrections

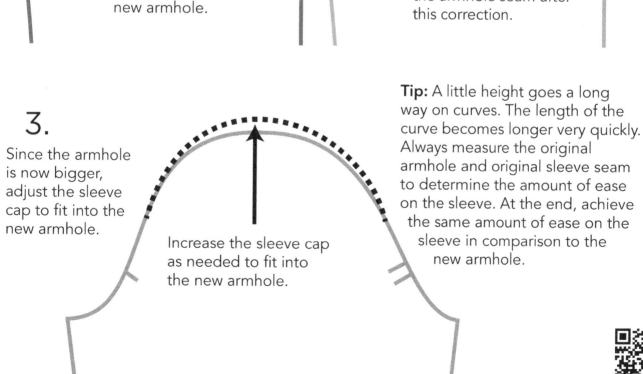

3.

Since the armhole is now bigger, adjust the sleeve cap to fit into the new armhole.

Increase the sleeve cap as needed to fit into the new armhole.

Tip: A little height goes a long way on curves. The length of the curve becomes longer very quickly. Always measure the original armhole and original sleeve seam to determine the amount of ease on the sleeve. At the end, achieve the same amount of ease on the sleeve in comparison to the new armhole.

Shoulders Too Narrow

Making the Shoulders Wider on the Garment - Options 1 & 2

This is also called a broad shoulder adjustment. There are two pattern correction options to increase the across shoulder measurement on your garment. Steps (A) and (B) are the same for both options. Both options for correcting the pattern are shown on the following pages.

A) Identifying the Issue - The armhole seam lies too high on the shoulder area. The armhole seam does not rest on the low point shoulder tip (LPS).

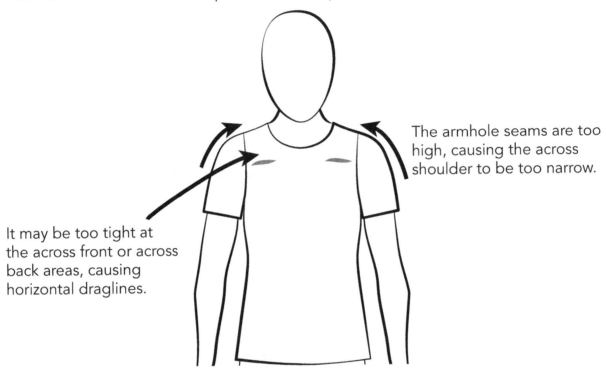

The armhole seams are too high, causing the across shoulder to be too narrow.

It may be too tight at the across front or across back areas, causing horizontal draglines.

B) Cutting the Sample - Cut the armhole at the LPS until you are happy with the location of the armhole seam. Cut the back armhole the same way to make the adjustment to both the front and the back panels. Tape it open, and measure the amount you opened.

Carefully move your arm around to feel the movement of the sleeve and shoulder area. You should be able to move comfortably.

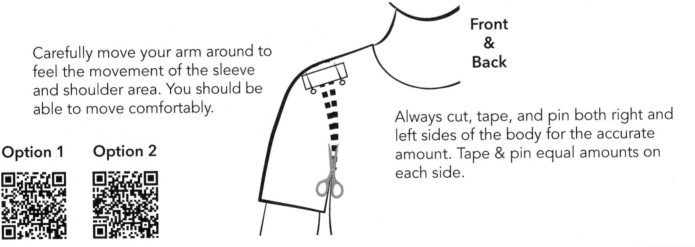

Front & Back

Always cut, tape, and pin both right and left sides of the body for the accurate amount. Tape & pin equal amounts on each side.

Option 1   **Option 2**

Shoulders Too Narrow

Making the Shoulders Wider on the Garment - Option 1
(continued)

This correction is great if you do not want to alter the armhole and sleeve. However, the downside is that the angle of the shoulder slope is slightly modified. Increasing more than 3/8" (1 cm) on each side could create new fitting issues due to the change of the shoulder slope. Consider doing Option 2 if you need to increase more than 3/8" (1 cm).

C) Correcting the Pattern - Option 1 - To properly increase the shoulder, cut the pattern as shown.

1. The same correction must be done on both the front and the back panels. Mark the pattern with a straight line starting about 1/3 of the way from the LPS along the shoulder seam. This longer line goes to the across front and back areas at the curve of the armhole.

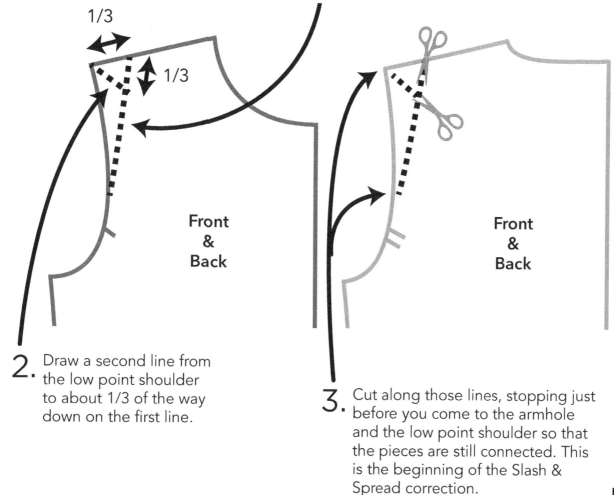

2. Draw a second line from the low point shoulder to about 1/3 of the way down on the first line.

3. Cut along those lines, stopping just before you come to the armhole and the low point shoulder so that the pieces are still connected. This is the beginning of the Slash & Spread correction.

(continued on next page)

Making the Shoulders Wider on the Garment - Option 1
(continued)

C) Correcting the Pattern - Option 1 *(continued)* - Continue the Slash & Spread correction on both the front and back pattern pieces.

4. Slash & Spread (cut and open) the pattern along the longer cut line the same amount you opened the sample. This is spreading the pattern and increasing the width of the shoulders on the pattern.

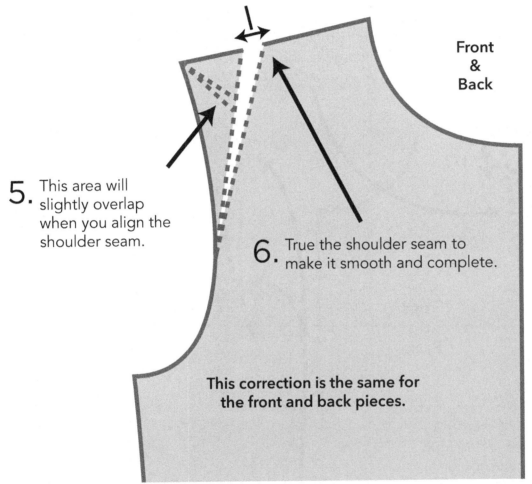

Front & Back

5. This area will slightly overlap when you align the shoulder seam.

6. True the shoulder seam to make it smooth and complete.

This correction is the same for the front and back pieces.

See page 96 to true the armhole seam after this correction.

For this correction, a sleeve correction is not required since the armhole measurement remains the same.

Shoulders Too Narrow

Making the Shoulders Wider on the Garment - Option 2
(continued from page 92)

This correction is used if you do not want to alter the angle of the shoulder slope. However, the downside is that the sleeve requires a minor correction because the armhole is slightly decreased. This is my preferred method.

C) Correcting the Pattern - Option 2 - Draw a new armhole position to reflect the new across shoulder measurement.

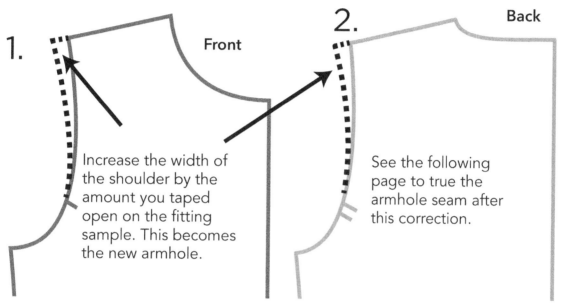

1. Front

Increase the width of the shoulder by the amount you taped open on the fitting sample. This becomes the new armhole.

2. Back

See the following page to true the armhole seam after this correction.

3.

Since the armhole is now smaller, adjust the sleeve cap to fit into the new armhole:

Slash & Close by overlapping the pattern the amount needed to fit into the new armhole.

Tip: Before the correction is made, measure the original armhole and original sleeve seam to determine the amount of ease on the sleeve. After the correction, achieve the same amount of ease on the sleeve in comparison to the new armhole.

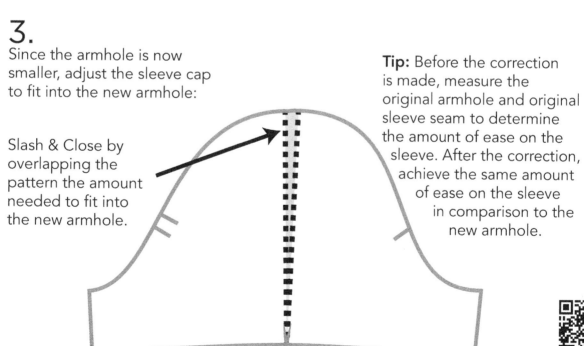

Across Shoulder Corrections

True the Armhole

After Any Shoulder Seam Correction

After you make a pattern correction to a seam that is sewn to an adjacent piece, always align the seams. The seam lengths must match. True the seams, making them continuous.

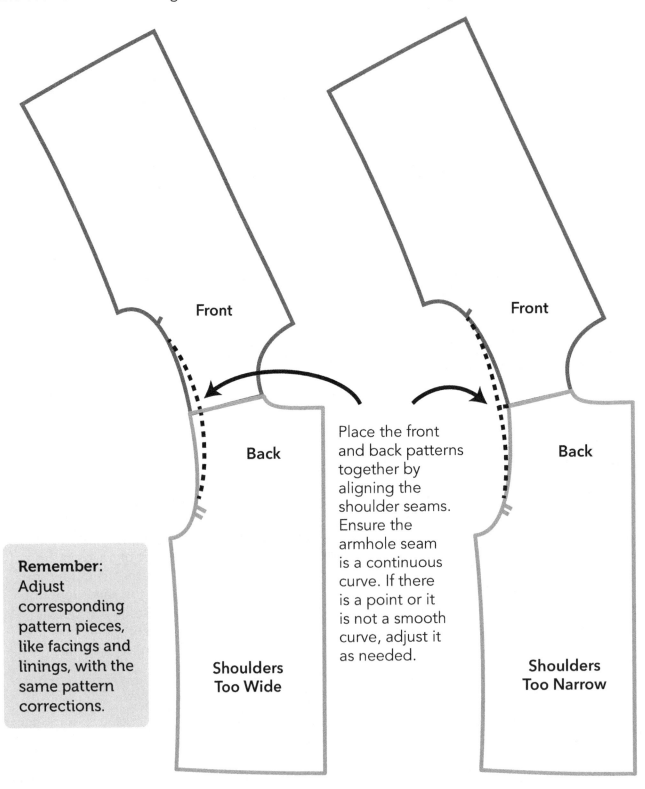

Front

Back

Place the front and back patterns together by aligning the shoulder seams. Ensure the armhole seam is a continuous curve. If there is a point or it is not a smooth curve, adjust it as needed.

Front

Back

Remember: Adjust corresponding pattern pieces, like facings and linings, with the same pattern corrections.

Shoulders Too Wide

Shoulders Too Narrow

Across Front & Across Back Corrections

The across front and across back refer to the measurements of the body from one armhole to the other armhole across the body. It affects the armhole shape and corresponds to the width of the body.

Since every person has a different shape, these two points of measure can vary significantly from person to person. The bust size and the rib cage also play a role in the amount of ease needed at the across front and across back to achieve ample movement of the arms.

To measure your body for the across front and across back points of measure, start from the crease of the armpit, and measure from one side of the body to the other. However, these positions can have various amounts of ease depending on the style pattern. Ease amounts and fabric characteristics play a huge role in obtaining the right fit. Therefore, unless you are making your patterns, skip the body measurements and base the corrections from the fitting samples.

If you are interested in learning all my techniques about how to measure yourself, my comprehensive patternmaking course covers this topic. Find out more at www.GRDMethod.com or through the QR code below.

Just a note: The most common corrections I have done in menswear have been the across back corrections shown in this chapter. Men, especially, want to have ample movement in the arms and back area!

Across Front Too Big

Reducing the Front Width from Armhole to Armhole

This correction is used when the across front on your garment is too big, but you are pleased with the placement of the shoulder seams. If the shoulders are also too big, you may make this correction in conjunction with the **"Shoulders Too Wide - Option 2"** correction on pages 88 and 91.

A) Identifying the Issue - The across front area feels or looks too big.

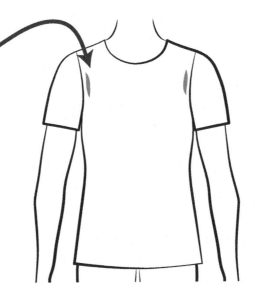

If it is too big at the across front area, you may have vertical draglines. The garment may feel too big when you move. Vertical draglines can indicate that the garment is too loose in that area.

B) Pinning the Sample - Pin the excess fabric at the across front area until you are happy with the way the garment feels when you move around.

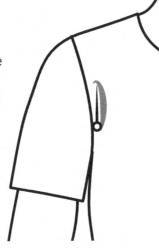

After you pinned the garment, carefully move your arm to see if you still have your preferred range of motion. If you cannot move around well, reduce the pinned amount until you are comfortable.

Always pin both right and left sides of the body for the accurate amount. Pin equal amounts on each side. Measure the amount you pinned on each side, and use this amount for the next step.

Across Front Too Big

Reducing the Front Width from Armhole to Armhole (*continued*)

C) Correcting the Pattern - Reduce the across front area at the armhole the same amount you pinned. This will make the across front smaller.

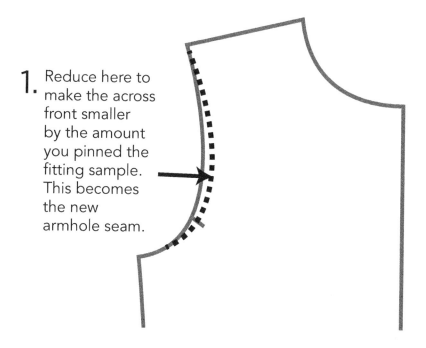

1. Reduce here to make the across front smaller by the amount you pinned the fitting sample. This becomes the new armhole seam.

Tip: Before the correction is made, measure the original armhole and original sleeve seam to determine the amount of ease on the sleeve. After the correction, achieve the same amount of ease on the sleeve in comparison to the new armhole.

Since this correction will enlarge the armhole slightly, you may need to adjust the sleeve. Follow this placement for a Slash & Spread correction.

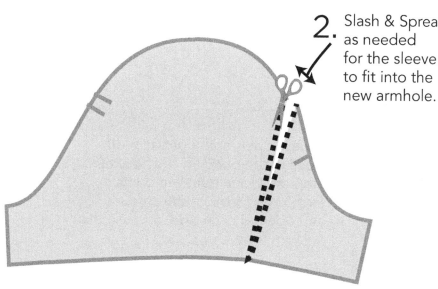

2. Slash & Spread as needed for the sleeve to fit into the new armhole.

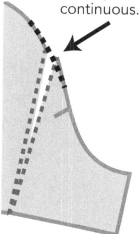

3. True the sleeve cap seam, making it complete and continuous.

Increasing the Front Width from Armhole to Armhole

This correction is used when the across front on your garment is too tight, but you are pleased with the placement of the shoulder seams. If the shoulders are also too narrow, you may make this correction in conjunction with the **"Shoulders Too Narrow - Option 2"** correction on pages 92 and 95.

A) Identifying the Issue - The across front feels or looks too small.

If it is too tight at the across front area, you may have horizontal draglines. The garment may feel too small when you move. Horizontal draglines can indicate that the garment is too tight.

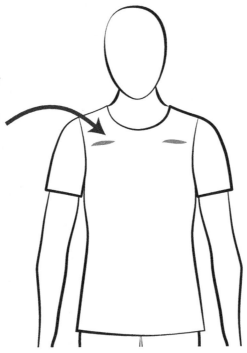

B) Pinning and Taping the Sample - Cut open the across front area at the armhole seams. When you are happy with the way the garment feels, tape and pin it in place.

After you taped and pinned the fitting sample, carefully move your arm to see if you have your preferred range of motion. If you cannot move around well, increase the opened amount until you are comfortable.

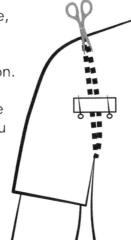

Always open both right and left sides of the body for the accurate amount. Open equal amounts on each side. Measure the amount you opened each side, and use this amount for the next step.

Across Front Too Small

Increasing the Front Width from Armhole to Armhole (continued)

C) Correcting the Pattern - Add to the across front area at the armhole the same amount you opened the fitting sample. This will make the across front larger.

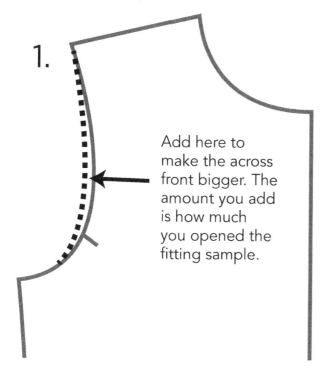

1.

Add here to make the across front bigger. The amount you add is how much you opened the fitting sample.

Tip: Before the correction is made, measure the original armhole and original sleeve seam to determine the amount of ease on the sleeve. After the correction, achieve the same amount of ease on the sleeve in comparison to the new armhole.

Since this correction will reduce the armhole slightly, you may need to adjust the sleeve. Follow this placement for a Slash & Close correction.

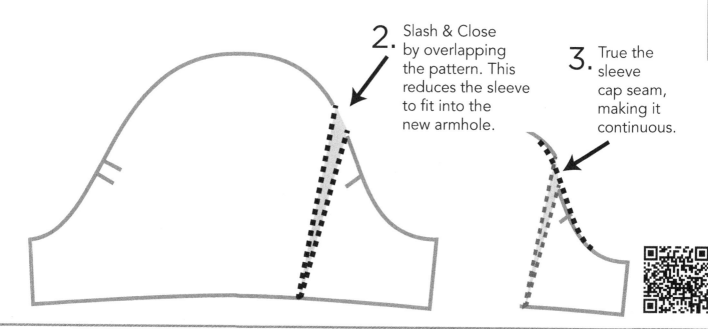

2. Slash & Close by overlapping the pattern. This reduces the sleeve to fit into the new armhole.

3. True the sleeve cap seam, making it continuous.

Reducing the Back Width from Armhole to Armhole

If the shoulders are also too big, you may make this correction in conjunction with the **"Shoulders Too Wide - Option 2"** correction on pages 88 and 91.

A) Identifying the Issue - The across back has excess fabric, or there is too much fabric when you reach forward.

There is excess fabric in the back area, and you do not need it to move comfortably. There may be vertical draglines.

B) Pinning the Sample - Pin the excess fabric at the across back area until you are happy with the way the garment feels when you move around. Carefully move your arm to see if you still have your preferred range of motion. If you cannot move around well, reduce the amount pinned until you are comfortable.

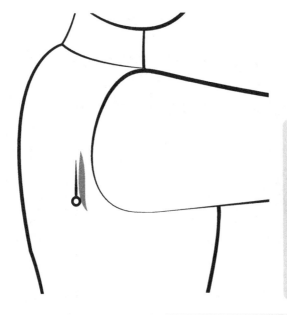

Always pin both right and left sides of the body for the accurate amount. Pin equal amounts on each side.

Tip: Before the correction is made, measure the original armhole and original sleeve seam on the patterns to determine the amount of ease on your sleeve. After the correction, achieve the same amount of ease on the sleeve in comparison to the new armhole.

Across Back Too Big

Reducing the Back Width from Armhole to Armhole
(continued)

C) Correcting the Pattern - Reduce the across back the same amount you pinned the fitting sample.

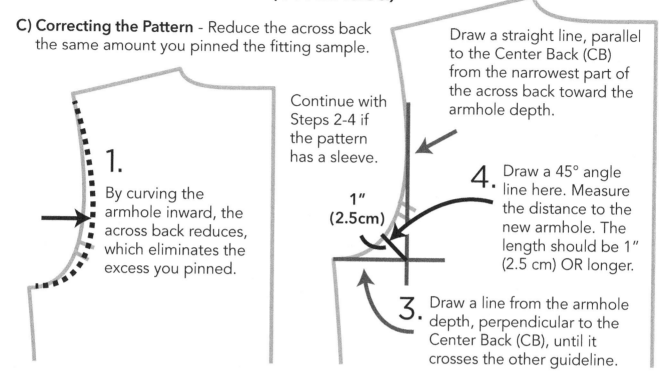

1. By curving the armhole inward, the across back reduces, which eliminates the excess you pinned.

Continue with Steps 2-4 if the pattern has a sleeve.

1"
(2.5cm)

Draw a straight line, parallel to the Center Back (CB) from the narrowest part of the across back toward the armhole depth.

4. Draw a 45° angle line here. Measure the distance to the new armhole. The length should be 1" (2.5 cm) OR longer.

3. Draw a line from the armhole depth, perpendicular to the Center Back (CB), until it crosses the other guideline.

The 45-degree Angle Rule: As shown in steps 2-4, achieve a 1" (2.5 cm) minimum for the 45-degree angle line when there is a sleeve. If there is no sleeve, the rule does not apply. In some patterns, the angle will not be exactly 45-degrees. Take the middle point between the guidelines for your angled line. You may break the rule for customized patterns, but it may restrict your arm movement.

Since this correction will enlarge the armhole slightly, you may need to adjust the sleeve to fit into the new armhole. Follow this placement for a Slash & Spread correction.

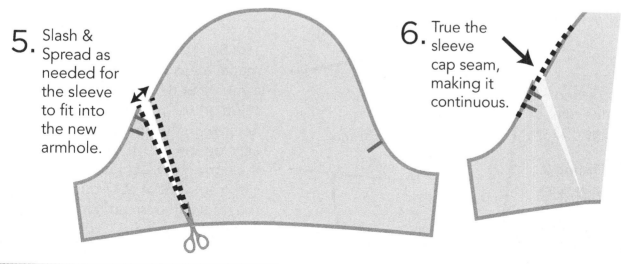

5. Slash & Spread as needed for the sleeve to fit into the new armhole.

6. True the sleeve cap seam, making it continuous.

Across Back Too Small

Increasing the Back Width from Armhole to Armhole - Options 1 & 2

There are several options for increasing the across back area. The following pages show the different options to choose from. Some corrections given are with design lines like yokes or CB seams. Choose the option you would like to try. Steps (A) and (B) are the same for Options 1 and 2.

A) Identifying the Issue - The across back feels too small, and it is tight when you reach forward.

There is excessive pulling across the back. It is too tight to move comfortably.

If you notice the back chest level is also too tight, see the correction on pages 109-110.

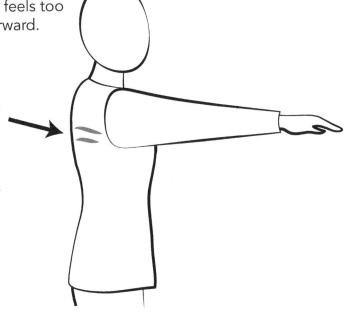

B) Cutting and Taping the Sample - Cut open the across back area at the armhole seams. Tape and pin it in place. Move around carefully to see how the garment feels. Adjust the amount opened, if necessary, to allow more movement.

Always open both right and left sides of the body for the accurate amount. Open equal amounts on each side.

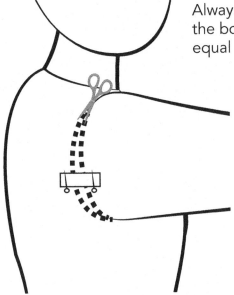

The Option 1 video begins with the rule shown on page 103.

Tip: Before the correction is made, measure the original armhole and original sleeve seam on the patterns to determine the amount of ease on the sleeve. After the correction, achieve the same amount of ease on the sleeve in comparison to the new armhole.

Option 1   Option 2

Across Back Too Small

Increasing the Back Width from Armhole to Armhole - Option 1 *(continued)*

This is the easiest option. It involves adding to the across back area at the armhole and to the sleeve for more movement. If the shoulders are also too narrow, you may make this correction in conjunction with the "**Shoulders Too Narrow - Option 2**" correction on pages 92 and 95.

C) Correcting the Pattern - Option 1 - Add to the across back the same amount you opened the fitting sample.

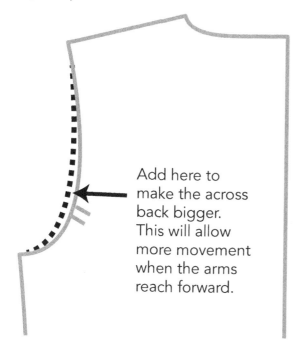

Add here to make the across back bigger. This will allow more movement when the arms reach forward.

Tip: Check the 45-degree Angle Rule shown on page 103. Achieve the 1" (2.5 cm) minimum distance for garments with sleeves.

Since this correction will reduce the armhole slightly, you may need to adjust the sleeve. If needed, do a Slash & Close correction.

Mark the pattern in this area, and Slash & Close it by overlapping the pattern for it to fit into the new armhole.

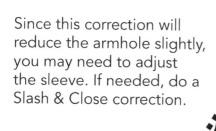

If you opened an excessive amount on the fitting sample, you could give some to the sleeve. This would distribute the amount you opened between both the sleeve and armhole, so the armhole does not become a strange shape.

Across Front & Across Back Corrections

Option 2 - Adding a Back Yoke and Pleats
(*continued from page 104*)

This option adds a yoke seam and pleats to allow for the movement of the across back and arms. This is a great option to obtain more movement, plus it is a nice design detail.

C) Correcting the Pattern - Option 2 - Add a yoke and pleats to allow for more movement.

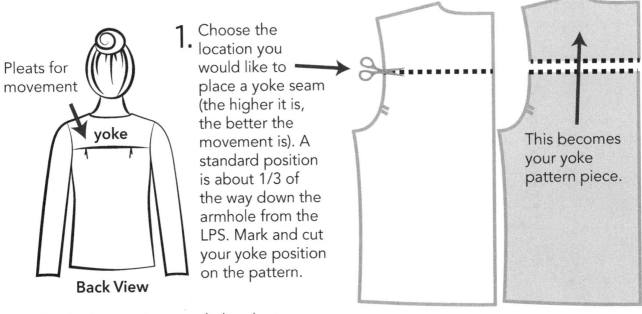

1. Choose the location you would like to place a yoke seam (the higher it is, the better the movement is). A standard position is about 1/3 of the way down the armhole from the LPS. Mark and cut your yoke position on the pattern.

Pleats for movement

yoke

Back View

This becomes your yoke pattern piece.

2. On the lower piece, mark the pleat position with a line down to the hem, leaving the bottom connected. The position can be 1/3 to 1/2 of the yoke seam length from the armhole.

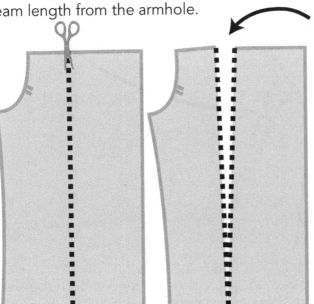

3. Slash & Spread the desired pleat depth. I suggest a minimum pleat depth of about 1/2" (1.3 cm) which is 1" (2.5 cm) total. The amount you opened the fitting sample is the minimum amount of your total pleat.

4. Draw the new pattern piece, accounting for the pleat. Mark the yoke seam with notches to indicate your pleat location.

The fold direction of the pleat.

Across Back Too Small

Option 3 - Adding a CB Seam for Movement

A) Identifying the Issue - The across back area is too tight. You may have back wrinkles or draglines indicating that it is too tight, you may have difficulty moving in the garment, or the garment may not feel right.

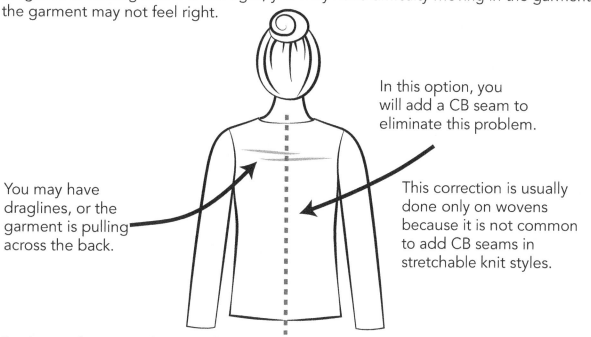

In this option, you will add a CB seam to eliminate this problem.

You may have draglines, or the garment is pulling across the back.

This correction is usually done only on wovens because it is not common to add CB seams in stretchable knit styles.

B) Cutting and Pinning the Sample - Choose the option below based on where the back neckline is lying.

Option 3A: Use this correction if you are happy with where the center back neckline sits. Cut a vertical slit at center back, near your shoulder blades.

Option 3B: Use this correction if the center back neckline sits too low or if the CB hemline is hiking up. Cut horizontally across the center back, perpendicular to your shoulder blades.

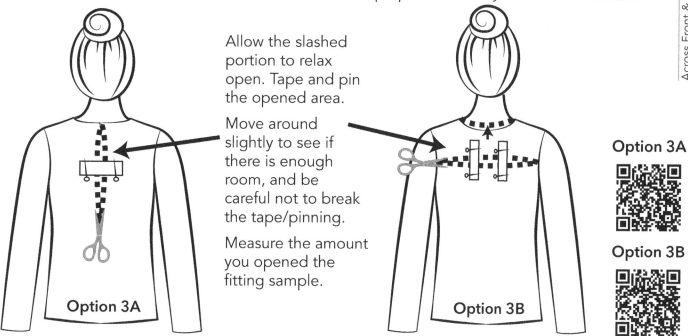

Allow the slashed portion to relax open. Tape and pin the opened area.

Move around slightly to see if there is enough room, and be careful not to break the tape/pinning.

Measure the amount you opened the fitting sample.

Option 3A

Option 3B

Option 3 - Adding a CB Seam for Movement (continued)

C) Correcting the Pattern - Option 3A - If the back neckline was sitting nicely, this is the correction to follow. Mark the pattern the same amount you opened the sample.

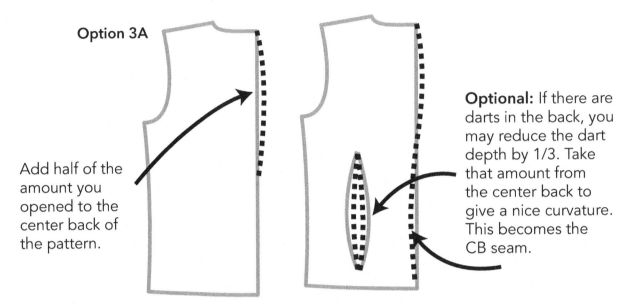

Option 3A

Add half of the amount you opened to the center back of the pattern.

Optional: If there are darts in the back, you may reduce the dart depth by 1/3. Take that amount from the center back to give a nice curvature. This becomes the CB seam.

C) Correcting the Pattern - Option 3B - If the back neckline is too low or the hemline is hiking up, this is the correction to follow. This is a Slash & Spread pattern correction. Cut horizontally from the center back, stopping just before you are at the armhole. Spread the amount you opened the fitting sample.

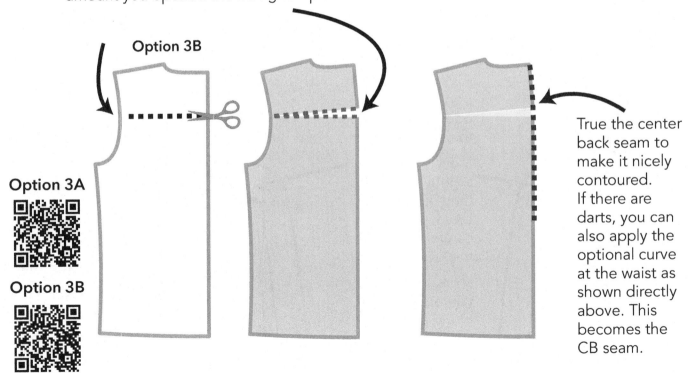

Option 3B

Option 3A

Option 3B

True the center back seam to make it nicely contoured. If there are darts, you can also apply the optional curve at the waist as shown directly above. This becomes the CB seam.

Across Back and Back Chest Level Too Tight

Increasing the Back Width

A) Identifying the Issue - The lower across back area and back chest/bust level are too tight or small. This can limit forward arm movement and feel tight in the across back and back area at the level of the chest/bust. The back chest/bust level refers to the lower back area below the armhole position and at the same level as the chest/bust circumference. This is a very common fitting correction in menswear.

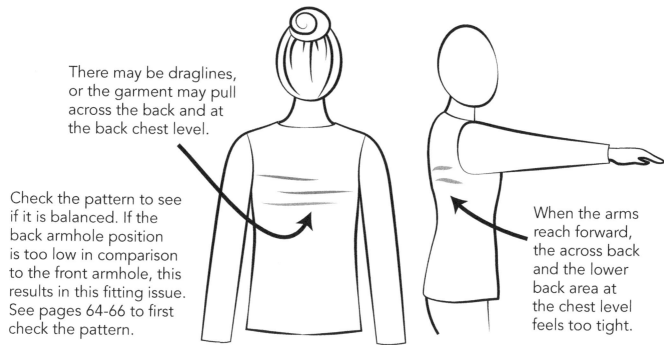

There may be draglines, or the garment may pull across the back and at the back chest level.

Check the pattern to see if it is balanced. If the back armhole position is too low in comparison to the front armhole, this results in this fitting issue. See pages 64-66 to first check the pattern.

When the arms reach forward, the across back and the lower back area at the chest level feels too tight.

B) Cutting and Pinning the Sample - Cut vertically at the center back area where the shoulder blades and center of the chest are. Stop before you come to the waist.

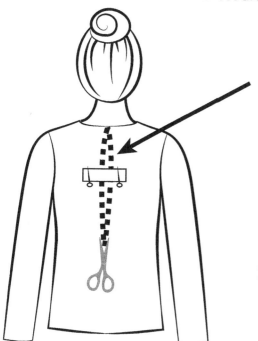

Allow the garment to open as needed so it is relaxed. Tape and pin the amount opened.

Move around slightly to see if there is enough room for movement, and be careful not to break the tape/pinning.

Measure the amount you opened the sample.

Tip: Check the 45-degree Angle Rule shown on page 103. Achieve the 1" (2.5 cm) minimum distance for garments with sleeves.

Increasing the Back Width (continued)

C) Correcting the Pattern - This is a Slash & Spread pattern correction. Cut the pattern as shown, about 2" (5 cm) below the armhole and about 2" (5 cm) up the shoulder seam. The exact location does not matter.

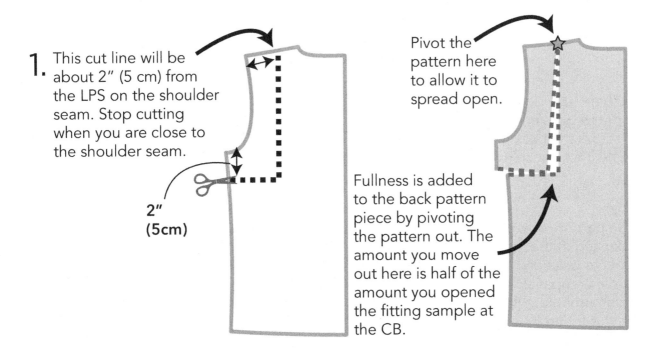

1. This cut line will be about 2" (5 cm) from the LPS on the shoulder seam. Stop cutting when you are close to the shoulder seam.

2" (5cm)

Pivot the pattern here to allow it to spread open.

Fullness is added to the back pattern piece by pivoting the pattern out. The amount you move out here is half of the amount you opened the fitting sample at the CB.

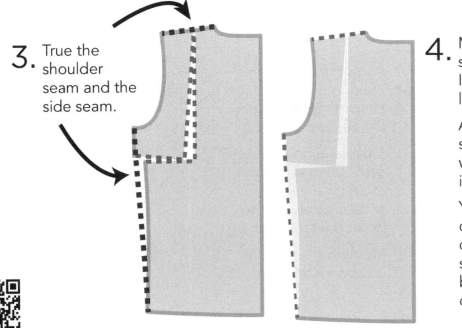

3. True the shoulder seam and the side seam.

4. Measure the new side seam on the back panel. It will likely become longer from pivoting out.

Add to the front side seam length at the waistline or hemline if needed.

You will notice that this correction breaks the rule of having mirrored side seams. It is acceptable to break the rules when you customize patterns.

Armhole & Raglan Sleeve Corrections

The infamous armhole - the woe of so many fitting issues! Why is it so tricky to achieve a nice fit along the armholes? Well, if you are using commercial or indie patterns, or if you are creating patterns with industry standard methods, you will likely run into fitting issues. The reason is due to the huge variance of body shapes, and the standard patterns simply cannot accommodate for the differences.

To really achieve a perfect armhole from the beginning, start with making a Moulage with The GRD Method™. This method gives you specific dart depths based on your body measurements, giving you accurate dart amounts in the areas where you need shaping. It is the only Moulage flat-pattern technique that is not based on industry standards for the dart depths and shoulder slopes.

However, when you find that perfect design in a commercial or an indie pattern and you have to make it, then it could be that these armhole corrections are just what you are looking for. The wonderful thing about making pattern corrections is that you can customize your patterns at any stage, as you have learned from the customization scale.

Throughout this book, remember: adjust corresponding pattern pieces, like facings and linings, with the same pattern corrections.

Let's jump right into the big armhole topic, and achieve the customized fit you desire!

Armhole Position Differences

Sleeveless Tops Versus Tops with Sleeves

Below are some of the main differences between a sleeveless top and a top with sleeves. A sleeveless top may also be called a tank top. The dotted line shows a top with sleeves. The solid line shows an example of a sleeveless top.

The necklines vary based on the design.

Dotted Line = Top with Sleeves

The shoulder width, across front, and across back are usually smaller on a sleeveless top.

Sleeveless tops normally have a lower armhole depth, between 1/4" - 1/2" (0.6 cm-1.6 cm).

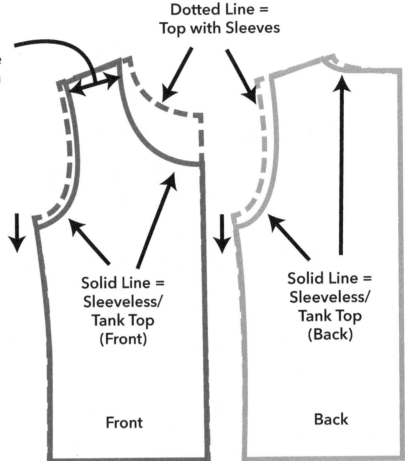

Solid Line = Sleeveless/ Tank Top (Front)

Solid Line = Sleeveless/ Tank Top (Back)

Front

Back

If you want to add a sleeve to a sleeveless top, raise the armhole and fill in the armhole area.

When adding a sleeve, always make a fitting sample to ensure the armhole position is in the correct location. This will allow you to check the fitting of the sleeve.

Armhole Gaping

Shoulder Slope Issue

There are many possible solutions for this issue, but this is the first correction to try. For garments with a princess seam or darts, or if you want to add a side dart in the garment, you may start with this correction. If it does not solve the issue, continue with the other options.

A) Identifying the Issue - The front armhole does not sit nicely against the body.

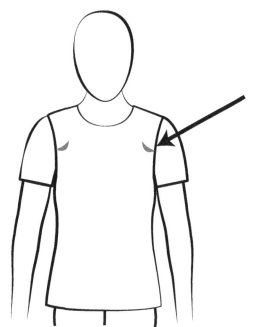

There is excess fabric at the front armhole, and the armhole does not rest well against the body.

When this issue exists, it is a sign that the front armhole should be reduced in length. The front armhole measurement is often shorter than the back armhole because the body can be more hollow in this area.

B) Pinning the Sample - Smooth the front fabric up toward the low point shoulder (LPS). Pin the excess on the front body panel only. Measure the amount you pinned. Stop pinning at the high point shoulder (HPS).

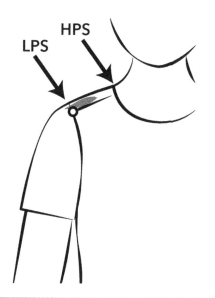

HPS

LPS

Note: If the garment does not look better after you pinned the shoulder slope, an alternative correction is to raise the front armhole only. If the front armhole is raised, the front reverse curve of the sleeve must also be raised, as shown on page 131. You could also add a side dart or princess seam to eliminate the excess. See the other options for more ideas.

Shoulder Slope Issue (*continued*)

C) Correcting the Pattern - Lower the front shoulder slope the amount you pinned the fitting sample. Draw the new shoulder slope. You will likely go to zero at the HPS, depending on how you pinned the garment.

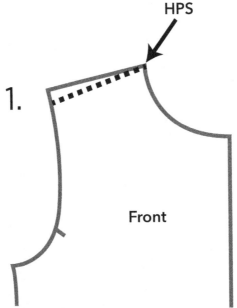

Since this correction reduces the armhole, adjust the sleeve to fit into the new armhole. To do this, use the Slash & Close method.

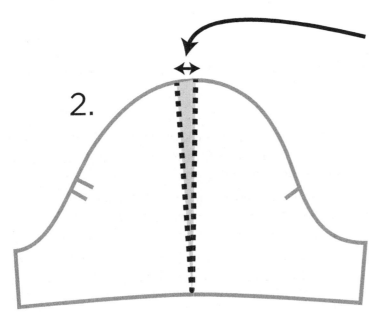

Mark the sleeve cap the same amount you lowered the shoulder slope. Draw two lines, going down to zero at the hem of the sleeve. Slash & Close the distance between the lines. True the sleeve cap seam, making it continuous.

After the correction, measure the armhole and sleeve to be sure they will fit together again. Account for the same amount of sleeve cap ease that the original pattern had.

Note: Instead of slashing out the sleeve as shown, you could reduce the cap height to fit into the new armhole.

Armhole Gaping

On a Style with Princess Seams

A) Identifying the Issue - There is gaping or extra fabric at the front armhole area on the side panel. Your princess seam location may vary from this image, but the concept for correcting the pattern is the same.

There is excess fabric in the armhole, and the armhole is not sitting flush against the body.

This issue may be a sign that a Full Bust Adjustment is needed. If there are additional draglines, see the Full Bust Adjustment corrections.

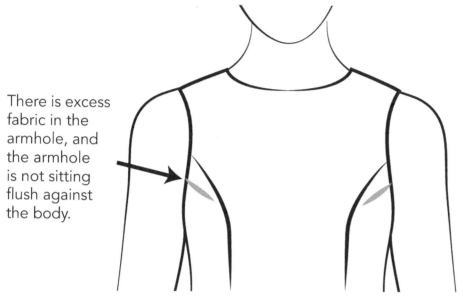

B) Pinning the Sample - Pin the excess fabric at the armhole toward the direction of the apex. Be sure your arm moves comfortably. If it is not comfortable, pin less. Measure the amount you pinned.

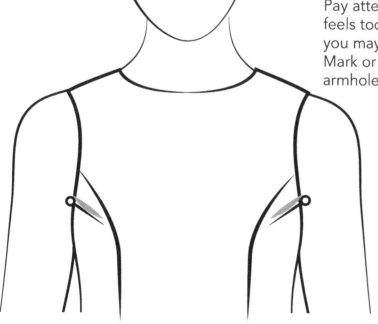

Pay attention to whether the armhole feels too high after pinning. If it does, you may need to lower the armhole. Mark or pin where you want the armhole lowered.

If the garment has a sleeve, see the sleeve correction on page 121. Fix the sleeve after you correct the bodice pattern.

On a Style with Princess Seams (*continued*)

C) Correcting the Pattern - This is a Slash & Close pattern correction.

On the side panel, mark the amount you pinned the sample at the armhole. Draw two lines in the direction of the apex. Go to zero at the princess seam.

1.

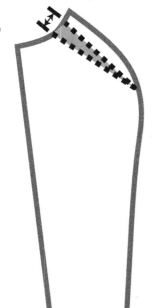

Slash & Close (fold out) the amount you marked.

2.

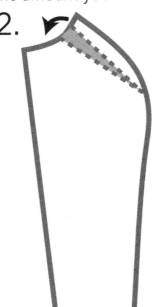

Notice that the armhole is no longer smooth.

3.

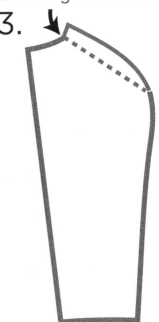

4.

Align the armhole pieces at the princess seam. True the armhole and princess seams, making them smooth contours.

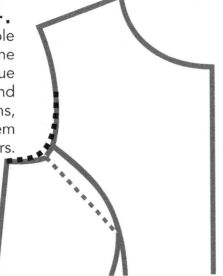

(Alternative for Step 4)
If the armhole was too high after you pinned, lower the armhole to true the armhole seam. Lower the back armhole the same amount to keep it balanced.

Armhole Gaping

On a Style with Side Darts

A) Identifying the Issue - There is gaping or extra fabric at the front armhole area.

There is excess fabric in the armhole, and the armhole is not sitting flush against the body.

This issue may be a sign that a Full Bust Adjustment is needed. If there are additional draglines, see the Full Bust Adjustment corrections.

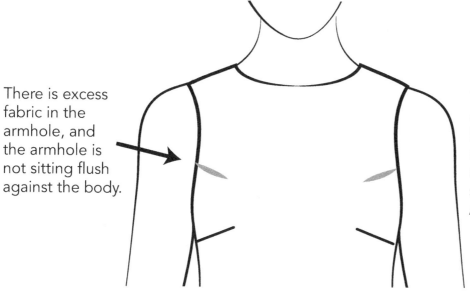

B) Pinning the Sample - Pin the excess fabric at the armhole toward the direction of the apex. Be sure your arm moves comfortably. If it is not comfortable, pin less. Measure the amount you pinned.

Pay attention to whether the armhole feels too high after pinning. If it does, you may need to lower the armhole. Mark or pin how much you want the armhole lowered.

If the garment has a sleeve, see the sleeve correction on page 121. Fix the sleeve after you correct the bodice pattern.

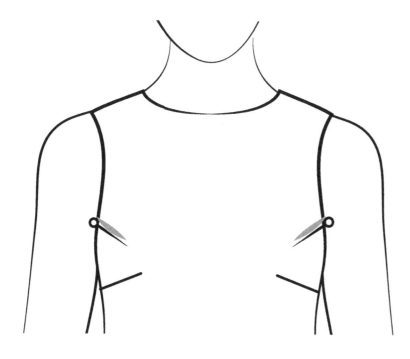

On a Style with Side Darts *(continued)*

C) Correcting the Pattern - This is a Slash & Close pattern correction but shown in a pivoting method.

Mark the amount you pinned the sample at the armhole. Draw two lines in the direction of the apex. Go to zero where you stopped pinning.

Extend the upper line in Step 1 toward the apex. Draw another line down the center of the dart to the apex until the two lines intersect.

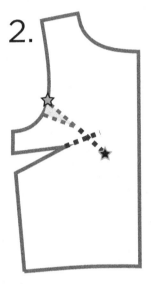

Draw around the edge of the pattern on a new piece of paper. Start at the top of the pinned area and finish at the point of the dart.

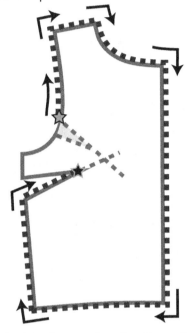

Pivot the pattern from the apex, at the intersection of the two lines. Pivot the pattern until the lower line of the armhole marked in Step 1 hits the traced armhole line in Step 3. Trace around the last part of the pattern.

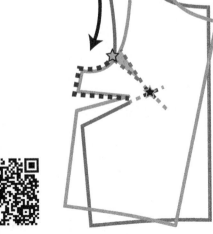

The dart is now deeper. True the armhole seam. Extend the dart lines until they create a dart point.

(Armhole Alternative for Step 5.) If the armhole was too high after you pinned it, lower the armhole to make it smooth. Lower the back armhole the same amount.

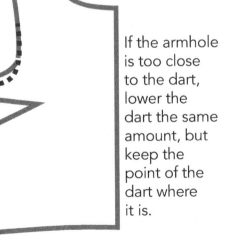

Adjust the dart distance from the apex based on your cup size, as found on page 41. Fold the dart closed, and true the side seam.

If the armhole is too close to the dart, lower the dart the same amount, but keep the point of the dart where it is.

Armhole Gaping - Adding a Side Dart

To a Style with No Darts

A) Identifying the Issue - There is gaping or extra fabric at the front armhole area.

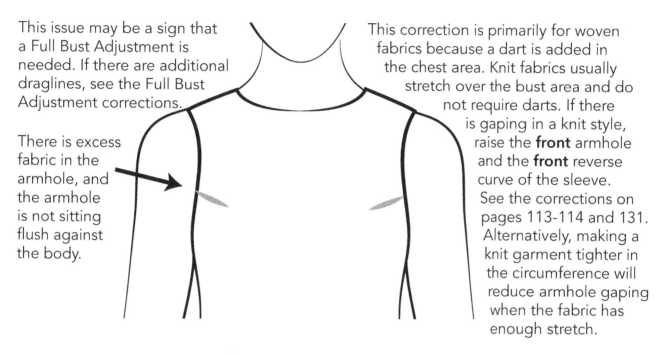

This issue may be a sign that a Full Bust Adjustment is needed. If there are additional draglines, see the Full Bust Adjustment corrections.

There is excess fabric in the armhole, and the armhole is not sitting flush against the body.

This correction is primarily for woven fabrics because a dart is added in the chest area. Knit fabrics usually stretch over the bust area and do not require darts. If there is gaping in a knit style, raise the **front** armhole and the **front** reverse curve of the sleeve. See the corrections on pages 113-114 and 131. Alternatively, making a knit garment tighter in the circumference will reduce armhole gaping when the fabric has enough stretch.

B) Pinning the Sample - Pin the excess fabric at the armhole toward the direction of the apex. Be sure your arm moves comfortably. If it is not comfortable, pin less. Measure the amount you pinned. Mark the apex position. You will be creating a dart to achieve a nicer fit.

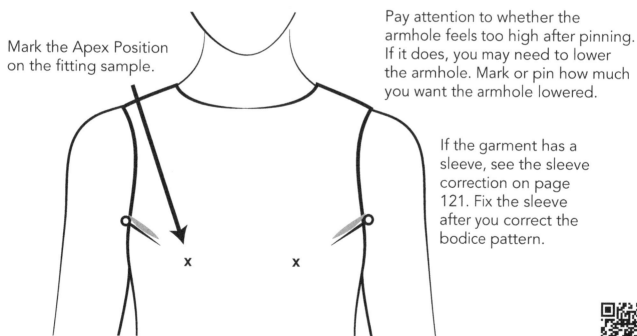

Mark the Apex Position on the fitting sample.

Pay attention to whether the armhole feels too high after pinning. If it does, you may need to lower the armhole. Mark or pin how much you want the armhole lowered.

If the garment has a sleeve, see the sleeve correction on page 121. Fix the sleeve after you correct the bodice pattern.

Armhole & Raglan Sleeve Corrections

To a Style with No Darts *(continued)*

C) Correcting the Pattern - The video for this fitting correction (found by scanning the QR code below) shows the Slash & Close pattern correction. However, the pivoting method is shown below. To see a fitting video with the pivoting method, see the previous correction's video on page 118. Both methods achieve the same result.

Mark the amount you pinned the sample at the armhole. Draw two lines in the direction of the apex. Go to zero where you stopped pinning.

Extend the upper line in Step 1 toward the apex. Draw a dart line from the side seam to the apex until the two lines intersect.

Draw around the edge of the pattern on a new piece of paper. Start at the top of the pinned area and finish at the line of the dart.

1.

2.

You may choose any position you want for your dart! **Get Creative!**

3.

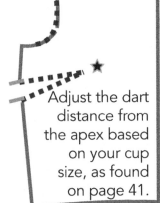

Mark a line here.

Pivot the pattern from the apex, at the intersection of the two lines. Pivot the pattern until the lower line of the armhole marked in Step 1 hits the traced armhole line in Step 3. Trace around the last part of the pattern.

Draw the dart lines from the side seam marks, going toward the apex, stopping before you come to the apex. True the armhole and side seams.

(Armhole Alternative to Step 5.) If the armhole was too high after you pinned it, lower the armhole to make it smooth. Lower the back armhole the same amount.

4.

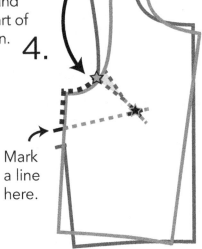

Mark a line here.

5.

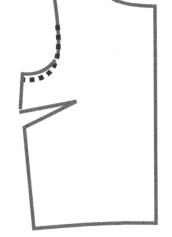

Adjust the dart distance from the apex based on your cup size, as found on page 41.

Armhole Gaping

Set-in Sleeve Correction

This is the sleeve correction for the previous three armhole gaping corrections. Since those corrections will reduce the armhole slightly, adjust the sleeve to fit into the new armhole.

Before the correction is made, measure the original armhole and original sleeve seam on the patterns to determine the amount of ease on the sleeve. After the correction, achieve the same amount of ease on the sleeve in comparison to the new armhole.

If you lowered the armhole, you may not need to reduce the sleeve. Alternatively, you may need to lower the reverse curve of the sleeve shown on page 134 in Step 3.

Option 1: This is a Slash & Close pattern correction. Pin the fitting sample the same amount you pinned the armhole on the sleeve. If there is enough movement in the bicep and cap width, you can do this correction.

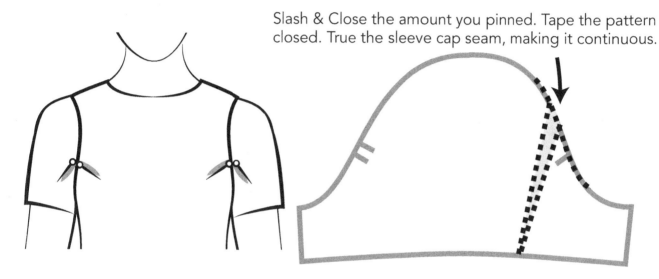

Slash & Close the amount you pinned. Tape the pattern closed. True the sleeve cap seam, making it continuous.

Option 2: If the bicep or sleeve cap width felt too tight when you pinned the sample as shown above, adjust the sleeve using this method of lowering the cap height.

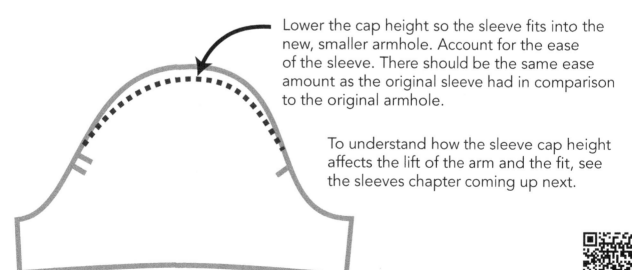

Lower the cap height so the sleeve fits into the new, smaller armhole. Account for the ease of the sleeve. There should be the same ease amount as the original sleeve had in comparison to the original armhole.

To understand how the sleeve cap height affects the lift of the arm and the fit, see the sleeves chapter coming up next.

Armhole & Raglan Sleeve Corrections

Armhole Gaping - Raglan Sleeves

With a Shoulder Dart or Knit Styles with No Darts - Option 1

This option deepens an existing shoulder dart. It can also be applied to knit styles without shoulder darts. If the low point shoulder tip feels too tight, try Option 2 for styles with darts.

A) Identifying the Issue - There is gaping or extra fabric at the front armhole of a raglan sleeve. The armhole seam does not lie well against the body.

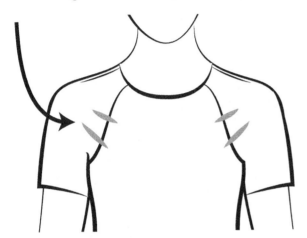

B) Pinning the Sample - Pin the excess fabric at the armhole toward the direction of the apex. Measure the amount you pinned. Do this correction if you pin less than 3/8" (1 cm) in total. If you pinned more than 3/8" (1 cm) or the low point shoulder tip feels too tight, try Option 2 for styles with darts. Additionally, you may pin on the sleeve along the armhole, as shown on pages 126-127. This helps eliminate gaping at the HPS.

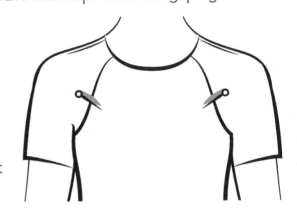

C) Correcting the Pattern - This is a Slash & Close pattern correction. Mark the pattern the amount you pinned at the armhole seam.

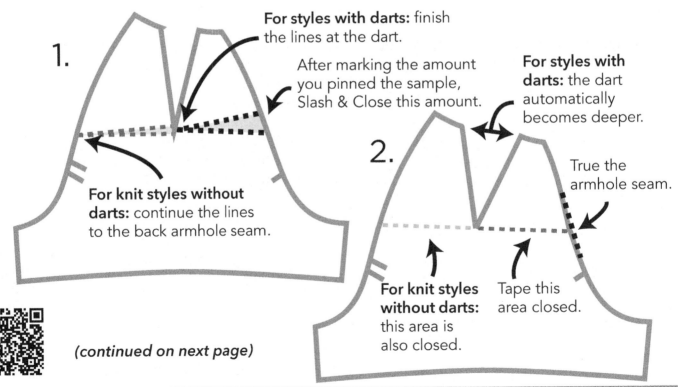

1.

For styles with darts: finish the lines at the dart.

After marking the amount you pinned the sample, Slash & Close this amount.

For knit styles without darts: continue the lines to the back armhole seam.

2.

For styles with darts: the dart automatically becomes deeper.

True the armhole seam.

For knit styles without darts: this area is also closed.

Tape this area closed.

(continued on next page)

Armhole Gaping - Raglan Sleeves

With a Shoulder Dart or Knit Styles with No Darts
Option 1 *(continued)*

C) Correcting the Pattern (*continued*) - The body needs to be adjusted to fit the new sleeve.

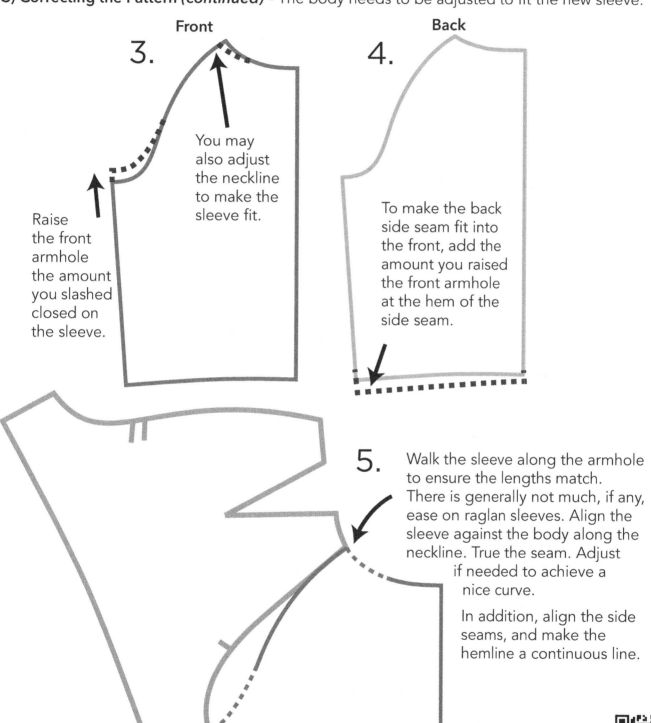

Front

3.

You may also adjust the neckline to make the sleeve fit.

Raise the front armhole the amount you slashed closed on the sleeve.

Back

4.

To make the back side seam fit into the front, add the amount you raised the front armhole at the hem of the side seam.

5. Walk the sleeve along the armhole to ensure the lengths match. There is generally not much, if any, ease on raglan sleeves. Align the sleeve against the body along the neckline. True the seam. Adjust if needed to achieve a nice curve.

In addition, align the side seams, and make the hemline a continuous line.

Armhole Gaping - Raglan Sleeves

With a Shoulder Dart - Option 2

This option deepens an existing shoulder dart, and it adds fullness to the low point shoulder tip. This is also called a broad shoulder adjustment.

A) Identifying the Issue - There is gaping or extra fabric at the front armhole of a raglan sleeve. The armhole seam does not lie well against the body.

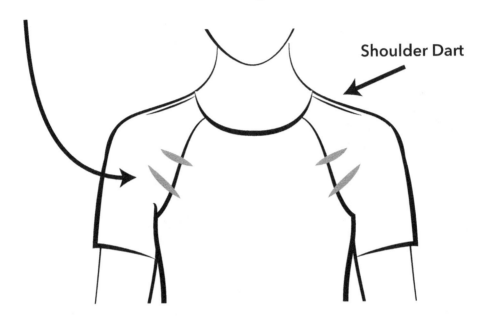

Shoulder Dart

B) Cutting the Sample - Cut each sleeve a different way to see which correction is better for you. Cut one sleeve vertically over the shoulder tip, and cut the other sleeve horizontally, extending all the way toward the back of the garment.

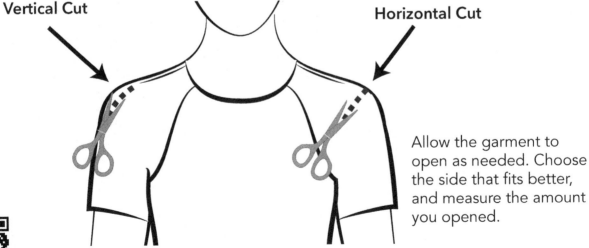

Vertical Cut

Horizontal Cut

Allow the garment to open as needed. Choose the side that fits better, and measure the amount you opened.

Armhole Gaping - Raglan Sleeves

With a Shoulder Dart - Option 2 *(continued)*

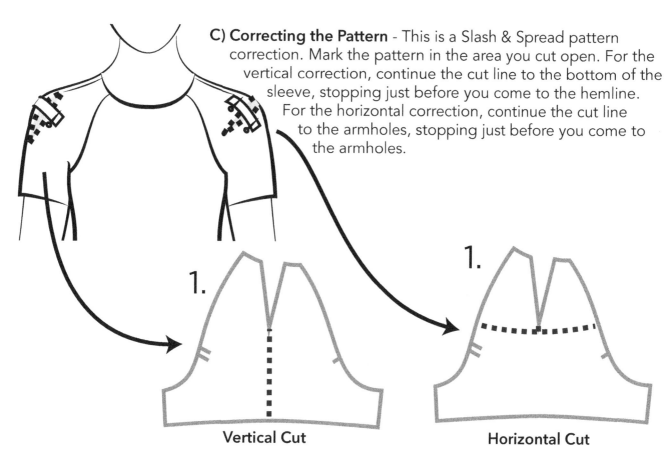

C) Correcting the Pattern - This is a Slash & Spread pattern correction. Mark the pattern in the area you cut open. For the vertical correction, continue the cut line to the bottom of the sleeve, stopping just before you come to the hemline. For the horizontal correction, continue the cut line to the armholes, stopping just before you come to the armholes.

1.

Vertical Cut

1.

Horizontal Cut

Slash & Spread the pattern the amount you opened the sample.

Allow the pattern to open at the shoulder tip the same amount you opened the sample. Extend the shoulder dart lines as needed to finish the dart point.

Allow the pattern to open at the shoulder tip the same amount you opened the sample.

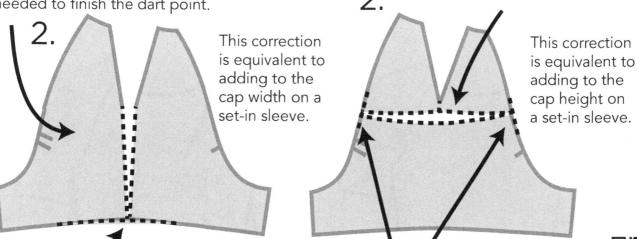

2.

This correction is equivalent to adding to the cap width on a set-in sleeve.

2.

This correction is equivalent to adding to the cap height on a set-in sleeve.

True the armhole seams or hemlines. The seam lines should be continuous, not coming to any points.

Armhole & Raglan Sleeve Corrections

Armhole Gaping - Raglan Sleeves

Adding a Shoulder Dart - Option 3

In this option, you will add shoulder darts to a style that does not already have them. Shoulder darts allow additional shaping which greatly improve the fit of woven and less stretchy knit tops.

A) Identifying the Issue - There is gaping or extra fabric at the front armhole of a raglan sleeve. The armhole seam does not lie well against the body.

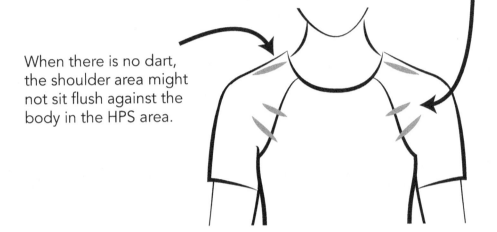

When there is no dart, the shoulder area might not sit flush against the body in the HPS area.

B) Cutting the Sample - Cut each sleeve two directions: vertically, over the low point shoulder (LPS), and horizontally, extending all the way toward the back of the garment.

Allow the garment to open until the shoulder area sits flush against the body, and the gaping is reduced. Tape and pin the opened areas. Measure the amounts opened both horizontally and vertically.

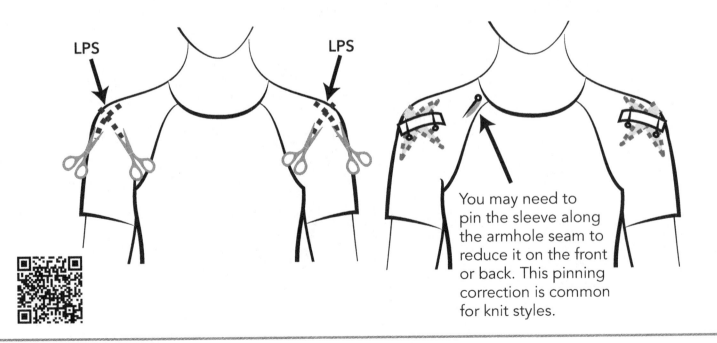

You may need to pin the sleeve along the armhole seam to reduce it on the front or back. This pinning correction is common for knit styles.

Armhole Gaping - Raglan Sleeves

Adding a Shoulder Dart - Option 3 *(continued)*

C) Correcting the Pattern - Slash & Spread the pattern the amount you opened the sample.

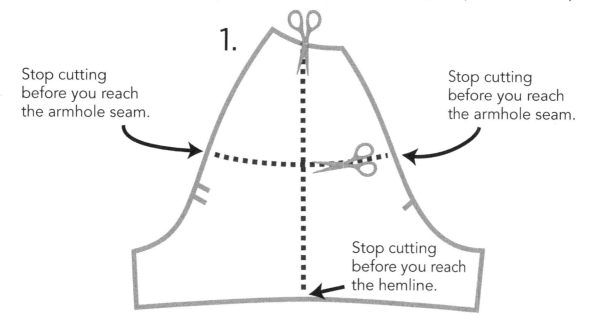

1.

Stop cutting before you reach the armhole seam.

Stop cutting before you reach the armhole seam.

Stop cutting before you reach the hemline.

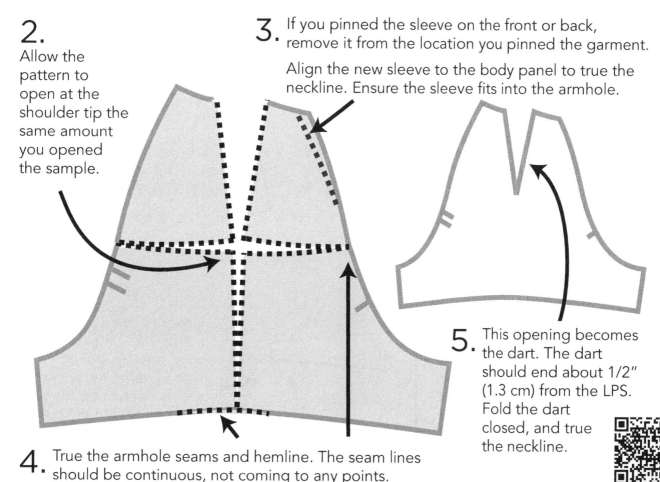

2. Allow the pattern to open at the shoulder tip the same amount you opened the sample.

3. If you pinned the sleeve on the front or back, remove it from the location you pinned the garment.

Align the new sleeve to the body panel to true the neckline. Ensure the sleeve fits into the armhole.

4. True the armhole seams and hemline. The seam lines should be continuous, not coming to any points.

5. This opening becomes the dart. The dart should end about 1/2" (1.3 cm) from the LPS. Fold the dart closed, and true the neckline.

Armhole & Raglan Sleeve Corrections

Low Armholes - Option 1

Adjusting the Shoulder Seam

This is a great quick fix if you have already cut out your garment in the final fabric and need to raise the armhole positions. Use this option if you notice the entire fitting sample is sitting too low, including dart positions, armholes, and necklines. This correction will raise the entire garment.

A) Identifying the Issue - Option 1 - The armhole position is too low and not sitting close enough to the armpit area. Often, the armhole feels low and a little loose.

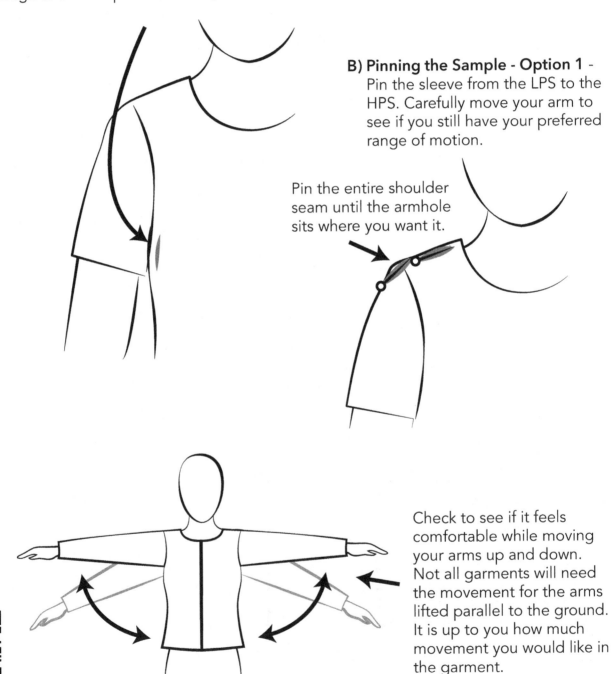

B) Pinning the Sample - Option 1 - Pin the sleeve from the LPS to the HPS. Carefully move your arm to see if you still have your preferred range of motion.

Pin the entire shoulder seam until the armhole sits where you want it.

Check to see if it feels comfortable while moving your arms up and down. Not all garments will need the movement for the arms lifted parallel to the ground. It is up to you how much movement you would like in the garment.

Adjusting the Shoulder Seam *(continued)*

C) Correcting the Pattern - Option 1 - Mark the pattern with the update you made, even if you already cut the final fabric and are doing it as a quick fix on your garment directly. Adjusting the armhole in this way means the entire garment is raised. You may have to readjust the neckline, collar, facing shapes, and dart positions. Consider this in your pattern corrections.

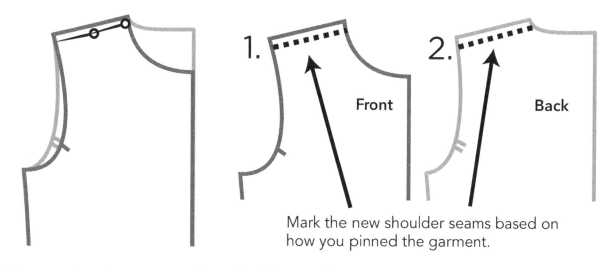

Front

Back

Mark the new shoulder seams based on how you pinned the garment.

Measure the sleeve to see if it will still fit into the new armhole. If it does not fit, Slash & Close the sleeve pattern the same amount you lowered the shoulder seams.

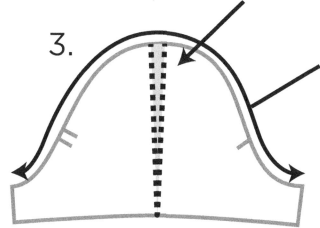

Account for the same amount of ease the sleeve had in comparison to the armhole before you did the correction.

Once you have adjusted the sleeve pattern piece, cut out the new sleeves in your final fabric and sew.

(Alternative for Step 3) If you do not have enough fabric to recut the sleeves with the Slash & Close method, you could reduce the height of the cap to make it fit into the new armhole. This would shorten the cap height which increases the lift of the arm movement. However, it may cause short sleeves to "wing" out as shown on page 147. For long sleeves, it may increase the underarm draglines, as shown on page 143.

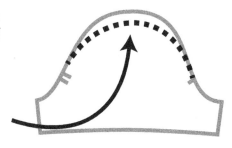

Armhole & Raglan Sleeve Corrections

Raising the Armhole

In Option 1, the entire garment is raised from the shoulder seam. The second option raises the armhole position only. The third option raises the garment from the across front area instead of at the shoulder seam. The advantage is that you would not have to adjust the necklines/neck facings when you use Options 2 & 3.

These two corrections will impact the waistline and dart positions. If you are pleased with the waistline and dart positions **before** pinning as shown below, follow Option 2. If you like the waistline and dart positions **after** pinning, follow Option 3. Steps (A) and (B) are the same for Options 2 and 3.

A) Identifying the Issue - The armhole position is too low and not sitting close enough to the armpit area.

Are you pleased with the waistline and dart positions?

If yes, proceed with Option 2 after completing Step (B).

If not, and you want the waistline and dart positions to rise with the armhole, proceed with Option 3 after completing Step (B).

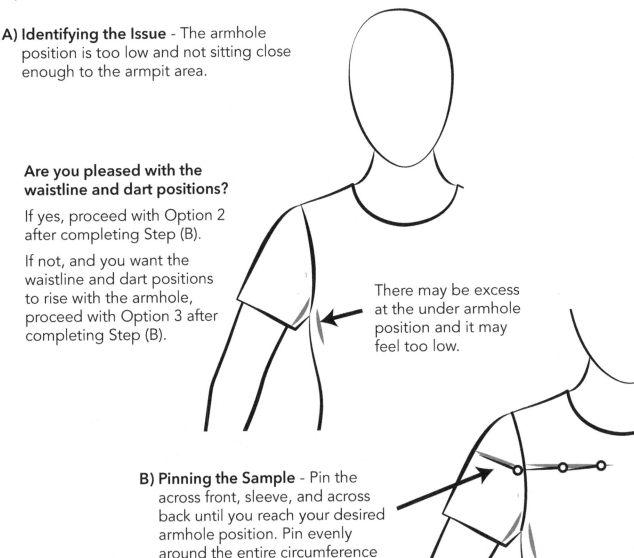

There may be excess at the under armhole position and it may feel too low.

B) Pinning the Sample - Pin the across front, sleeve, and across back until you reach your desired armhole position. Pin evenly around the entire circumference of the garment. Measure the amount you pinned around the across front, across back, and sleeve.

Option 2   Option 3

Raising the Armhole (*continued*)

After you pinned the across front, across back, and sleeve, you will notice that the darts, princess line, and waistline rise after pinning. If you preferred how it looked **before** pinning and do **NOT** want to raise these positions, this is the correction for you. This will only raise the armhole.

C) Correcting the Pattern - Option 2 - Raise the armhole positions on the front/back body panels and on the sleeve.

Note: Other corrections in this book refer to this page to raise the front armhole, back armhole, or reverse curve of the sleeve. If you are directed to this page from other corrections in the book, refer to only the instructed pattern pieces. On occasion, you may raise just the front or back armhole, changing the balance. If only one side is raised, shorten that side seam length at the hemline for the side seams to match. If the front or back armhole is raised, the reverse curve on the sleeve must also be raised on the corresponding front/back side. If the sleeve reverse curve is raised on only one side, you must ensure the underarm seam shortens to match the corresponding underarm seam.

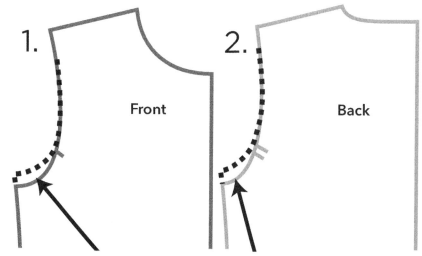

Raise the front and back armholes the same amount you pinned the fitting sample.

Mark the reverse curve of the sleeve pattern higher by the same amount you raised the armholes on the pattern. Go to zero at the curve.

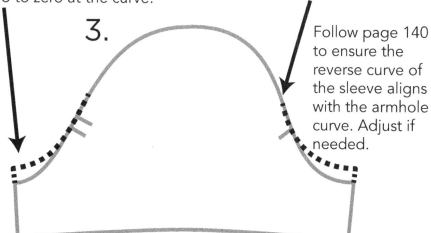

Follow page 140 to ensure the reverse curve of the sleeve aligns with the armhole curve. Adjust if needed.

After the correction, measure the armhole and sleeve to be sure they will fit together again. Account for the same amount of sleeve cap ease that the original pattern had.

Armhole & Raglan Sleeve Corrections

Raising the Armhole (*continued from page 130*)

After you pinned the across front, across back, and sleeve, you will notice that the darts, princess line, and waistline rise after pinning. If you are happy with the new positions **after** pinning, this is the right correction for you.

C) Correcting the Pattern - Option 3 - Raise the armhole positions on the front/back body panels and on the sleeve using the Slash & Close method.

Measure the amount you pinned around the across front, across back, and sleeve in the previous Step (B). Also, measure the positions where you pinned the sample.

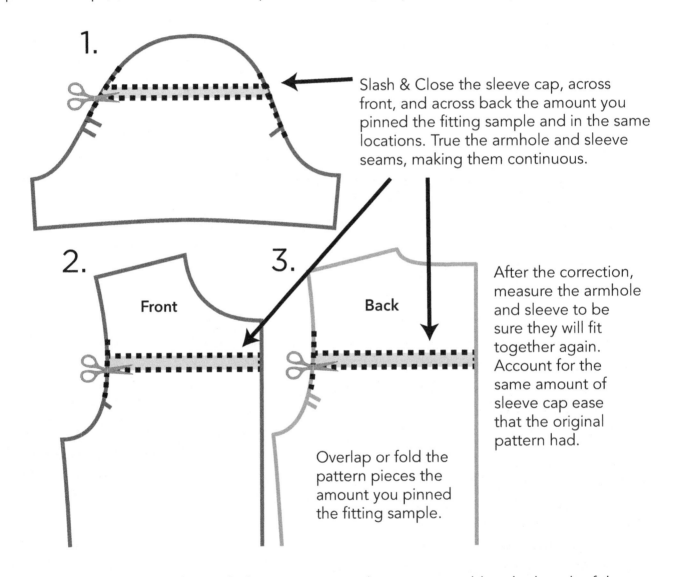

Slash & Close the sleeve cap, across front, and across back the amount you pinned the fitting sample and in the same locations. True the armhole and sleeve seams, making them continuous.

After the correction, measure the armhole and sleeve to be sure they will fit together again. Account for the same amount of sleeve cap ease that the original pattern had.

Overlap or fold the pattern pieces the amount you pinned the fitting sample.

Since adjusting the armhole means raising the garment, add to the length of the garment at the hem and sleeve for all the pieces to keep the original length. If you do not lengthen the garment, the garment will be shorter than the intended length, since you Slashed & Closed the pattern.

High Armholes - Options 1 & 2

Lowering the Armhole

There are three options for correcting a pattern with a high armhole issue. Depending on which option you chose, it may impact the waistline and dart positions. If you are pleased with the waistline and dart/princess line positions, follow Option 1.

If you feel the waistline and dart/princess line positions could be moved down the same amount as the armhole, follow Option 2. Step (A) is the same for both Options 1 & 2.

If you are noticing a diagonal dragline in the armhole area, follow Option 3, which is a shoulder slope correction. Option 3 can often be used in conjunction with Option 1, meaning you could do both corrections if needed.

A) Identifying the Issue - The armhole position feels too high when you are wearing the garment, or there are draglines along the curve of the armhole.

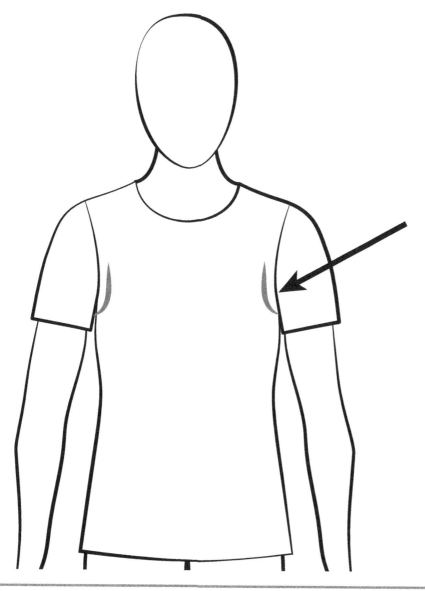

The armhole feels high, and you may have draglines around the under armhole area. The garment may not feel comfortable, and the garment may rub in the armpit area.

Lowering the Armhole (*continued*)

After identifying that the armhole position is too high, look at the darts/princess lines, and waistline. If you think they are in the correct positions, this is the right correction for you. This correction will not affect the dart/princess lines and waistline positions.

B) Pinning the Sample - Option 1 - Pin the dragline/bunched fabric at the under-armhole area, near the side seam. Measure the amount you pinned.

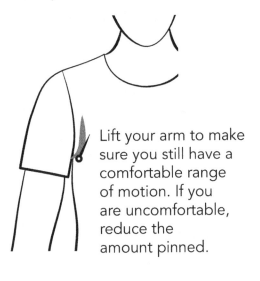

Lift your arm to make sure you still have a comfortable range of motion. If you are uncomfortable, reduce the amount pinned.

C) Correcting the Pattern - Lower the front and back armholes the same amount and the same positions you pinned the fitting sample.

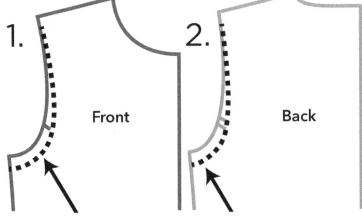

Lower both the front and back body panels to keep the pattern balanced.

3. Lower the reverse curve area on the sleeve the same amount you lowered the armhole on the pattern.

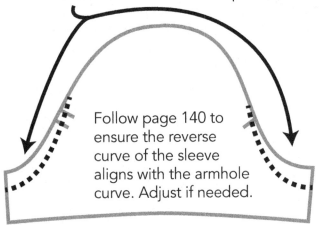

Follow page 140 to ensure the reverse curve of the sleeve aligns with the armhole curve. Adjust if needed.

After the correction, measure the armhole and sleeve to be sure they will fit together. Account for the same amount of sleeve cap ease that the original pattern had.

Note: Other corrections in this book refer to this page to lower the front armhole, back armhole, or reverse curve of the sleeve. If you are directed to this page from other corrections in the book, refer to only the instructed pattern pieces. On occasion, you may lower just the front or back armhole, changing the balance. If only one side is lowered, lengthen that side seam length at the hemline for the side seams to match. If the front or back armhole is lowered, the reverse curve on the sleeve must also be lowered on the corresponding front/back side. If the sleeve reverse curve is lowered on only one side, you must ensure the underarm seam lengthens to match the corresponding underarm seam.

High Armholes - Option 2

Lowering the Armhole (*continued from page 133*)

After identifying that the armhole position is too high, look at the darts/princess lines and waistline. If you think all of these positions are too high, this is the right correction for you.

B) Cutting and Taping the Sample - Option 2 - Take the garment off to cut the across front, sleeve, and across back. Start by cutting only half (wearer's right or left side) of the garment. Start taping and pinning the upper portion and lower portions together until you reach your desired armhole position. Try on the garment before you continue with the entire circumference of the garment.

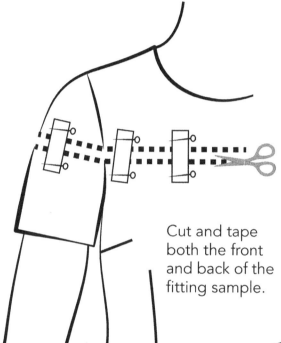

> **Note:** You cannot do this correction while wearing the garment because it is very difficult to tape and pin the two parts on the body (especially since the lower part falls down). Take the garment off to cut and tape it. Try it on carefully to check the fit, and adjust accordingly until you are pleased.

Cut and tape both the front and back of the fitting sample.

Measure the amount you opened the sample. Measure the position where you opened, from the high point shoulder (HPS) to the cut line. This will be the same placement on the body pattern. Measure the distance from the LPS to the cut line for the correct position on the sleeve pattern.

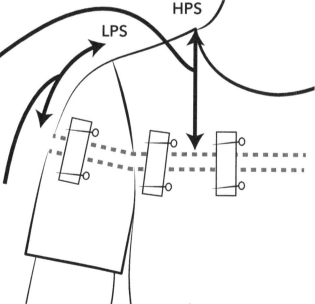

Armhole & Raglan Sleeve Corrections

High Armholes - Option 2

Lowering the Armhole (continued)

C) Correcting the Pattern - Option 2 - Slash & Spread the pattern pieces the amount you taped and pinned the fitting sample. To keep the pattern balanced, do this correction on the front and back panels.

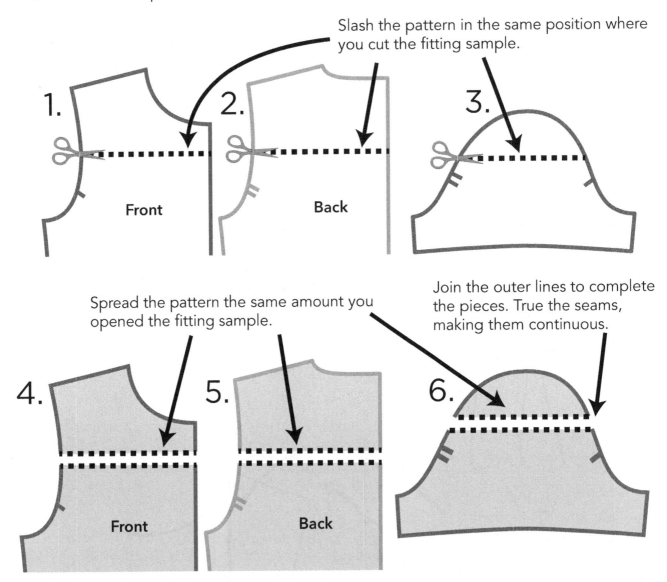

Slash the pattern in the same position where you cut the fitting sample.

Spread the pattern the same amount you opened the fitting sample.

Join the outer lines to complete the pieces. True the seams, making them continuous.

1.

2. Front

3. Back

4. Front

5. Back

6.

After the correction, measure the armhole and sleeve to be sure they will fit together. Account for the same amount of sleeve cap ease that the original pattern had.

> Whenever you Slash & Spread the pattern pieces, tape a piece of paper underneath the gap, filling in the spread area.

Shoulder Slope Issue

If there is a diagonal dragline from the armhole area toward the HPS, this correction is for you. According to The GRD Method™ in fitting, diagonal draglines generally point down toward the area that should be raised and pinned up. Here, this results in a shoulder slope correction. This correction (Option 3) is often done in conjunction with Option 1 or 2.

A) Identifying the Issue - There are excessive diagonal draglines near the armhole. The draglines are pointing up toward the high point shoulder and pointing down toward the armhole.

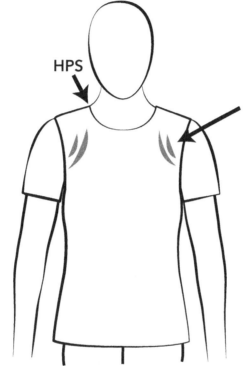

HPS

This fitting issue may appear in the front, back, or on both sides of the garment.

As you will learn in the last chapter of this book, "Diagonal Draglines Demystified," the garment must be raised and pinned above the bottom point of a diagonal dragline.

B) Pinning the Sample - Smooth the draglines upward as much as possible, pinning them at the low point shoulder (LPS) along the shoulder seam.

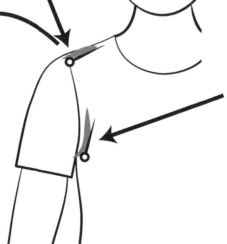

We "pick up" the shoulder slope in the area above the bottom of the draglines. Depending on the sample, you may pin on the front only, or on the back panel, too.

The shoulder slope correction may be all you need. However, if you notice the armhole feels too high, continue with the previous two options after you make this correction.

Armhole & Raglan Sleeve Corrections

Shoulder Slope Issue (continued)

C) Correcting the Pattern - Measure the amount you pinned at the LPS and lower that amount on the pattern. Draw the new shoulder slope. You will likely go to zero at the HPS, depending on how you pinned the garment.

Lower the shoulder slope the amount you pinned the sample.
Adjust only the panels you pinned on the fitting sample.

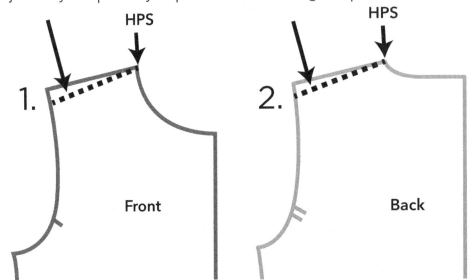

Since this correction reduces the armhole, the sleeve needs to be adjusted to fit into the new armhole. Use the Slash & Close method.

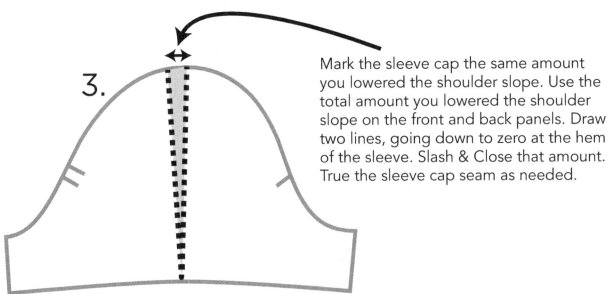

Mark the sleeve cap the same amount you lowered the shoulder slope. Use the total amount you lowered the shoulder slope on the front and back panels. Draw two lines, going down to zero at the hem of the sleeve. Slash & Close that amount. True the sleeve cap seam as needed.

After the correction, measure the armhole and sleeve to ensure they fit together. Account for the same amount of sleeve cap ease that the original pattern had.

Set-in Sleeve Topics & Corrections

It is important to identify armhole issues before moving to sleeve corrections. When the across shoulder, across front, or across back position changes, it can affect the fit of a sleeve. Once you are pleased with the complete armhole, you will more easily identify if sleeve fitting issues exist.

The first important topic to check is the sleeve shape in comparison to the front and back body panels, as found on the following page. This is always the starting point in checking commercial or indie patterns, and you would be amazed how many patterns do not follow this rule. A mismatched sleeve curvature to the body panels is one of the biggest issues I have seen from garment factory patterns while working in the clothing industry. Many ready-to-wear garments do not follow this rule. It is often the first sign of an ill-fitting armhole and sleeve to the wearer. I cannot overstress the importance of checking this before and after sleeve and armhole corrections.

Additional topics in this chapter include sleeve terminology, how the sleeve cap height affects the fit of the garment, and general sleeve fitting corrections. The correction, "Sleeves Peaking Out or Hiking Up," in this chapter had over 68,800 views on the video I posted on Instagram®. This is a hot topic and one which many people do not know how to correct. It is the most common fitting correction in tee-shirts for both men and women.

Remember: sleeve corrections come after armhole corrections, as shown in the order of this book.

Signs of Nicely-Fitting Sleeves

Checking the Sleeve Pattern

Check that the sleeve pattern is well-balanced. These are critical points to check on the pattern to achieve the best fit. When customizing your fit with your moulage and slopers, you may break these rules after you fit your garments, but always start with a balanced pattern.

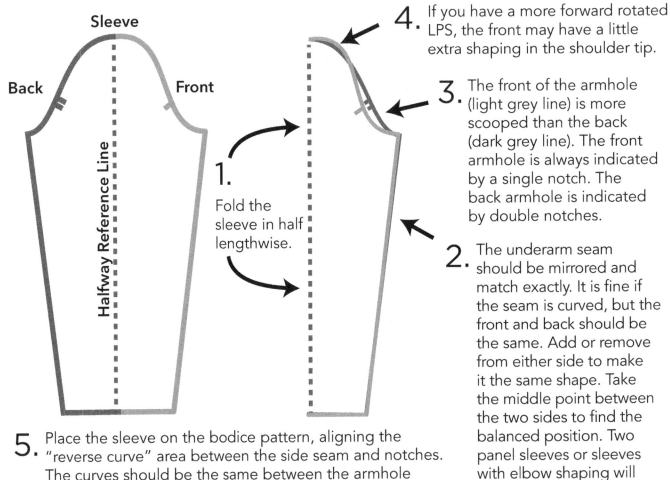

4. If you have a more forward rotated LPS, the front may have a little extra shaping in the shoulder tip.

3. The front of the armhole (light grey line) is more scooped than the back (dark grey line). The front armhole is always indicated by a single notch. The back armhole is indicated by double notches.

1. Fold the sleeve in half lengthwise.

2. The underarm seam should be mirrored and match exactly. It is fine if the seam is curved, but the front and back should be the same. Add or remove from either side to make it the same shape. Take the middle point between the two sides to find the balanced position. Two panel sleeves or sleeves with elbow shaping will not follow this rule.

5. Place the sleeve on the bodice pattern, aligning the "reverse curve" area between the side seam and notches. The curves should be the same between the armhole and the sleeve in this "reverse curve" area. If the curve shapes do not match, find the halfway point between the two lines. Redraw both lines to the halfway point. This rule also applies to raglan sleeves.

If you have ever worn a garment and the armhole or sleeve did not feel right, the curves probably did not line up in this area.

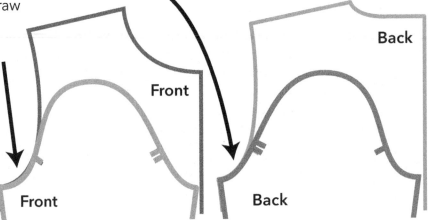

Sleeve Cap Heights Explained

How the Sleeve Cap Affects Movement

Refer to page 16 for sleeve terminology. The height between the armhole position line and the LPS line on a sleeve is called a sleeve cap. The height of the sleeve cap can be different from garment to garment. The taller the sleeve cap height, the more the garment rises when the arms are lifted, and there is less movement in the garment. The shorter the cap height, the less the garment rises when the arms lift, and it is easier to move in the garment.

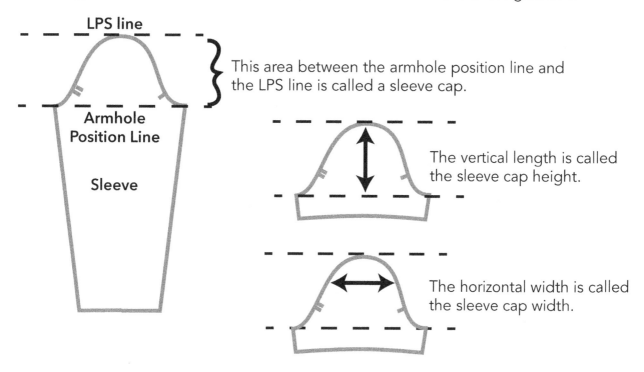

LPS line

This area between the armhole position line and the LPS line is called a sleeve cap.

Armhole Position Line

Sleeve

The vertical length is called the sleeve cap height.

The horizontal width is called the sleeve cap width.

Below are two examples of sleeve cap heights. These measurements are purely for the purpose of demonstration and are not standards to use in patternmaking.

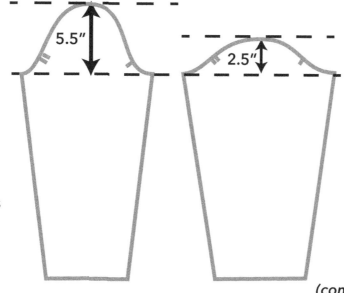

A sleeve with a taller cap height is generally used in garments like blazers, coats, jackets, button-down shirts, blouses and dresses. Most garments will have a sleeve cap height which has this appearance.

5.5"

2.5"

A sleeve with a shorter cap height is generally used in garments like ski, snowboard, climbing jackets, and other activewear garments. The shorter cap height allows for movement to raise the arms in sports. It creates a more functional garment.

(continued on next page)

Sleeve Cap Heights Explained

How the Sleeve Cap Affects Movement (continued)

When you raise your arms, the bottom of the garment will rise more with a taller sleeve cap height. This is called the "lift" of the garment, specifically referring to the sleeve lift. It is expected that the garment will rise, or "lift" more when the arms are raised due to the restriction of the arm movement with the taller cap height.

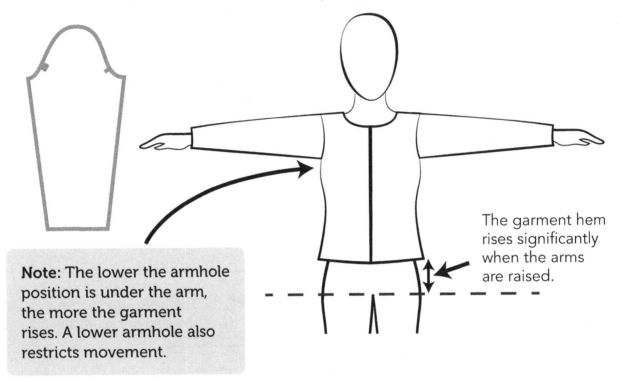

Note: The lower the armhole position is under the arm, the more the garment rises. A lower armhole also restricts movement.

The garment hem rises significantly when the arms are raised.

A shorter cap height is normally used in ski, snowboarding, climbing jackets, and other activewear garments. When you raise your arms, the bottom of the garment will not rise as much.

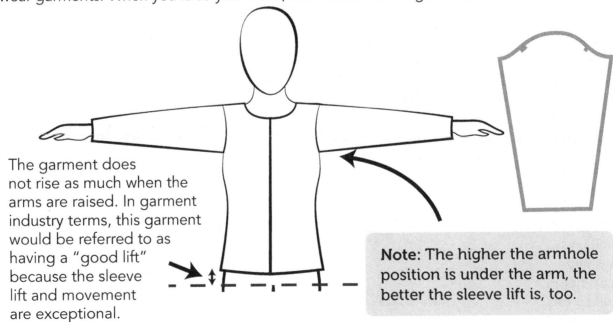

The garment does not rise as much when the arms are raised. In garment industry terms, this garment would be referred to as having a "good lift" because the sleeve lift and movement are exceptional.

Note: The higher the armhole position is under the arm, the better the sleeve lift is, too.

Sleeve Cap Heights Explained

How the Sleeve Cap Affects Draglines

A standard or taller cap height creates a more attractive appearance when your arms are down at your sides. Finding the perfect cap height will take trial and error until you are pleased with both the lift of the garment and the appearance when the arms are down.

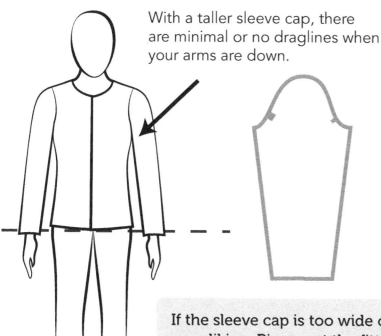

With a taller sleeve cap, there are minimal or no draglines when your arms are down.

If the sleeve cap is too wide or too high, adjust it according to your liking. Pin or cut the fitting sample and apply the changes to the exact locations on the pattern. The sleeve must fit into the armhole with the appropriate amount of ease.

With a shorter sleeve cap, draglines are more prominent when your arms are down.

The shorter the cap height, the wider the bicep and cap width are. This must be wider to fit into the armhole of the front and back pieces.

Note: Raglan sleeves without shoulder darts often have more draglines under the arms like the image on the left. They are unavoidable when there is no shoulder dart. This is why, as patternmakers, we try to keep the shoulder dart in raglan sleeves on woven styles.

Sleeve Cap Height

How To Measure Your Sleeve Cap Height

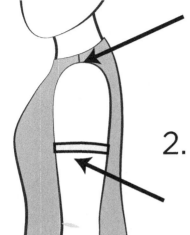

1. If you have a sleeveless fitting sample, wear it. Use the LPS of the fitting sample as the top of the cap position. If you do not have a fitting sample, follow the instructions found on pages 86-87, **"How to Find the Perfect Across Shoulder Width,"** to mark your LPS.

2. Sew an elastic band that will fit around your bicep. Put the elastic on your arm, parallel to the bottom of the under armhole position when your arms are relaxed. Check its positioning in the mirror. Reference a fitting sample for the under armhole position. If you do not have a fitting sample, place the elastic about 3/4" (2 cm) below your armpit as a starting point.

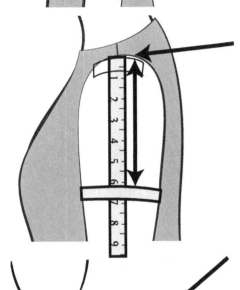

3. Using adhesive tape, attach the end of a tape measure to your LPS at the top of your arm. When the arm is relaxed, the measurement will be longer. You could use this as a starting point if you want a little more fullness in the look of the cap height. However, this will not allow the arms to rise well. A term often used in patternmaking is the "lift," which refers to how easily the arm "lifts" in comparison to how much the garment "lifts." The measurement determined with this arm position is used more for tailored suits and coats.

4. Keeping the tape measure adhered to your LPS, raise your arm out to the side at a 45-degree angle. Measure from the top of your arm to the top of the elastic around your bicep. As you lift the arm, the measurement reduces. This measurement is a good starting point for blouses or garments when you need more movement because you will have better arm "lift."

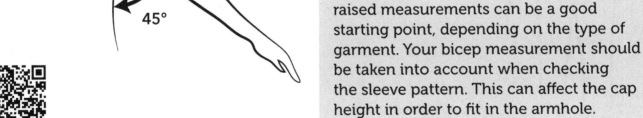

Tip: Any point between the relaxed and raised measurements can be a good starting point, depending on the type of garment. Your bicep measurement should be taken into account when checking the sleeve pattern. This can affect the cap height in order to fit in the armhole.

How To Measure Your Sleeve Cap Width

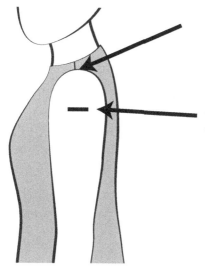

1. Refer to the same position for your LPS as mentioned on the previous page.

2. Mark between 2-3" (5-7.5 cm) down from your shoulder tip (LPS). Write down the amount you have chosen to measure as reference to mark the pattern later. This will be your positioning for the cap width.

3. You may want help with this step. Mark your "across back" area at the same position as the cap width but on the back armhole area. If you have a fitting sample, use the fitting sample position. If you do not have a fitting sample, mark your body where the imaginary armhole will be. It is generally above the crease from the armhole. Alternatively, mark a sticker, and place that on your body.

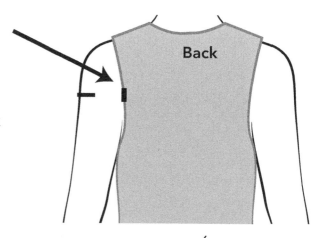

4. Place a piece of tape on the end of a measuring tape, and tape it to the across back area.

5. Wrap it around to the across front area. Pull the tape measure close to the arm, so it is resting against the arm completely.

When the arm is relaxed, the measurement will be shorter. This is your sleeve cap width measurement that could be used for knit tops with a fair amount of stretch.

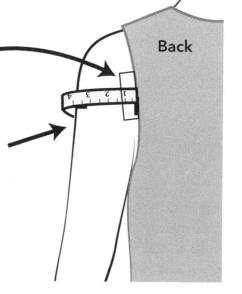

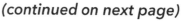

(continued on next page)

How To Measure Your Sleeve Cap Width (*continued*)

Keeping the tape measure adhered to your across back marking, raise your arm out to the side at a 45-degree angle. Measure from the across back area all the way around your arm to the across front area.

The across front area is where your armhole seam will be. For a garment with sleeves, it is usually directly above the armpit crease and over the cap width position you marked in Step 2.

As the arm lifts, the measurement increases. Hold the measuring tape at the across front and move the arm around to ensure ample movement. The measurement at your across front is a good starting point for your sleeve cap width.

The measurement determined is for woven blouses or garments needing movement since woven materials have no stretch and require this ease. The measurement may be smaller for fabrics that stretch.

Add ease to this amount measured if it is for a coat or jacket.

A point of measure that can affect the sleeve cap width is the bicep. If there is a large bicep, the sleeve cap width may be larger than the measurement to accommodate the arm.

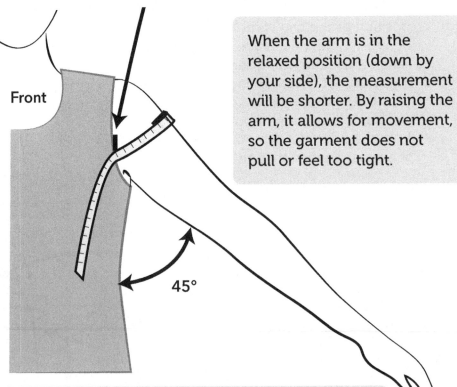

When the arm is in the relaxed position (down by your side), the measurement will be shorter. By raising the arm, it allows for movement, so the garment does not pull or feel too tight.

Front

45°

Use your body measurements for the sleeve cap height and width to compare to the sleeve pattern. If the sleeve cap is too wide or too high, adjust it according to your liking. Pin or cut the fitting sample and apply the changes to the exact locations on the pattern. The sleeve must fit into the armhole with the appropriate amount of ease.

Sleeves Peaking Out or Hiking Up

Short Sleeves - Part 1

A) Identifying the Issue - The sleeve hem is too slanted and angles up. It looks like it is peaking out or hiking up on the side.

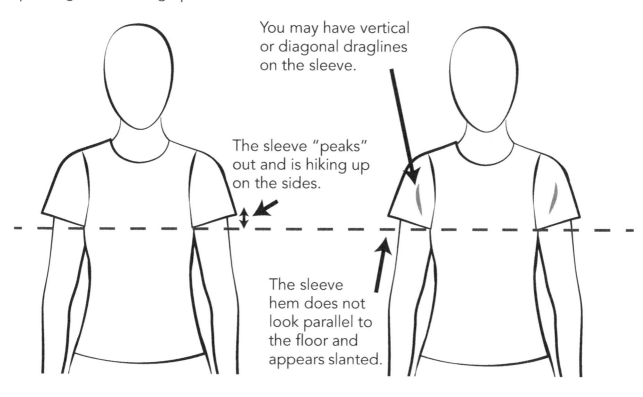

You may have vertical or diagonal draglines on the sleeve.

The sleeve "peaks" out and is hiking up on the sides.

The sleeve hem does not look parallel to the floor and appears slanted.

B) Cutting and Taping the Sample - Cut or unpick the armhole on the fitting sample, starting at the across front area and stopping at the across back area. Allow the sleeve to lower until the hemline appears parallel with the floor.

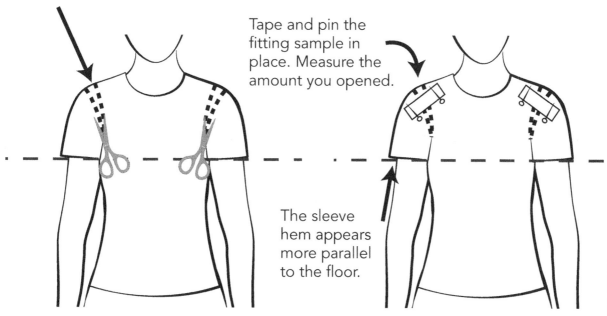

Tape and pin the fitting sample in place. Measure the amount you opened.

The sleeve hem appears more parallel to the floor.

Short Sleeves - Part 1 *(continued)*

C) Correcting the Pattern - Increase the cap height the same amount you opened in the shoulder area. If the across shoulder is too narrow, this correction can be done in conjunction with **"Shoulders Too Narrow - Option 2"** on pages 92 and 95. Then the amount opened would be split between the cap height and the armhole body panels. It is great to combine the corrections so the sleeve does not become too large.

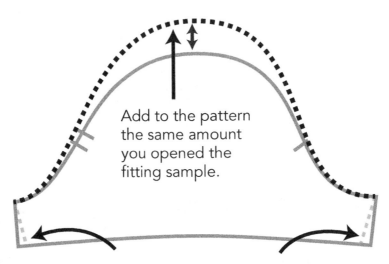

Add to the pattern the same amount you opened the fitting sample.

You may choose to reduce the bottom opening of the sleeve if you felt it was too loose and winging out too much. This is optional.

This correction makes the sleeve longer along the cap seam. You may either lower the armhole to fit the new sleeve or reduce the sleeve to fit into the existing armhole. To lower the armhole on the front and back body panels for the new sleeve, follow the front/back body panel corrections for **"High Armholes"** on page 134 in Steps 1 and 2.

A little curve on the cap can add a lot to the sleeve seam measurement. It is always trial and error until you find a sleeve cap height with minimal underarm draglines, no hiking-up issues, and allows the arm to lift easily. Do not add too much because the armhole will become too big to accommodate the larger sleeve. It is a tricky balance to find!

Alternatively, see the continuation of this correction on pages 150-151 for **"Reducing the Sleeve pattern to Fit into the Armhole - Part 2."** This correction shows how to reduce the new sleeve to fit the existing armhole. This will reduce the sleeve cap width, bicep, and possibly bottom hem opening, depending on how you Slash & Close.

After the correction, measure the armhole and sleeve to be sure they will fit together. Account for the same amount of sleeve cap ease that the original pattern had.

Sleeves Peaking Out or Hiking Up

Long Sleeves - Part 1

The issue of sleeves peaking out or hiking up appears slightly different in long sleeves. The issues appear in the form of excessive draglines under the arm. Notice that Steps (B) and (C) are the same correction as short sleeves on the previous pages.

A) Identifying the Issue - There are diagonal draglines on the underarm area of the sleeves. According to The GRD Method™ in fitting, diagonal draglines point up toward the area that should be cut open and lowered. This will be explained in the last chapter of this book. In this situation, the cap height needs to be opened and lowered.

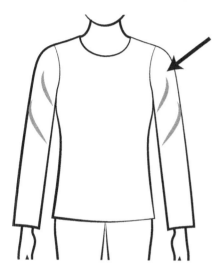

The diagonal draglines at the underarm area point up toward the cap height, indicating that the cap height should be opened. These draglines are a sign that the cap height is too short.

B) Cutting and Taping the Sample - Cut or unpick the sleeve on the fitting sample, starting at the across front area and stopping at the across back area. Allow the sleeves to lower until the draglines are reduced.

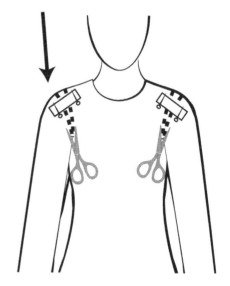

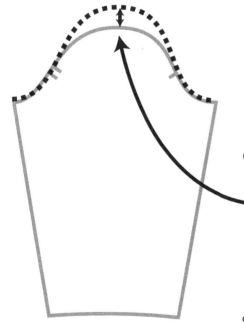

C) Correcting the Pattern - Increase the cap height the same amount you opened in the shoulder area. If the across shoulder is too narrow, this correction can be done in conjunction with **"Shoulders Too Narrow - Option 2"** on pages 92 and 95. Then the amount opened would be split between the cap height and the armhole body panels. It is great to combine the corrections so the sleeve does not become too large.

See the Part 2 continuation of this correction on the following pages. Refer to the fitting video from pages 147-148 for this pattern correction.

Reducing the Sleeve To Fit into the Armhole
Part 2 - Short and Long Sleeves (*continued from Part 1*)

Since the sleeve cap height is now taller, the sleeve will likely be too large for the armhole. The same method can apply to both long and short sleeves. The goal is to make the sleeve fit into the armhole with the same amount of ease before the correction. To do this, the two options are:

Option 1 - Lower the armhole, making it bigger. Follow the front/back body panel corrections for **"High Armholes,"** found on page 134 in Steps 1 and 2.

Option 2 - Slash & Close in several areas, reducing the sleeve measurement to fit into the armhole. The following correction shows this option.

1. Place the sleeve on the bodice pattern, aligning the "reverse curve" area between the side seam and notches. The curves should be the same on the armhole and the sleeve in this "reverse curve" area. If the sleeve's curve is too wide, Slash & Close in this reverse curve area until it matches. If it fits well, you do not need to Slash & Close in this specific area. If the curve shapes do not match, find the halfway point between the two lines. Redraw both lines to the halfway point.

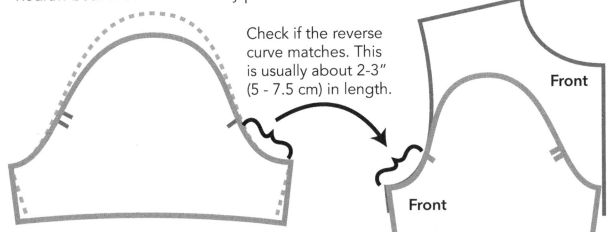

Check if the reverse curve matches. This is usually about 2-3" (5 - 7.5 cm) in length.

Front

Front

2. Determine the amount to slash the sleeve closed.

   • Start by measuring the seam line of the armhole on the front and back body panels. For this example, let's say the armhole measures 19" (48.2 cm).

   • Measure the original sleeve pattern along the armhole seam line, prior to the correction.

   Example: 19 1/2" (49.5 cm). This means there is 1/2" (1.3 cm) of ease on the sleeve.

   • Measure the new sleeve pattern with the taller cap height.

   Example: 20 1/2" (52 cm). This means a total of 1" (2.5 cm) should be slashed out to achieve the original sleeve measurement. The amount to slash out will be spread over several areas on the sleeve. Please consider that this will reduce the cap width and the bicep.

Reducing the Sleeve To Fit into the Armhole
Part 2 *(continued)*

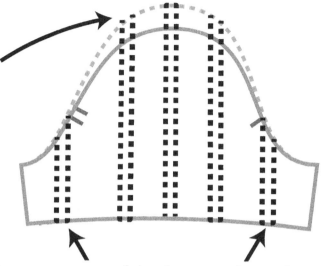

3. Mark vertical lines on the sleeve pattern where you will Slash & Close. The small distance between each vertical line adds up to the total amount you will close. The goal is to achieve the same length of the armhole plus the ease amount. Consider that this correction reduces the cap width and bicep. If you have a fitting sample, it is a good idea to pin the amount you are slashing closed to double-check it. If you do not have a fitting sample, achieve the cap width measurement from pages 145-146.

Only if the reverse curve of the sleeve was larger than the armhole curve, would you Slash & Close in the appropriate reverse curve area. If the sleeve was not matching and too short in this area, Slash & Spread in this area to make it fit the body reverse curves.

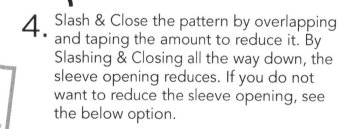

4. Slash & Close the pattern by overlapping and taping the amount to reduce it. By Slashing & Closing all the way down, the sleeve opening reduces. If you do not want to reduce the sleeve opening, see the below option.

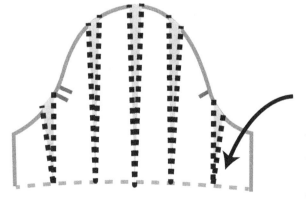

Alternatively, if you do not want to Slash & Close the bottom sleeve opening, go to zero. This would maintain the bottom sleeve opening as the original pattern, and you would only overlap the top sleeve portion to achieve the measurement of the armhole. It would also keep the bicep bigger than slashing out the full amount in that area.

(continued on next page)

Reducing the Sleeve To Fit into the Armhole
Part 2 (continued)

5. Once you Slashed & Closed the pattern, the sleeve curve will not be smooth. True the line, making the curve continuous.

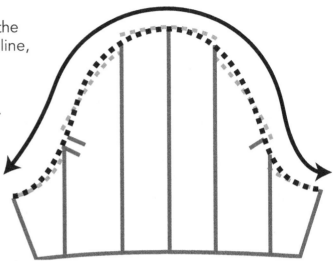

After the correction, measure the armhole and sleeve to be sure they will fit together. Account for the same amount of sleeve cap ease that the original pattern had.

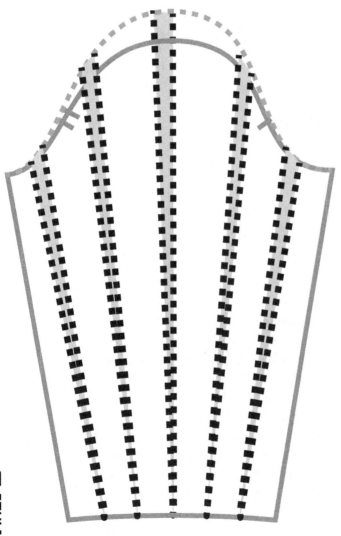

Long Sleeves: Follow the same method for long sleeves. You may choose to go to zero at the bottom opening to maintain the original sleeve hem opening. Also, consider that this correction will reduce the bicep, elbow, and sleeve cap width according to the amount you Slash & Close in those areas. If you have a fitting sample, pin the amount on the bicep, elbow, and sleeve cap width to check it before you adjust the pattern.

Bicep Too Big on a Sleeve

How To Reduce a Bicep on the Pattern

A) Identifying the Issue - The bicep area is too loose on the fitting sample. This might be indicated by vertical draglines or a loose feeling of too much fabric in the bicep area.

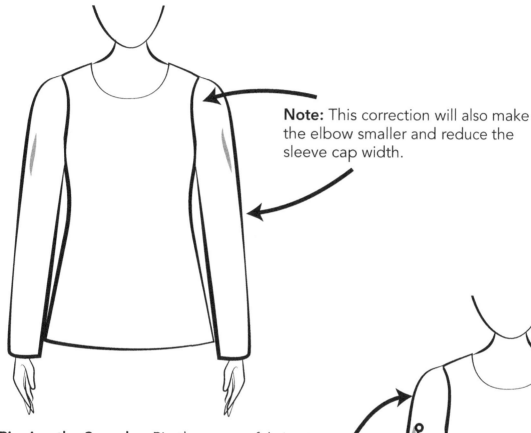

Note: This correction will also make the elbow smaller and reduce the sleeve cap width.

B) Pinning the Sample - Pin the excess fabric at the bicep. Measure the amount you pinned.

If the sleeve cap width is also loose, pin this area. If it is too tight when you pin the sleeve cap width, note the original sleeve cap width to achieve on the pattern correction.

The pattern corrections shown on pages 153-156 can be done in the opposite ways: Slash & Spread or Slash & Close. I have shown a different option for each fitting issue as an example for the slashing positions. In other words, you may use the correction from page 156 for this fitting issue, but close the pattern instead of opening it. Then, no adjustment to the sleeve cap is needed. Follow either option for slashing positions.

How To Reduce a Bicep on the Pattern (continued)

C) Correcting the Pattern - This is a Slash & Close pattern correction.

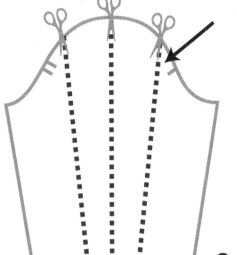

1. Cut three long lines vertically on the sleeve. The lines should be distributed along the sleeve as shown.

4. Add to the cap height and width to fit into the armhole pattern. Alternatively, reduce the armhole pattern by raising the armhole position on the body pattern pieces (as shown on page 131 in Steps 1 and 2). After the correction, measure the armhole and sleeve to be sure they will fit together. Account for the same amount of sleeve cap ease that the original pattern had.

2. Stop cutting before you reach the sleeve edge.

5. After you Slash & Close the bicep area, measure the width of the sleeve cap. Make sure you achieve the desired measurement that you noted during Step (B) - Pinning the Sample. If the measurement is too small, add to the sleeve cap width. By adding to the width of the sleeve cap in this area, the bicep and the lower part of the sleeve remain smaller, while the sleeve cap still achieves your desired amount for movement.

3. Distribute the amount to reduce the bicep among all three lines. Draw the secondary lines indicating the amount to close. Slash & Close the vertical lines.

6. If you need to reduce the bicep by a significant amount, reduce additionally at the underarm seam. Check the reverse curves again to the armhole pattern to ensure that they match (as shown on page 140). If you only want to reduce a small amount on the bicep without reducing the cap width, reduce here at the underarm seams only. Alternatively, you may reduce the sleeve by curving the underarm seam as shown on page 156.

Bicep Too Small on a Sleeve

How To Increase a Bicep on the Pattern

A) Identifying the Issue - The bicep area is too tight on the fitting sample. This might be indicated by horizontal draglines or a tight, uncomfortable feeling.

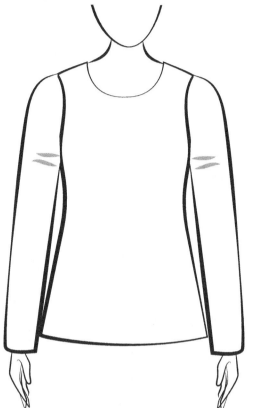

Note: This correction will also make the elbow bigger. However, you can reduce the elbow after the correction to keep it the same size. It will also increase the sleeve cap width.

The pattern corrections shown on pages 153-156 can be done in the opposite ways: Slash & Spread or Slash & Close. I have shown a different option for each fitting issue as an example for the slashing positions. In other words, you may use the correction from page 154 for this fitting issue, but open the pattern instead of closing it. Then reduce the cap height to fit in the armhole. Follow either option for slashing positions.

B) Cutting the Sample - Open the underarm seam to see how much to add to the bicep area. Continue cutting down to the elbow if needed. In some cases, you may need to also open the side seam at the chest to allow enough room for the bicep.

Tape and pin the opened area. Measure the amount you opened.

Bicep Too Small on a Sleeve

How To Increase a Bicep on the Pattern (continued)

C) Correcting the Pattern - This is a Slash & Spread pattern correction.

Cut the pattern as shown.

2. Stop cutting before you reach the sleeve cap edges.

6. True the sleeve cap seam, making it continuous.

3. Stop cutting before you reach the hemline edge.

5. Allow this area of the sleeve cap to overlap.

4. Allow the pattern to open the same amount you opened the sample. This is the amount the bicep will increase. If you want to keep the elbow the same size, add a slight curve on the underarm seams to reduce the elbow as needed.

The great thing about this correction is that the sleeve will still fit into the armhole without adjusting the armhole pattern. This correction shortens the cap height, which improves the arm lift and increases the sleeve cap width.

The downside to this correction: since the cap height is shorter, it could increase some diagonal draglines in the undersleeve area. If you want to avoid this and go back to the original sleeve cap height, increase the armhole by lowering the armhole position on the body panels, as shown on page 134 in Steps 1 and 2.

Bust Corrections

Many people struggle with how garments fit in the bust area. If your bust size is not a B-cup, you will likely be using this chapter at some point in your customization process. These are more complex corrections, but with practice, it becomes easier.

I break down the options in this chapter by the type of style you chose. Whether your style has princess seams, side darts, french darts, or no darts, you will find an option to follow here. Do not let all the options overwhelm you. Pick the option based on the criteria of the style: location of darts, princess seams, or no darts.

The first section explains a way to check the measurements of the pattern. This is a more advanced method since it requires understanding desired ease amounts. If you are not ready for this, just read it, and know it is here when you are more advanced in pattern corrections.

This chapter covers both Full and Small Bust Adjustments. These corrections are done only in womenswear. The options with darts are generally only for woven styles. For knit styles, follow the option without darts.

If you notice the bustline in the wrong position, mark the fitting sample and move all the darts/apex points as needed.

It is time to have that perfectly-fitting bodice to show off your lovely style! Let's start with the bust adjustments!

Bust Adjustments

Checking the Pattern

A bust adjustment is needed when the person has a larger or smaller bra cup size than the sewing pattern. Most pattern companies create their sewing patterns based on a standard B-cup bust size. If you are not a B-cup or are between cup sizes in standard, ready-to-wear bras, you will likely need an adjustment.

Sizes larger than B-cup require a Full Bust Adjustment (FBA). Sizes smaller than B-cup require a Small Bust Adjustment (SBA).

There are many different ways of approaching bust adjustments because every style has different design lines (such as dart placements or princess seams). The most common corrections require either the Slash & Spread method for a Full Bust Adjustment or the Slash & Close option for a Small Bust Adjustment.

If you already have a fitting sample, skip these steps in the next three pages. Follow the rest of the chapter for your adjustments.

However, advanced sewists may make the pattern corrections before making the first fitting sample. This is done by measuring the patterns, determining wearing ease, and figuring out if the pattern measurements are correct for your body.

The following example shows how to determine if the pattern needs a bust adjustment before making a sample. This method is more difficult because you need to understand wearing ease in order to do it.

Many patterns give the finished garment measurements, or you can find them by measuring the pattern yourself. Check the following body and pattern measurements with the method shown.

If there are multiple pattern pieces in the front and back panels, join them together at the seam lines to create a complete front and complete back panel.

1) Above Bust: Measure the smallest circumference above the breasts and under the armhole. This is generally tilted upward in the front of the body and NOT parallel to the floor.

Above Bust Body Measurement:

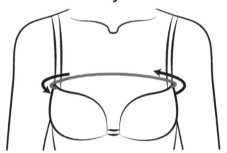

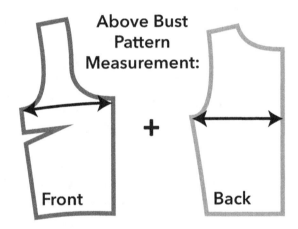

Above Bust Pattern Measurement:

Front

Back

Measure the pattern pieces at the under armhole to the CF or CB.

(Front + Back Pattern Amounts) x 2 = the Above Bust Circumference

All formulas are multiplied by two because only half of the pattern was measured (to the CF and CB).

An alternative method to measuring the above bust is to measure the under bust. However, this method is harder to compare to the full bust measurement because garments tend to be less-fitted under the bust, which gives different proportional amounts in ease.

Bust Adjustments

Checking the Pattern *(continued)*

When measuring your body, it is CRITICAL that you are relaxed with your arms at your sides. If your arms and elbows are up, your circumference measurements will be smaller and inaccurate. To learn how to self-measure, sign up for my free mini-course series through the QR code below. Always double-check your body measurements for accuracy.

2) Bust: Measure the largest circumference of the bust going over the apex area. This should be parallel to the floor. Measure the apex position from the HPS.

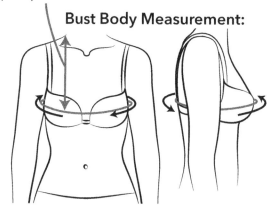

Bust Body Measurement:

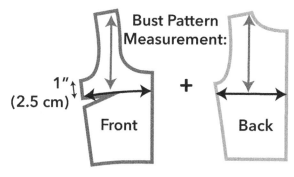

Bust Pattern Measurement:

1" (2.5 cm)

Front + Back

Measure the pattern pieces at the bustline. This is typically about 1" (2.5 cm) below the armhole at the side seam, then go to the CF or CB. Make sure the distance from the apex to the high point shoulder is the same on the pattern and on your body.

(Front + Back Pattern Amounts) x 2 = the Full Bust Circumference

If the bust or waist position is incorrect on the pattern in comparison to the body measurements, raise or lower the positions on the pattern as needed.

3) Waist: Measure the smallest part of the waist, usually slightly higher than the belly button. This should be parallel to the floor. If you are unsure where your waistline is, lean to the side; your waist is where your torso bends. Measure the waist position from the HPS.

Waist Body Measurement:

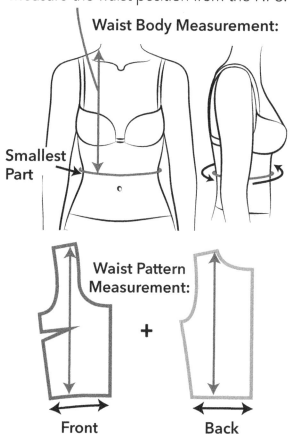

Smallest Part

Waist Pattern Measurement:

Front + Back

Measure the pattern pieces at the waistline, from the side seam to the CF or CB. Make sure the distance from the waist to the high point shoulder is the same on the pattern and on your body.

(Front + Back Pattern Amounts) x 2 = the True Waist Circumference

(continued on next page)

Bust Corrections

Bust Adjustments

Checking the Pattern (*continued*)

The next step is to compare the pattern measurements to your body. You must consider the wearing ease and design ease included in a pattern. This determines the finished garment's measurements. The ease amounts can vary from style to style. The below example shows the calculation in imperial units. However, you can enter any unit of measurement (inches or centimeters) into the formulas.

Let's say the pattern measures **33" for the *above bust*** and **34" for the bust**. Because you are measuring a pattern, these amounts include wearing ease.

The body measurements are **32" for the *above bust* measurement** and **35" for the bust**. Because they are the body measurements, no ease is included. Consider how much ease you would like.

For this example, you want to have 1" of wearing ease. Therefore, add 1" to your body measurements: **(32" + 1" ease = 33" *above bust*)** and **(35" + 1" ease = 36" bust)**.

Therefore, the pattern is fine with the 33" *above bust* since it is the same as the body measurement + ease. However, your bust body measurement + ease = 36", which is 2" bigger than the pattern's 34" bust measurement.

(Bust Body Measurement + Ease) - Bust Pattern Measurement = Amount Needed for the Bust Adjustment

Because the target 36" bust measurement is 2" larger than the pattern piece, an adjustment is needed. To do this, slash the pattern open 1" at the apex area (for a total of 2" added when both bodice pieces are cut). This is an example of a Full Bust Adjustment with a side dart. Follow the other corrections in this book for styles with princess seams, french darts, or no darts.

If the pattern and the body do not have the same above bust measurement when ease is considered, measure other pattern sizes to see if they are closer to your body + ease amount. If the above bust pattern is bigger than your body + ease amount, there will be armhole gaping.

The waist increases the amount you opened at the apex. If you do not need the extra waist amount, reduce the waist circumference on the side seams. Alternatively, you could add/eliminate waist darts or adjust existing waist darts/princess lines if they are on the pattern, to achieve your desired waist measurement.

Follow this chapter for a more detailed explanation to execute the pattern correction.

For this example, the amount you need to open the apex would be 1" here. The amount is measured horizontally, perpendicular to the CF line.

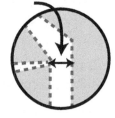

If your body measurement of the bust is smaller than the pattern measurement, this will result in a negative number using the formulas above. Therefore, it will require a Small Bust Adjustment with the Slash & Close method. The correction is the same as above. Instead of opening the pattern at the apex, you will close it by overlapping the pieces.

Full Bust Adjustment (FBA)

Side Darts or Adding Side Darts

Follow this correction for styles with side darts. Alternatively, follow this correction to add darts to a woven style that does not already have them. Adding darts will achieve a nicer fit.

A) Identifying the Issue - The bust is tight or pulling. There may be gaping at the neckline or armhole. There are often draglines from multiple locations pointing toward the apex area.

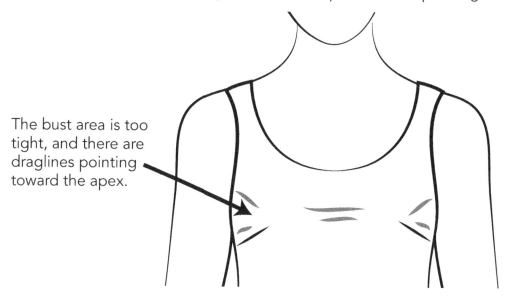

The bust area is too tight, and there are draglines pointing toward the apex.

B) Cutting, Taping, and Pinning the Sample - From the waistline, cut vertically along the front bust to the apex. Continue cutting toward the armhole, but stop cutting 1/16" (2 mm) from the armhole edge. Allow the slashed portion to relax open. Tape the opened portion at the apex, and measure the distance horizontally. This is the amount to open the pattern at the apex. Mark the apex location on the fitting sample or a piece of tape. If the style has no darts and you would like to add darts, draw a line indicating the desired dart position.

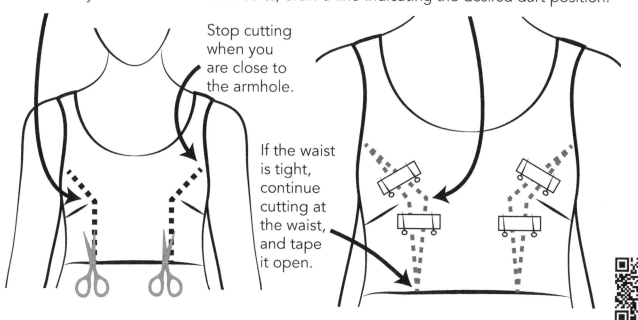

Stop cutting when you are close to the armhole.

If the waist is tight, continue cutting at the waist, and tape it open.

Bust Corrections

Full Bust Adjustment (FBA)

Side Darts or Adding Side Darts *(continued)*

C) Correcting the Pattern - This is a Slash & Spread pattern correction in which you will cut the pattern and open it. Always make pattern corrections to the seam line, not to the seam allowance cut line. Check the seam allowances after changes are completed, and adjust them if needed.

When using the Slash & Spread method, it is easiest to place a fresh piece of paper underneath the pattern. Tape the cut pieces to it, creating the new pattern piece.

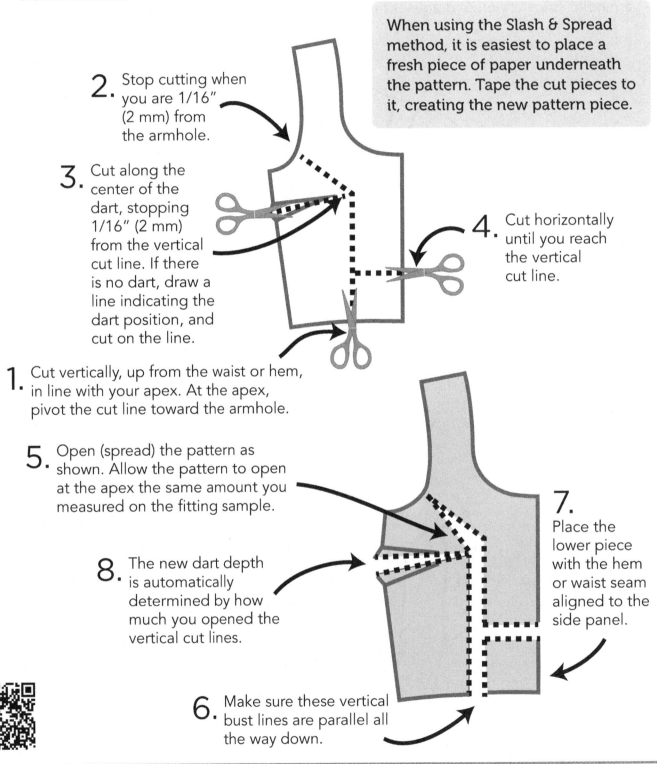

2. Stop cutting when you are 1/16" (2 mm) from the armhole.

3. Cut along the center of the dart, stopping 1/16" (2 mm) from the vertical cut line. If there is no dart, draw a line indicating the dart position, and cut on the line.

4. Cut horizontally until you reach the vertical cut line.

1. Cut vertically, up from the waist or hem, in line with your apex. At the apex, pivot the cut line toward the armhole.

5. Open (spread) the pattern as shown. Allow the pattern to open at the apex the same amount you measured on the fitting sample.

7. Place the lower piece with the hem or waist seam aligned to the side panel.

8. The new dart depth is automatically determined by how much you opened the vertical cut lines.

6. Make sure these vertical bust lines are parallel all the way down.

Side Darts or Adding Side Darts (continued)

9. On the new pattern piece, mark the apex. The location of your apex may require you to change the angle or position of the dart. If you need to adjust the dart position, keep the same depth at the side seam, and move it as needed. Draw the new dart point away from the apex the following amounts according to your cup size:

1" (2.5 cm) = B cup

1 1/4" (3 cm) = C cup

1 1/2" (3.5 cm) = D cup

1 3/4" (4.5 cm) = E cup

2" (5 cm) = + E cup

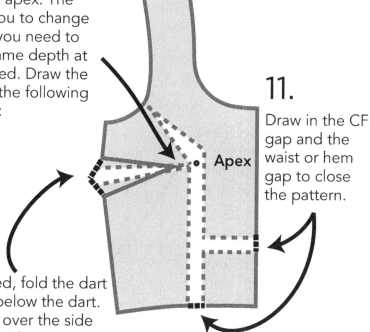

11. Draw in the CF gap and the waist or hem gap to close the pattern.

Apex

10. After the dart legs are marked, fold the dart closed with the folded part below the dart. Run a pointed tracing wheel over the side seam. This will give the new side seam dart shaping when the dart unfolds.

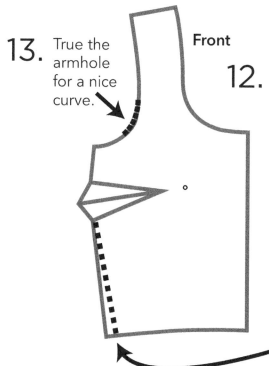

Front

Back

13. True the armhole for a nice curve.

12. The waist became bigger since the front vertical lines spread apart the pattern. To reduce the waist, remove half of the vertical amount from the front pattern and half from the back pattern at the side seams. Go to zero at the dart or armhole position. Alternatively, you may add waist darts to reduce the waist. If the waist was too tight on the fitting sample, skip this step of adjusting the waist.

Your pattern is ready to go! Great work on your Full Bust Adjustment!

Bust Corrections

Full Bust Adjustment (FBA)

Princess Seams

A) Identifying the Issue - The bust is tight or pulling. There may be gaping at the neckline or armhole. There are often draglines pointing toward the apex area and specifically diagonal draglines on the side panel.

The bust area is too tight, and there are diagonal draglines on the side panel.

This correction can also be done on a style with a princess seam coming from the armhole. For this, cut below the princess seam at the armhole.

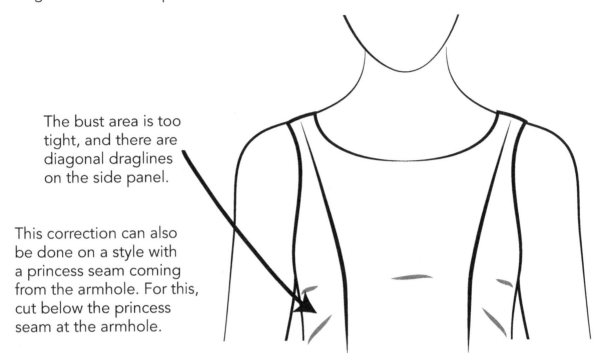

B) Cutting, Taping, and Pinning the Sample - Cut horizontally between the apex positions. Continue cutting toward the armhole, but stop cutting 1/16" (2 mm) from the armhole edge. Allow the slashed portion to relax open. Tape the opened portion at the apex, and measure the distance vertically. This is the amount to open the pattern at the apex. Mark the apex location on the fitting sample or a piece of tape.

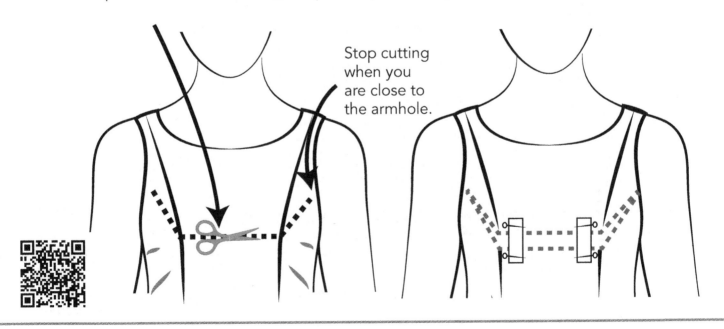

Stop cutting when you are close to the armhole.

Full Bust Adjustment (FBA)

Princess Seams *(continued)*

C) Correcting the Pattern - This is a Slash & Spread pattern correction in which you will cut the pattern and open it. Always make pattern corrections to the seam line, not to the seam allowance cut line. Check the seam allowances after changes are completed, and adjust them if needed.

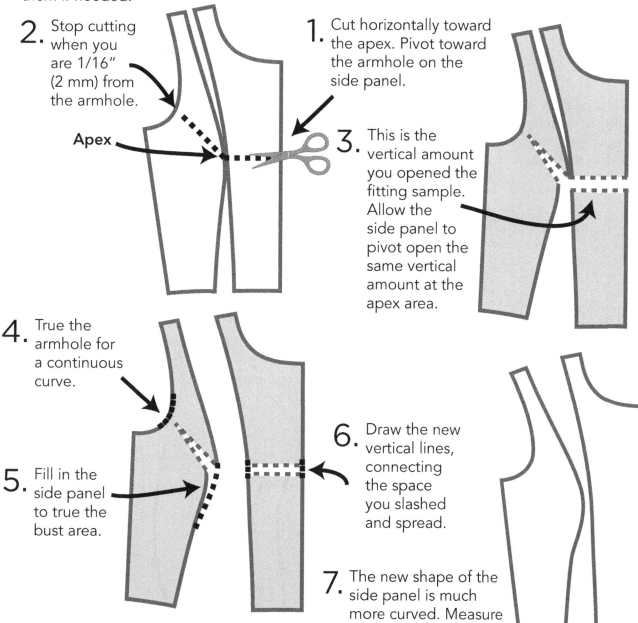

2. Stop cutting when you are 1/16" (2 mm) from the armhole.

Apex

1. Cut horizontally toward the apex. Pivot toward the armhole on the side panel.

3. This is the vertical amount you opened the fitting sample. Allow the side panel to pivot open the same vertical amount at the apex area.

4. True the armhole for a continuous curve.

5. Fill in the side panel to true the bust area.

6. Draw the new vertical lines, connecting the space you slashed and spread.

7. The new shape of the side panel is much more curved. Measure both panels along the princess seams to ensure they fit together. Place a notch on the seam allowances, indicating the apex position (this is not shown in the images above since there are no seam allowances on these sketches).

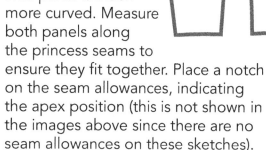

When using the Slash & Spread method, it is easiest to place a fresh piece of paper underneath the pattern. Tape the cut pieces to it, creating the new pattern piece.

Bust Corrections

Full Bust Adjustment (FBA)

French Darts

A) Identifying the Issue - The bust is tight or pulling. There may be gaping at the neckline or armhole. There are often draglines from multiple locations pointing toward the apex area.

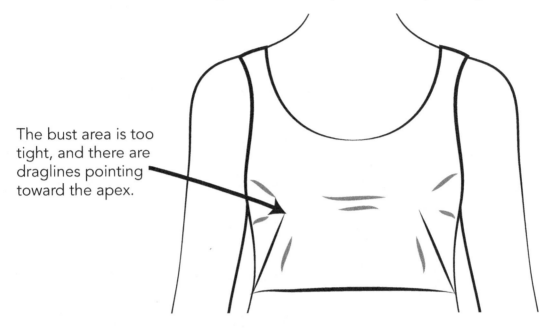

The bust area is too tight, and there are draglines pointing toward the apex.

B) Cutting, Taping, and Pinning the Sample - From the waistline, cut vertically along the front bust to the apex. Continue cutting toward the armhole, but stop cutting 1/16" (2 mm) from the armhole edge. Allow the slashed portion to relax open. Tape the opened portion at the apex, and measure the distance horizontally. This is the amount to open the pattern at the apex. Mark the apex location on the fitting sample or a piece of tape.

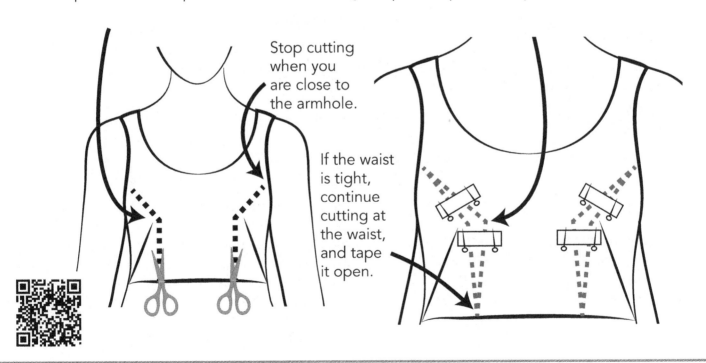

Stop cutting when you are close to the armhole.

If the waist is tight, continue cutting at the waist, and tape it open.

Full Bust Adjustment (FBA)

French Darts *(continued)*

C) Correcting the Pattern - This is a Slash & Spread pattern correction in which you will cut the pattern and open it. Always make pattern corrections to the seam line, not to the seam allowance cut line. Check the seam allowances after changes are completed, and adjust them if needed.

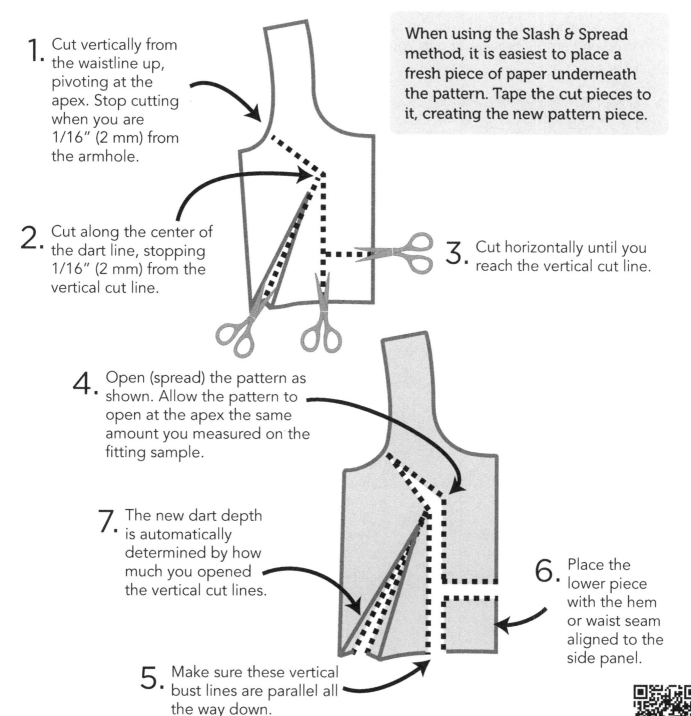

1. Cut vertically from the waistline up, pivoting at the apex. Stop cutting when you are 1/16" (2 mm) from the armhole.

When using the Slash & Spread method, it is easiest to place a fresh piece of paper underneath the pattern. Tape the cut pieces to it, creating the new pattern piece.

2. Cut along the center of the dart line, stopping 1/16" (2 mm) from the vertical cut line.

3. Cut horizontally until you reach the vertical cut line.

4. Open (spread) the pattern as shown. Allow the pattern to open at the apex the same amount you measured on the fitting sample.

7. The new dart depth is automatically determined by how much you opened the vertical cut lines.

6. Place the lower piece with the hem or waist seam aligned to the side panel.

5. Make sure these vertical bust lines are parallel all the way down.

(continued on next page)

Bust Corrections

Full Bust Adjustment (FBA)

French Darts (*continued*)

8. On the new pattern piece, mark the apex. The location of your apex may require you to change the angle or position of the dart. If you need to adjust the dart position, keep the same depth at the waist seam, and move it as needed. Draw the new dart point away from the apex the following amounts according to your cup size:

1" (2.5 cm) = B cup

1 1/4" (3 cm)= C cup

1 1/2" (3.5 cm) = D cup

1 3/4" (4.5 cm) = E cup

2" (5 cm) = + E cup

9. After the dart legs are marked, fold the dart closed with the folded part toward the CF. Run a pointed tracing wheel over the waist seam. This will give the new dart shaping along the waist seam when the dart unfolds.

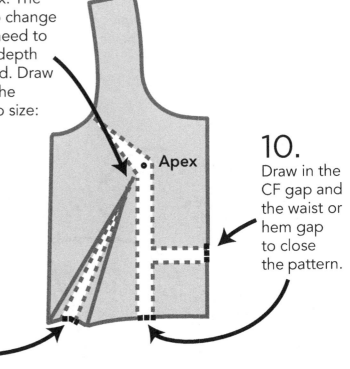

Apex

10. Draw in the CF gap and the waist or hem gap to close the pattern.

12. True the armhole seam, making it continuous.

Front

11. The waist became bigger since the front vertical lines spread apart the pattern. To reduce the waist, remove half of the vertical amount from the front pattern and half from the back pattern at the side seams. Go to zero at the dart or armhole position. If the waist was too tight on the fitting sample, skip this step of adjusting the waist.

Back

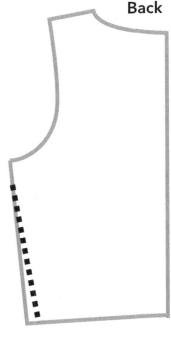

13. If you want the dart to be directly in the corner of the side seam and waist seam, pivot the dart the amount you are reducing the side seam on the front.

Full Bust Adjustment (FBA)

No Darts or Princess Seams

A) Identifying the Issue - The bust is tight or pulling. There may be gaping at the neckline or armhole. There are often draglines from multiple locations pointing toward the apex area.

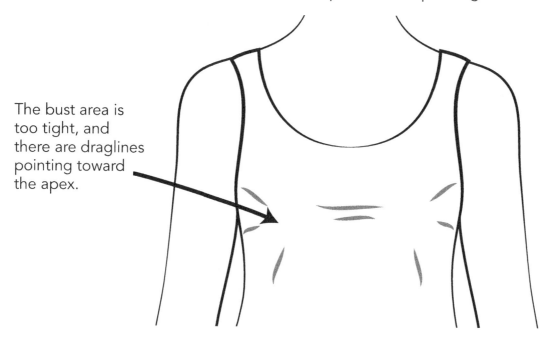

The bust area is too tight, and there are draglines pointing toward the apex.

B) Cutting, Taping, and Pinning the Sample - From the waistline, cut vertically along the front bust to the apex. Continue cutting toward the armhole, but stop cutting 1/16" (2 mm) from the armhole edge. Allow the slashed portion to relax open. Tape the opened portion at the apex, and measure the distance horizontally. This is the amount to open the pattern at the apex.

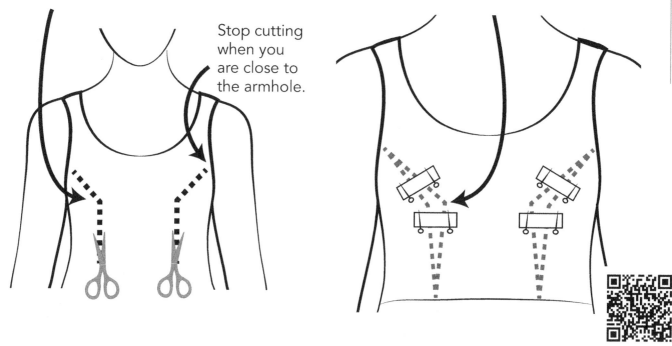

Stop cutting when you are close to the armhole.

Full Bust Adjustment (FBA)

No Darts or Princess Seams (*continued*)

C) Correcting the pattern - This is a pivoting pattern correction. Place a piece of patternmaking paper under the pattern piece.

1. Using the amount you opened the fitting sample at the apex, mark that distance away from the armhole at the side seam.

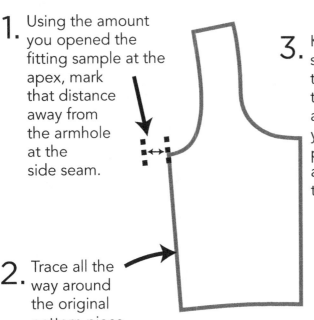

2. Trace all the way around the original pattern piece for reference.

3. Keeping the low point shoulder aligned, pivot the pattern piece until the armhole edge aligns with the mark you made. Trace the pattern for the new armhole from the LPS to the mark.

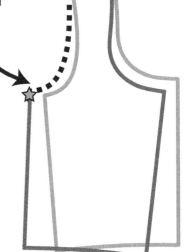

4. Using the new under armhole position as a pivot point, move the pattern piece until the side seam aligns with the waist. Connect these points to make a new side seam.

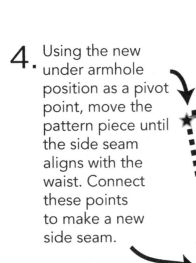

5. The new pattern will look like this. The dotted lines are the adjusted pattern lines. Ignore the old side seam and armhole lines from Step 2.

The waistline may need to be raised slightly to keep the same side seam length. Align the front and back pattern pieces along the side seams, and true the waist or hem seams.

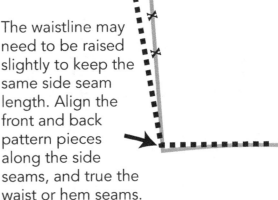

Another option is to add a side dart to your style. For this option, follow the correction to add a side dart as shown on pages 161-163.

Small Bust Adjustment (SBA)

Side Darts

Follow this correction for styles with side darts.

A) Identifying the Issue - The fitting sample is too loose at the bust area, and there is excess fabric. The garment does not lie well against the body along the front bust area.

The bust area is too loose. You may have vertical draglines, which are a sign that the garment is too big.

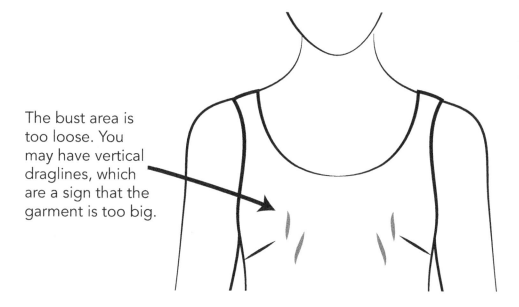

B) Pinning the Problem - Pin the excess fabric vertically in the front bust area, and measure the amount you pinned. Mark the apex location on the fitting sample.

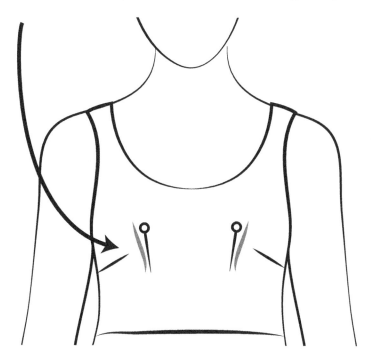

Small Bust Adjustment (SBA)

Side Darts *(continued)*

C) Correcting the Pattern - This is a Slash & Close pattern correction in which you will cut the pattern and overlap it to close it. Always make pattern corrections to the seam line, not to the seam allowance cut line. Check the seam allowances after changes are completed, and adjust them if needed.

2. Stop cutting when you are 1/16" (2 mm) from the armhole.

4. Cut horizontally until you reach the vertical cut line.

5. The pieces will separate like this, though you are NOT spreading the pattern. In the next steps, you will close the pattern.

3. Cut along the center of the dart. Stop cutting 1/16" (2 mm) from the vertical cut line.

1. Cut vertically, up from the waist or hem, in line with your apex. At the apex, pivot the cut line toward the armhole.

6. Close the pattern as shown by overlapping the vertical bust lines the amount you pinned and measured on the fitting sample.

9. The new dart depth is automatically determined from the overlapping of the vertical bust lines. You will keep the original dart leg lines. They will be closer together, making the dart less deep.

8. Overlap the lower piece. The hem or waist seam should align with the side panel.

7. Make sure these vertical bust lines are parallel all the way down as they overlap each other.

Small Bust Adjustment (SBA)

Side Darts *(continued)*

10. Mark the apex position. The location of your apex may require you to change the angle or position of the dart. If you need to adjust the dart position, keep the same depth at the side seam, and move it as needed. Draw the new dart legs with the dart point 3/4" (2 cm) from the apex.

Apex

Tape the overlapping pieces together, and make sure all the outer edges are smooth.

11. After the dart legs are marked, fold the dart closed with the folded part below the dart. Run a pointed tracing wheel over the side seam. This will give the new side seam dart shaping when the dart unfolds.

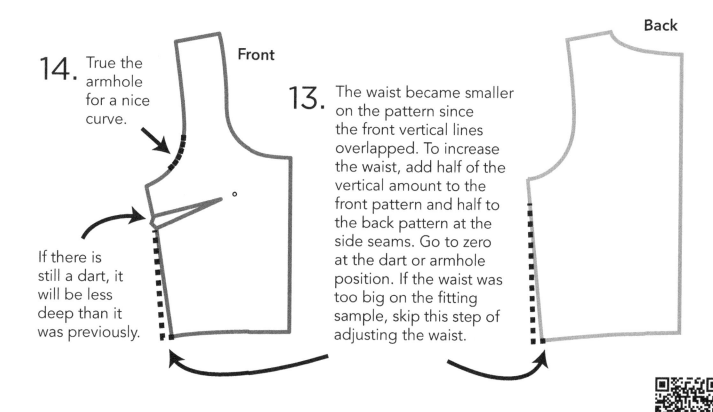

Back

Front

14. True the armhole for a nice curve.

If there is still a dart, it will be less deep than it was previously.

13. The waist became smaller on the pattern since the front vertical lines overlapped. To increase the waist, add half of the vertical amount to the front pattern and half to the back pattern at the side seams. Go to zero at the dart or armhole position. If the waist was too big on the fitting sample, skip this step of adjusting the waist.

Small Bust Adjustment (SBA)

Princess Seams

A) Identifying the Issue - The fitting sample is too loose at the bust area, and there is excess fabric. The garment does not lie well against the body along the front bust area.

The bust area is too loose. You may have vertical draglines, which are a sign that the garment is too big.

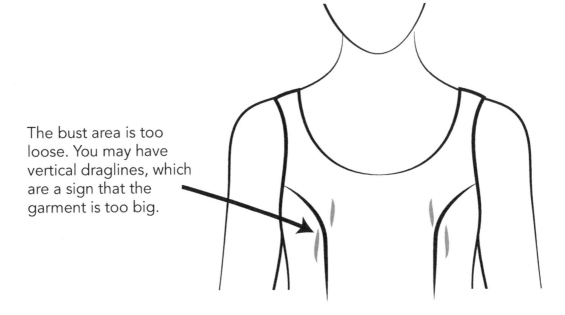

B) Pinning the Problem - Pin the excess fabric horizontally in the front bust area, and measure the amount you pinned.

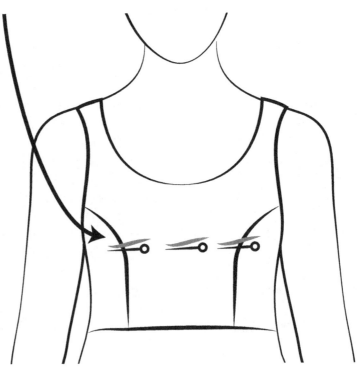

Small Bust Adjustment (SBA)

Princess Seams (continued)

C) Correcting the Pattern - This is a Slash & Close pattern correction where you cut the pattern and overlap to close it. Always make pattern corrections to the seam line, not to the seam allowance cut line. Check the seam allowances after changes are completed, and adjust them if needed.

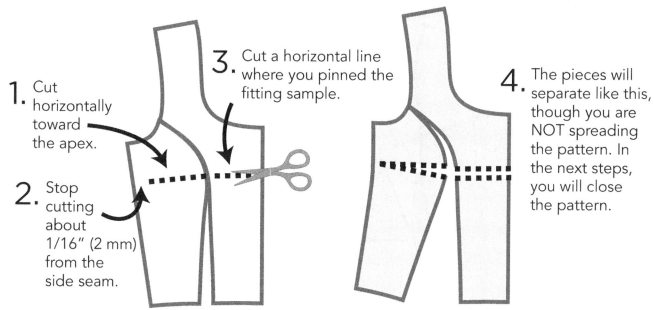

1. Cut horizontally toward the apex.

2. Stop cutting about 1/16" (2 mm) from the side seam.

3. Cut a horizontal line where you pinned the fitting sample.

4. The pieces will separate like this, though you are NOT spreading the pattern. In the next steps, you will close the pattern.

5. Now, close the slashed lines by overlapping the pattern pieces the amount you pinned.

6. The black dotted lines show how the piece shifts when the slashed lines are closed.

7. True the new princess line and the side seam.

8. Overlap the pieces of the front panel to fit with the side panel.

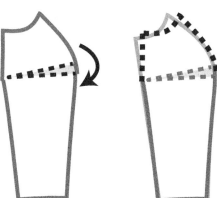

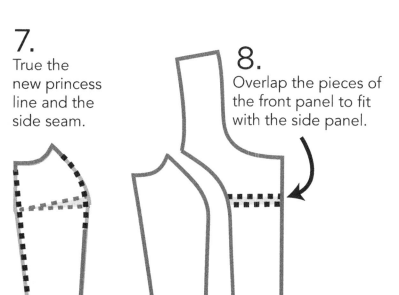

Measure the pattern pieces to be sure they fit together after the correction.

9. Place a notch on the seam allowances, indicating the apex position (this is not shown in the images since there are no seam allowances on these sketches).

Bust Corrections

Small Bust Adjustment (SBA)

French Darts

A) Identifying the Issue - The fitting sample is too loose at the bust area, and there is excess fabric. The garment does not lie well against the body along the front bust area.

The bust area is too loose. You may have vertical draglines, which are a sign that the garment is too big.

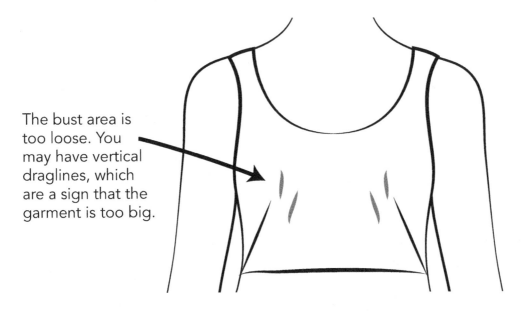

B) Pinning the Problem - Pin the excess fabric vertically in the front bust area, and measure the amount you pinned. Mark the apex location on the fitting sample.

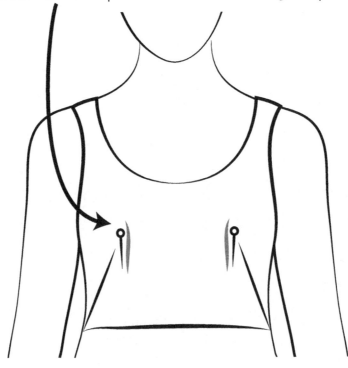

Small Bust Adjustment (SBA)

French Darts (continued)

C) Correcting the Pattern - This is a Slash & Close pattern correction where you cut the pattern and overlap it to close it. Always make pattern corrections to the seam line, not to the seam allowance cut line. Check the seam allowances after changes are completed, and adjust them if needed.

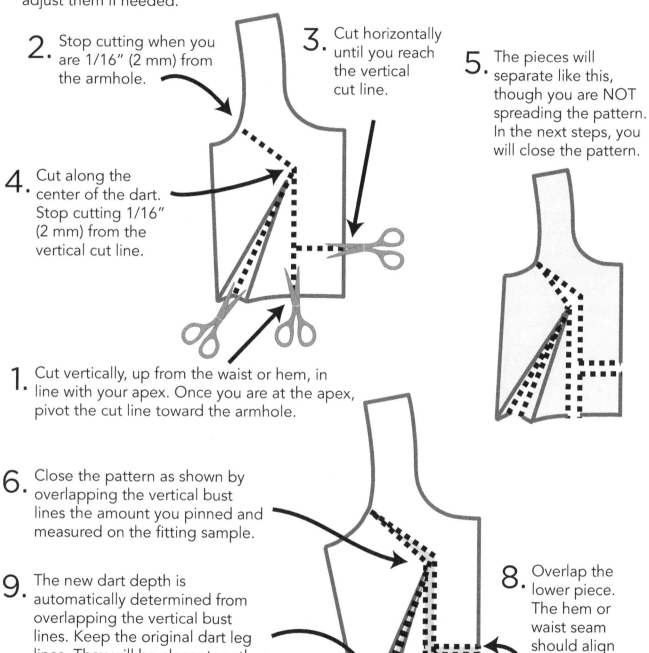

2. Stop cutting when you are 1/16" (2 mm) from the armhole.

3. Cut horizontally until you reach the vertical cut line.

5. The pieces will separate like this, though you are NOT spreading the pattern. In the next steps, you will close the pattern.

4. Cut along the center of the dart. Stop cutting 1/16" (2 mm) from the vertical cut line.

1. Cut vertically, up from the waist or hem, in line with your apex. Once you are at the apex, pivot the cut line toward the armhole.

6. Close the pattern as shown by overlapping the vertical bust lines the amount you pinned and measured on the fitting sample.

9. The new dart depth is automatically determined from overlapping the vertical bust lines. Keep the original dart leg lines. They will be closer together, making the dart less deep.

7. Make sure these vertical bust lines are parallel all the way down as they overlap each other.

8. Overlap the lower piece. The hem or waist seam should align with the side panel.

(continued on next page)

Bust Corrections

French Darts *(continued)*

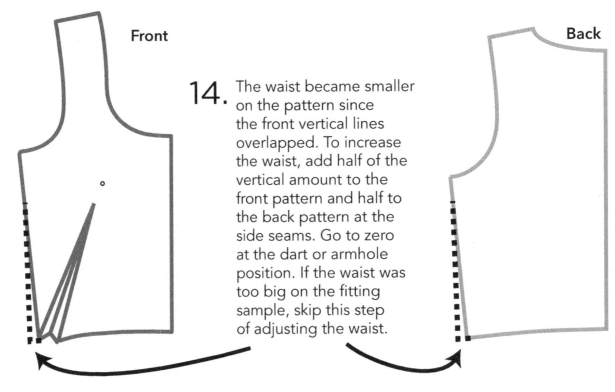

10. True the armhole for a continuous curve.

11. Mark the apex position. The location of your apex may require you to change the angle or position of the dart. If you need to adjust the dart position, keep the same depth at the waist seam, and move it as needed. Draw the new dart legs with the dart point 3/4" (2 cm) from the apex.

12. If you still have a dart, it will be less deep than it was previously. After the dart legs are marked, fold the dart closed with the folded part toward the CF. Run a pointed tracing wheel over the waist seam. This will give the new dart shaping along the waist seam when the dart unfolds.

Apex

13. Tape the overlapping pieces together, and make sure all the outer edges are smooth.

Front

Back

14. The waist became smaller on the pattern since the front vertical lines overlapped. To increase the waist, add half of the vertical amount to the front pattern and half to the back pattern at the side seams. Go to zero at the dart or armhole position. If the waist was too big on the fitting sample, skip this step of adjusting the waist.

15. If you want the dart to be directly in the corner of the side seam and waist seam, pivot the dart the amount you are adding to the side seam on the front.

Small Bust Adjustment (SBA)

No Darts or Princess Seams

A) Identifying the Issue - The fitting sample is too loose at the bust area, and there is excess fabric. The garment does not lie well against the body along the front bust area.

The bust area is too loose. You may have vertical draglines, which are a sign that the garment is too big.

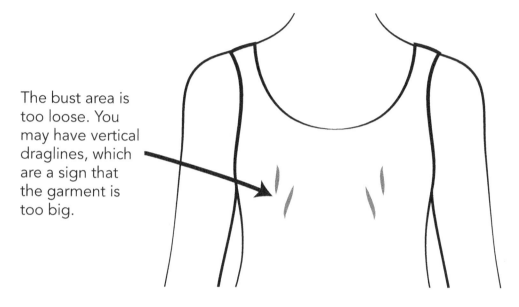

B) Pinning the Problem - Pin the excess fabric vertically in the front bust area, and measure the amount you pinned.

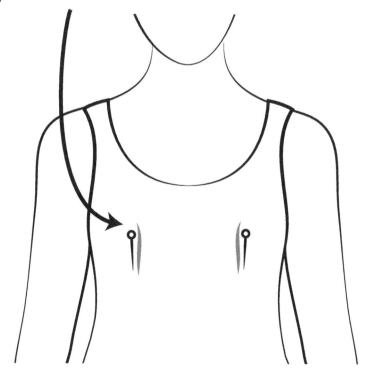

Small Bust Adjustment (SBA)

No Darts or Princess Seams *(continued)*

C) Correcting the pattern - This is a pivoting pattern correction. Place a piece of patternmaking paper under the pattern piece.

1. Mark the amount you pinned inward from the armhole at the side seam. Use a pointed tracing wheel to go through the pattern piece to the layer of paper underneath. Trace with a pencil all the way around the original pattern piece for reference of the original pattern.

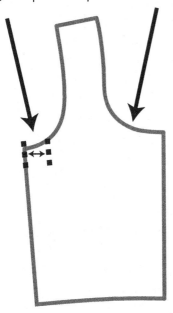

2. Keeping the low point shoulder aligned, pivot the pattern piece until the armhole edge aligns with the mark you made. Trace the pattern to create the new armhole from the LPS to the mark.

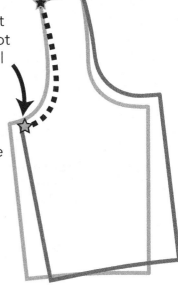

3. Using the new under armhole position as a pivot point, move the pattern piece until the side seam aligns with the waist. Connect these points to make a new side seam.

4. The new pattern will look like this. The dotted lines are the adjusted pattern lines. Ignore the old side seam and armhole lines from Step 1.

The waistline may need to be raised slightly on the back panel to match this side seam length. Align the front and back pattern pieces along the side seams, and true the waist or hem seams.

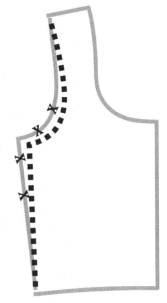

Back Draglines & Hemline Corrections

Often when the hemline is not lying well, the problem lies in the upper portion of the garment. However, it is not always intuitive to know where the issue is. This chapter shows the most common pattern corrections when there are back hemline or dragline issues.

If there is a hemline issue in the front of the garment, and it is rising or not lying parallel to the floor, it is a sign that you may need a bust adjustment.

Incorrect bust shaping is the most common reason for uneven hemlines in the front. If the front hemline is rising a lot, you may need a Full Bust Adjustment. If the front hemline is dipping down a lot, you may need a Small Bust Adjustment. If a bust adjustment is needed, you will likely see the additional symptoms to identify the fitting issues.

Back draglines often occur due to the curvature of the spine or the roundness of the shoulder blades. In addition to the corrections shown in this chapter, you can add to the garment length, adjusting the hemline to be curved or dropped as you wish.

There are many options in this chapter. Some of the options are more creative, like adding design lines. Be creative with your design lines! Many people do not know that the purpose of many design lines is to achieve a perfect fit!

Back Waist Draglines

Step (A) for Options 1-4

A) Identifying the Issue - The back waist has excess fabric. The back hemline may be hiking upward and not parallel to the floor. When this issue occurs, check the pattern to see if it is balanced. An unbalanced pattern, specifically at the armhole positions, may cause back draglines. Refer to pages 62-66 to ensure the back armhole position is not too low in comparison to the front armhole position.

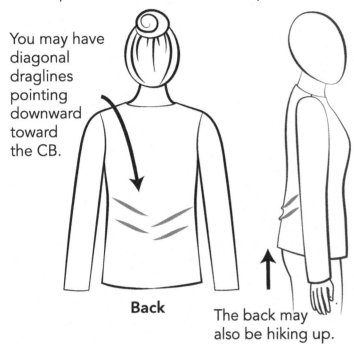

You may have diagonal draglines pointing downward toward the CB.

Back

The back may also be hiking up.

Additionally, a common reason for this fitting issue is that the hip area on the garment is not big enough to accommodate the curves of the body. To check if this is the issue, open the side seams from the waist down to allow the garment to relax and hang down. If this corrects the issue, measure the amount you have opened, and add it to the side seams in the waist and hip area. If this does not correct the issue, and there are back darts in the garment, increase the dart depths by pinning the garment at the back darts in the waist area. If this improves the issue, adjust the back darts to the new depth you pinned. Then, give the amount you've pinned to the side seam at the waist, achieving the original waist measurement if desired. Additional options for correcting this issue are found on the following pages.

There are several options for fixing the problem:

Option 1 (page 183) - For either woven fabrics or knits.

Add a horizontal design line from the waistline up, like a yoke or peplum seam. This correction follows The GRD Method™ in fitting. Diagonal draglines generally point down toward the area that should be raised and pinned up (as explained in the final chapter of the book). If there are diagonal draglines, this is the best option.

Option 2 (page 184) - Recommended mainly for woven fabrics but can also be done on knit styles.

Add vertical darts or princess seams. This correction often will not eliminate the problem if there are diagonal draglines. If the draglines are more vertical, it will help the issue.

Option 3 (pages 185-186) - Recommended only for woven fabrics.

Add vertical darts or princess seams and a center back seam.

Option 4 (page 187) - Recommended only for knit fabrics.

Make the garment tighter, reducing the side seams.

Back Waist Draglines

Option 1 - Adding a Horizontal Design Line

B) Pinning the Problem - Pin horizontally wherever you want to add a design line. The most common locations are a yoke seam or a peplum seam. However, you can choose any location you want at the waist or above. This correction follows The GRD Method™ in fitting. Diagonal draglines generally point down toward the area that should be raised and pinned up (as explained in the final chapter of the book).

To add a yoke, pin at shoulder blade area. Pin a deeper amount at the center back. Stop pinning when you come close to the armhole.

To add a peplum seam, pin the waist area. Pin a deeper amount at the center back, and stop when you are close to the side seams. It is most common to continue the peplum seam around to the front pattern too. However, only mark the position in the front, and do not pin.

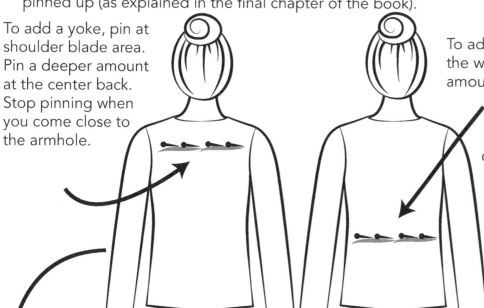

C) Correcting the Pattern - Mark the pattern the same amount you pinned the sample. In many cases, the lines will be curved with a fish-eye appearance.

1.

Yoke

Get creative with your yoke design lines! This is a standard location and shape.

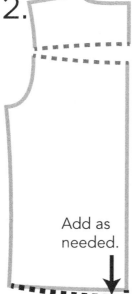

2.

Add as needed.

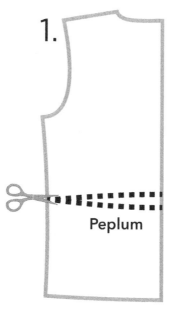

1.

Peplum

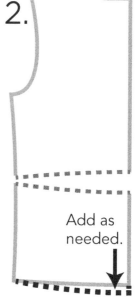

2.

Add as needed.

Cut the pattern along the yoke or peplum line. These are the new pattern pieces. If needed, add to the back length to ensure the hemline is parallel to the ground.

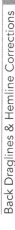

Back Waist Draglines

Option 2 - Adding Darts or Princess Seams

B) Pinning the Problem - Pin vertically along each side on the back of the garment, where darts or princess seams would be. The dart option is recommended only for woven fabrics because knits usually do not require darts. However, you may consider doing this option for knits if you turn the dart into a princess seam or a design line, as shown in Steps 2-3.

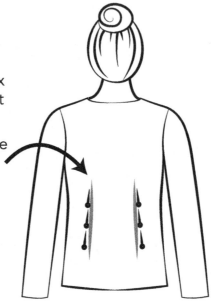

To determine the distance between darts, measure the front of your body from apex to apex (from one high point of one breast to the other).

This measurement will be the distance between darts or princess seams on the back panel of the garment. The dart position will begin 1" (2.5 cm) below the bustline.

This correction often will not eliminate the problem if there are diagonal draglines. If the draglines are more vertical, it will help the issue. There is also a continuation option on the next page which can be used in conjunction with this correction.

C) Correcting the Pattern - Mark the pattern the same amount you pinned the sample. The dart should have a fish-eye appearance.

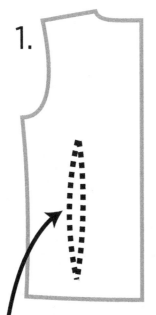

1.

This is the dart added to the pattern. You can either stop here, or continue to turn the dart into a princess seam or design line.

A further option could be to turn the dart into a princess seam or design line. Draw the location you want for the seam. Be creative with your design lines. The example below shows a traditional placement. Eliminate the inside of the dart, cut the pieces apart, and true the lines.

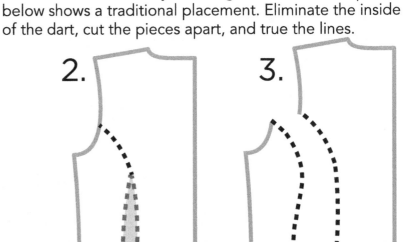

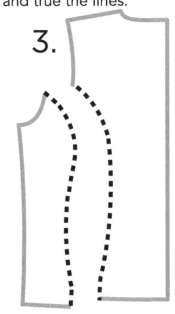

2.

3.

Back Waist Draglines

Option 3 - Adding a CB Seam

B) Pinning the Problem - If there are still draglines at the waist from Option 2, do this correction in conjunction with it, and add a center back seam. This option can be done on its own without doing Option 2. However, it is only recommended for woven styles.

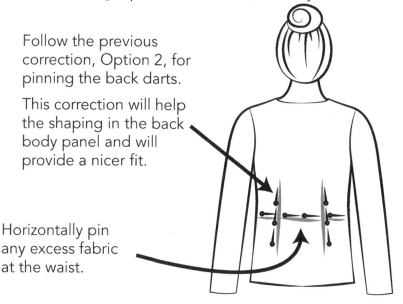

Follow the previous correction, Option 2, for pinning the back darts.

This correction will help the shaping in the back body panel and will provide a nicer fit.

Horizontally pin any excess fabric at the waist.

Pinning vertically and horizontally can be tricky so do your best.

C) Correcting the Pattern - Follow Option 2 for adding the dart if you choose.
Slash & Close the amount you pinned at the waistline, and reshape the CB seam.

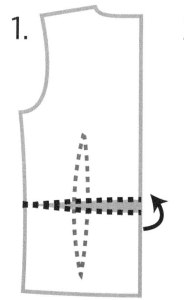

1.

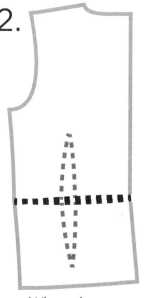

2.

Add 1/4" (6 mm) to the across back area, making a slight curve.

3.

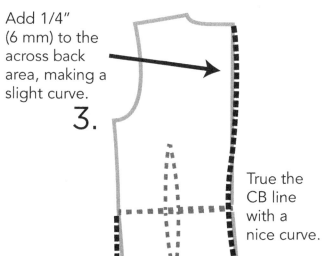

True the CB line with a nice curve.

Mark the pattern horizontally as you pinned. Slash & Close by folding the lower horizontal line up to the upper horizontal line, closing the waist.

When the horizontal lines are folded, it will look like this.

Rebalance the side seam. (See the next page for my method of rebalancing.) Add to the CB length to prevent hiking up.

Back Draglines & Hemline Corrections

Back Waist Draglines

Option 3 *(continued)* Rebalancing the Side Seams

In order to rebalance the side seams, use this method for bodices and dresses.

4. Draw a vertical guideline parallel to the CF. Align the front and back HPS positions on the vertical guideline.

Other pages in the book refer to this page to rebalance a bodice pattern. Follow the steps (4-7) on this page for balancing a pattern.

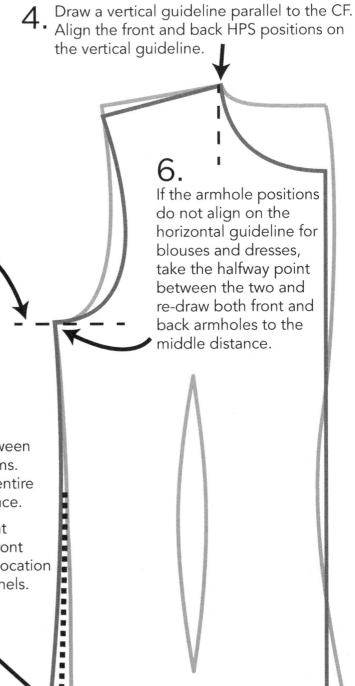

5. Draw a horizontal guideline perpendicular to the CF, going through the front armhole position. Lay the front pattern (darker grey line) on the back pattern (lighter grey line), aligning the armhole position on the horizontal guideline. The armhole positions should touch anywhere on this horizontal guideline. This means the armhole positions are the same depth from the HPS on both the front and back panels.

6. If the armhole positions do not align on the horizontal guideline for blouses and dresses, take the halfway point between the two and re-draw both front and back armholes to the middle distance.

7. Measure the halfway distance between the two panels along the side seams. Mark the halfway point along the entire side seam where there is a difference.

The dotted line is the halfway point between the back panel and the front panel. This is the NEW side seam location for both the front and the back panels.

Rebalancing is that easy!

Back Waist Draglines

Option 4 - Making the Garment Tighter

B) Pinning the Sample - This option is for knits and will make the garment more fitted. Pin vertically along each side seam, making the garment tighter. You may pin the back only or both the front and back panels.

There will still be some wrinkles, but they will be tighter and straighter.

Tip: Before adjusting the pattern, make sure the pattern is balanced. When the HPS is aligned, the armhole positions should be the same from the front to the back patterns for stretchable knit styles (as shown on page 64).

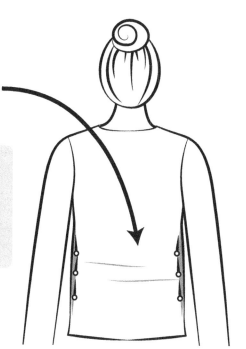

C) Correcting the Pattern - Mark the pattern the same amount you pinned the sample on the front and back side seams.

If you pinned on both the front and back side seams, make sure the side seams mirror each other. Mark the new seams on the front and back panels.

If you only pinned on the back panel, it will not be mirrored. This is acceptable when it comes to customized patterns.

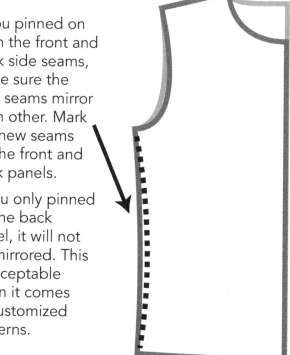

While making the garment tighter will not eliminate the draglines completely, it will make them less visible. The tighter a knit garment is, the better the draglines look. If you want to completely eliminate them, go back to Option 1 to add a yoke or design line to the garment. However, with knits, be cautious when sewing horizontal design lines because the fabric stretches and can give a wavy appearance.

For fitted knit styles, it is generally acceptable to have some draglines in the back waist area when there are no design lines.

Back Draglines & Hemline Corrections

Center Back Hiking Up

With a Yoke or Adding a Yoke

A) Identifying the Issue - The back hem is hiking up and not parallel to the floor. You may have vertical draglines in the back of the garment, causing the garment to stand away from the body.

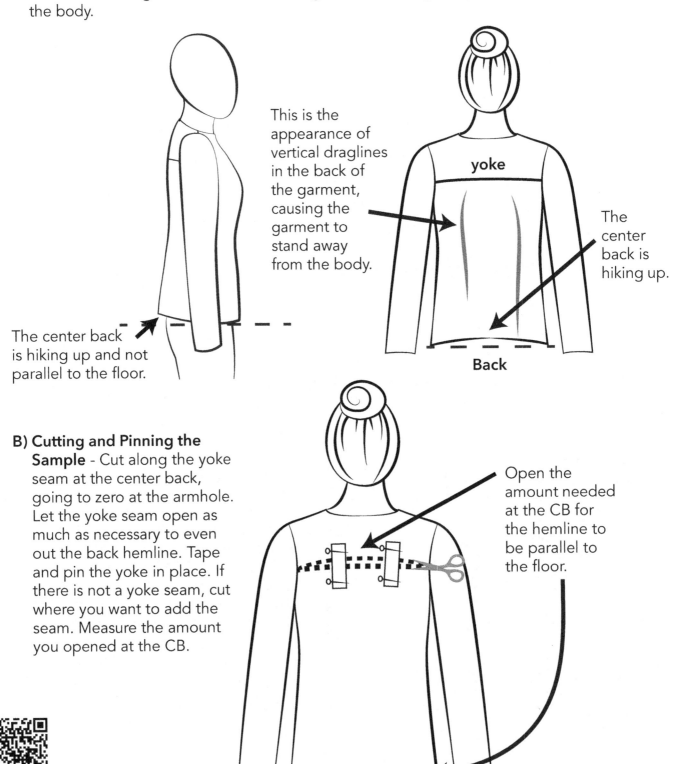

This is the appearance of vertical draglines in the back of the garment, causing the garment to stand away from the body.

yoke

The center back is hiking up.

Back

The center back is hiking up and not parallel to the floor.

B) Cutting and Pinning the Sample - Cut along the yoke seam at the center back, going to zero at the armhole. Let the yoke seam open as much as necessary to even out the back hemline. Tape and pin the yoke in place. If there is not a yoke seam, cut where you want to add the seam. Measure the amount you opened at the CB.

Open the amount needed at the CB for the hemline to be parallel to the floor.

With a Yoke or Adding a Yoke (continued)

C) Correcting the Pattern - Add to the yoke seam on the body panel the amount you opened the sample. If you are adding a yoke seam, mark a straight line on the pattern in the location where you cut the fitting sample. Then separate the pattern pieces.

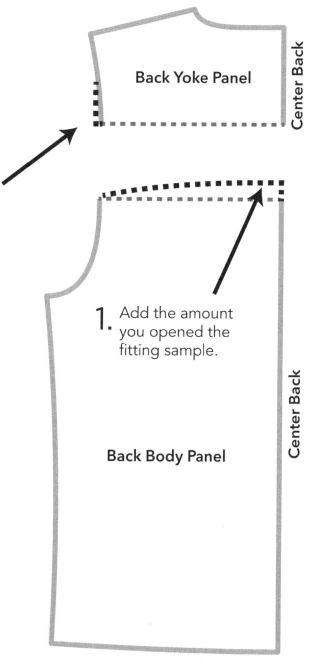

2. Since the body panel will be longer, make sure the yoke fits the new measurement. Add to the yoke seam at the armhole as needed to fit.

1. Add the amount you opened the fitting sample.

3. The hem usually has a slight curve on the pattern, but it appears parallel to the floor when worn.

4. Add seam allowances to the new yoke seams on the body and the yoke panels.

Center Back Hiking Up

No Yoke on the Garment

A) Identifying the Issue - The back hem is hiking up and not parallel to the floor. You may have vertical draglines in the back of the fitting sample, causing the garment to stand away from the body.

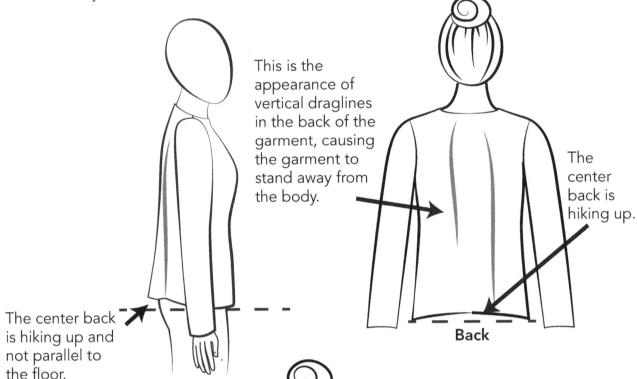

This is the appearance of vertical draglines in the back of the garment, causing the garment to stand away from the body.

The center back is hiking up.

The center back is hiking up and not parallel to the floor.

Back

B) Cutting and Pinning the Sample - Cut along the shoulder seams between the neckline and the armhole. Tape and pin the shoulder seams open at the HPS, allowing the garment to drop down and relax.

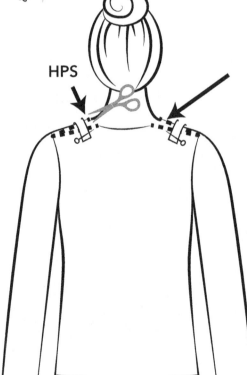

HPS

Open the shoulder seam at the HPS the amount needed for the hemline to be parallel to the floor. Go to zero at the LPS, where the armhole is.

NOTE: If you do not see an improvement in the back hem after cutting the sample, you do not need to adjust the shoulder slope. Instead, add to the center back length at the hemline.

Center Back Hiking Up

No Yoke on the Garment (continued)

C) Correcting the Pattern - Add the amount you opened the fitting sample at the HPS by raising the shoulder seam angle and the back neckline. This makes the shoulder slope more drastic. As you can see, the shoulder slope was the actual fit issue that needed to be corrected.

Most of the time, the shoulder slope is adjusted only on the back panel for this correction. When you open the fitting sample, look at the shoulder seam and imagine adding to the back shoulder seam as shown in this correction.

In some cases, you may choose to give to the front shoulder slope too, to have the shoulder seam in the correct position. You can choose to split the amount you are adding to the front and back.

If you need to add to the front shoulder slope, in addition to the back, follow the correction below.

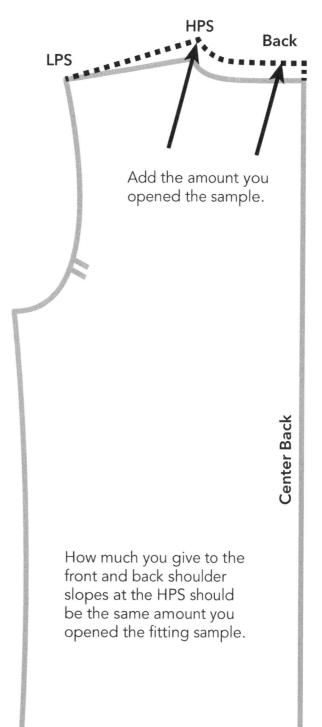

Add the amount you opened the sample.

How much you give to the front and back shoulder slopes at the HPS should be the same amount you opened the fitting sample.

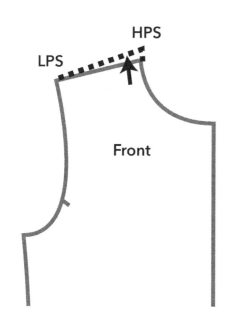

FITTING SKIRTS & PANTS

Skirts, Dresses, & Pants Corrections

We have covered many fitting corrections for tops. Now it is time to move to the lower portion of your outfit, which includes skirts, dresses, and pants.

Though the images show skirts in this chapter, the corrections can be applied to dresses and pants. Apply the same logic to correct dress and pants patterns with these techniques.

In some situations, you may want to tackle the hip and waist corrections before adjusting some of the bodice corrections for dresses. The main reason: if the hip and waist are not lying correctly, it could cause the garment to creep up or not lie in the correct position for the upper portion of the garment. As a general rule, if I ever notice something on the garment that is too tight, I first open the side seams, then assess the fit, as we covered in the beginning of the "Fitting Tops" section. If it is too loose, reduce the side seams until you are pleased with the fullness.

A helpful correction that is easy and achieves a superb fit for a full abdomen or shapely backside is at the end of this chapter called "Draglines toward the Abdomen or Backside." It is such a simple correction, and it can offer curvier women a wonderful option to achieve a nice fit.

Try these corrections on pants and dress patterns too! The next chapter will go deeper into pants topics and corrections.

Hips Too Tight

On a Skirt, Dress, or Pants Pattern

A) Identifying the Issue - The front or back hip area is tight. This is often signified by horizontal draglines in the front or back of the garment.

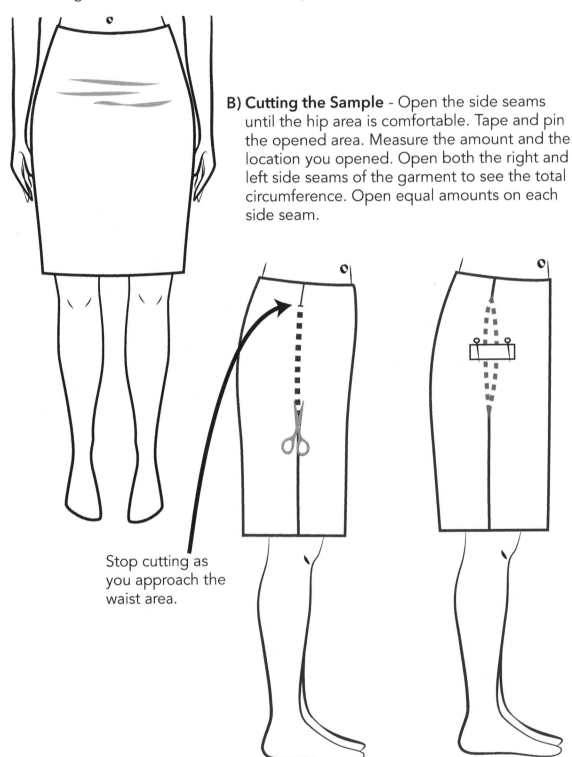

B) Cutting the Sample - Open the side seams until the hip area is comfortable. Tape and pin the opened area. Measure the amount and the location you opened. Open both the right and left side seams of the garment to see the total circumference. Open equal amounts on each side seam.

Stop cutting as you approach the waist area.

Hips Too Tight

On a Skirt, Dress, or Pants Pattern *(continued)*

C) Correcting the Pattern - Add to the side seams the amount you opened on one side of the sample, giving half of that amount to the front and half to the back panels.

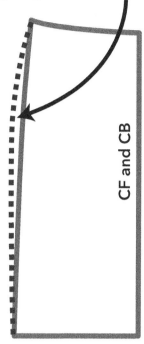

1. The back and front panels should have the same correction. By giving the same amount to the front and back, the side seams remain mirrored and balanced.

If the side seam becomes too curved, you may deepen existing waist darts, or add a waist dart as shown below.

4. Make the side seam less curved by extending the waist seam. Create a dart or deepen an existing dart by the amount you added to the waistline at the side seam.

3.

This example shows a very drastic hip curve, which will not give a nice shape.

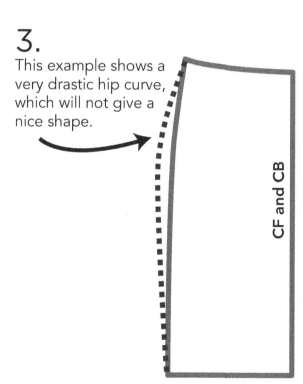

5.

The same correction can be done on both the front and back patterns. If a dart is unwanted on the front panel, the entire amount added along the waistline may be added to the back dart depth. Note, the back side seam can be straighter above the hip in comparison to the front side seam due to the back waist dart depth.

Skirts, Dresses, & Pants Corrections

Waist Too Tight

On a Skirt, Dress, or Pants Pattern

A) Identifying the Issue - The front or back waist area is tight. This is often signified by horizontal draglines, as in the left image, or wrinkles toward the darts, shown in the right image.

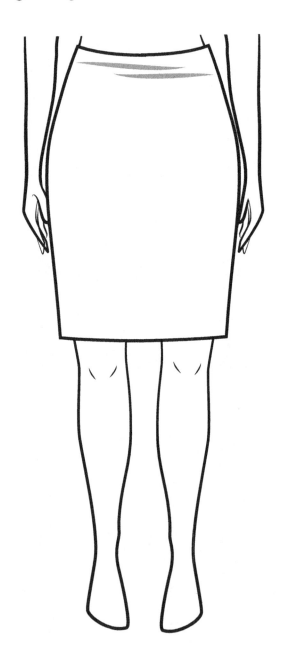 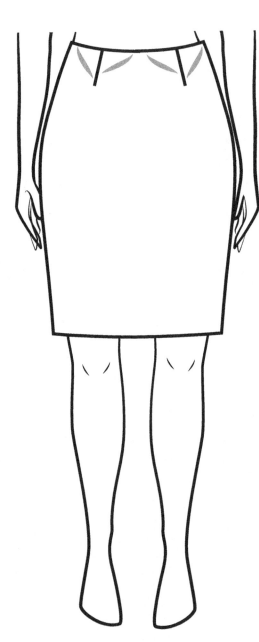

You may have draglines on the front panel, back panel, or both.

Alternatively, you may feel that the waist is too tight.

Waist Too Tight

On a Skirt, Dress, or Pants Pattern *(continued)*

B) Cutting the Sample - Open the side seams until the waist is comfortable. Tape and pin the opened area. Measure the amount you opened. Open both the right and left side seams of the garment to see the total circumference. Open equal amounts on each side seam.

Stop cutting where the garment is not too tight.

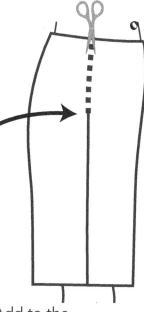
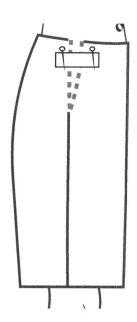

C) Correcting the Pattern - Add to the side seams the amount you opened on one side of the sample, giving half of that amount to the front and half to the back panels.

If the garment has darts, you may reduce the dart depths. This is another way of increasing the waist. You may also remove front darts completely.

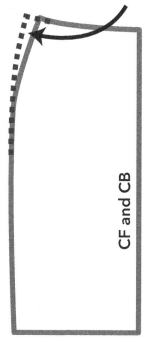

The back and front panels have the same correction. Giving the same amount to the front and back keeps the pattern balanced. Note, the back side seam can be straighter along the upper waist portion in comparison to the front side seam due to the back waist dart depth.

CF and CB

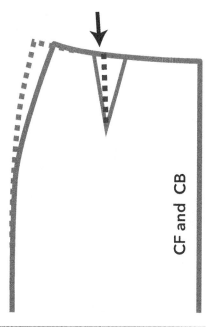

CF and CB

Skirts, Dresses, & Pants Corrections

On a Skirt or Dress Pattern

This issue is commonly due to the curvature of the spine (sway back) or due to curves of the body. This correction shows the fitting issue of the skirt tilting toward the back. If the skirt is tilting toward the front, pin and correct the back panel.

A) Identifying the Issue - The skirt or dress is tilting toward the back in the profile view.

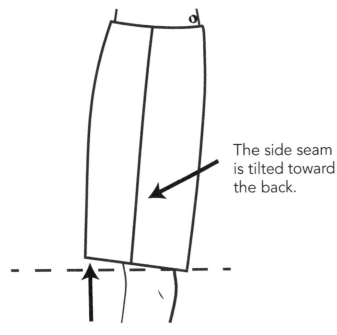

The side seam is tilted toward the back.

The goal is to have the skirt sitting more level to the floor, as shown below.

The hem is hiking up in the back and is not parallel to the floor.

B) Pinning the Sample - Pin the center front waistline horizontally until the hemline appears parallel to the floor. Stop pinning when you reach the side seams. Measure the amount you pinned.

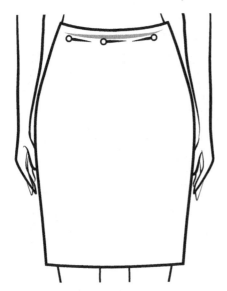

Tilting toward the Back or Front

On a Skirt or Dress Pattern *(continued)*

C) Correcting the Pattern - Take off the amount you pinned at the front waistline.

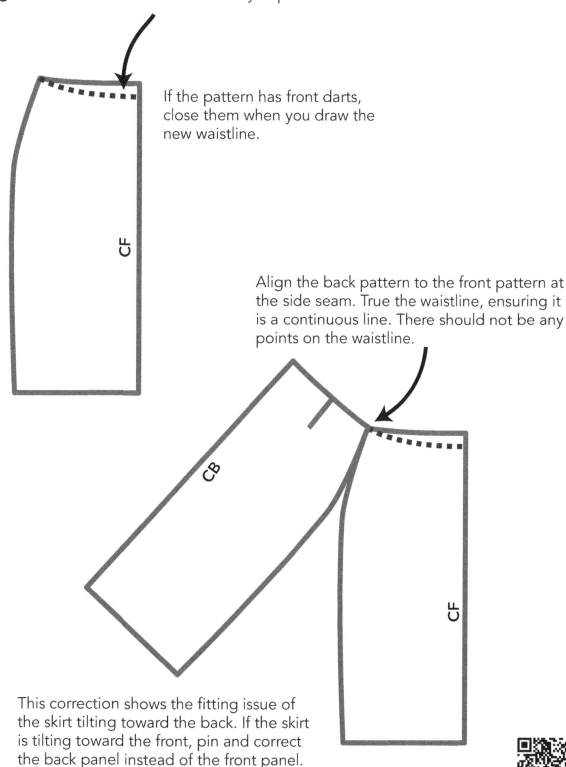

If the pattern has front darts, close them when you draw the new waistline.

Align the back pattern to the front pattern at the side seam. True the waistline, ensuring it is a continuous line. There should not be any points on the waistline.

This correction shows the fitting issue of the skirt tilting toward the back. If the skirt is tilting toward the front, pin and correct the back panel instead of the front panel.

Draglines toward the Abdomen or Backside

On a Skirt, Dress, or Pants Pattern

This is also referred to as a full abdomen or full backside correction. Use this correction for the front panel, back panel, or both. This correction can also be used for pants.

A) Identifying the Issue - There are draglines coming from multiple locations toward the abdomen or backside. The draglines are pointing toward the fullness of the body shapes.

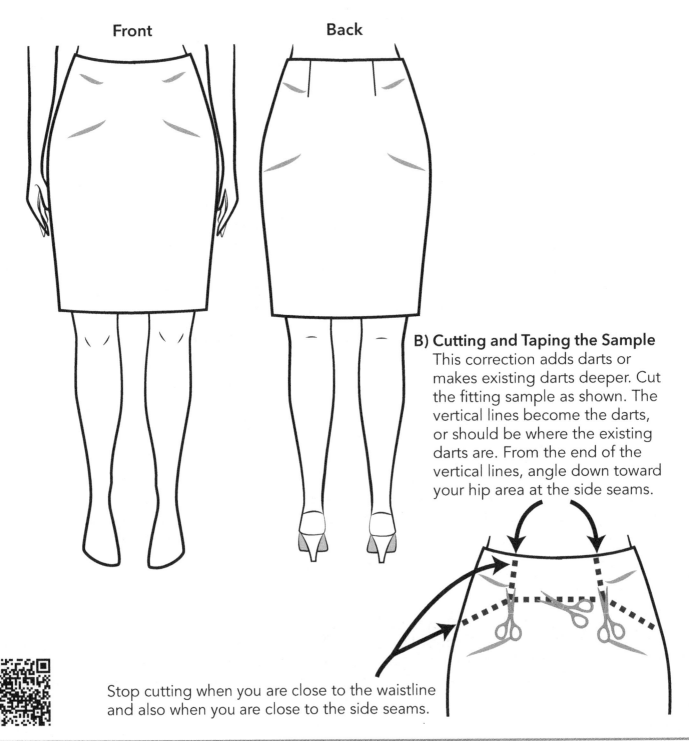

Front

Back

B) Cutting and Taping the Sample
This correction adds darts or makes existing darts deeper. Cut the fitting sample as shown. The vertical lines become the darts, or should be where the existing darts are. From the end of the vertical lines, angle down toward your hip area at the side seams.

Stop cutting when you are close to the waistline and also when you are close to the side seams.

Draglines toward the Abdomen or Backside

On a Skirt, Dress, or Pants Pattern (*continued*)

B) Cutting and Taping the Sample (*continued*) - Allow the fitting sample to open until the draglines disappear. Tape and pin the horizontal opening first, then tape and pin the vertical amount.

C) Correcting the Pattern - This is a Slash & Spread correction. Cut the pattern in the same location as you cut the fitting sample, but also cut the vertical lines through the waistline to allow a dart to form. Shift the horizontal line up the amount you opened the fitting sample.

The vertical cut lines spread to become the new dart. True the side seams, center back, and center front. Fold the dart closed and align the side seams of the front and back panels. True the waistline so it is a continuous curve.

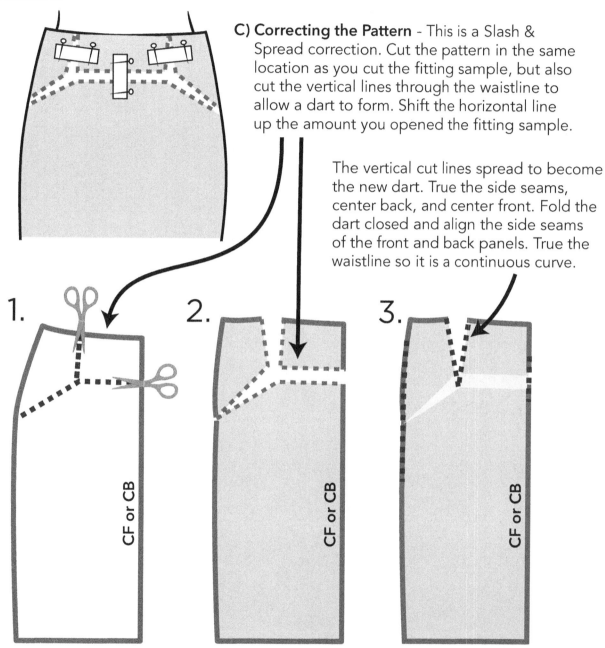

If the garment already has darts, cut the vertical line in the same location as the existing dart. This correction will make existing darts deeper.

If the waistline was tight on the fitting sample and was opened, measure the distance opened. This amount can reduce the depth of the new dart to make the waist larger. In some cases, this may eliminate the need for a dart.

Fitting Pants

This book started with this chapter. In the Fall of 2018, I posted a video about fitting pants that went viral on Instagram®. There were 41,000 views on that video in just a few days, and I quickly realized how important the fitting topic was in the sewing community.

This led me on a journey of creating 110+ videos for Instagram®. They are short due to the previous 1-minute Instagram® time limit. They are the same fitting videos posted on my YouTube® channel to which the QR codes in this book direct you. After I finished the pants video series, I created this fitting chapter.

After the pants-fitting video series, I knew there was so much more about fit that I wanted to teach. I kept going with the series, moving to tops. I spent two and a half years creating videos, coming back to the book to draw the sketches and write the supporting instructions. And here we are! Your fitting book with the most common pattern corrections at your fingertips.

My primary job in the garment industry has been to make clothes fit. Many people who have worked with me know that pants are my favorite clothes to fit. When you follow the corrections in this chapter, you are sure to achieve a nicely-fitted garment. These are techniques that I have used while working in the garment industry. They are the most common fitting issues when it comes to pants. You may also want to refer to the previous chapter about skirts & dresses since many of those corrections can be applied to pants, too.

Pants silhouettes, balanced patterns, and fitting issues are all covered in this chapter.

Womenswear Pants Silhouettes

The images below show how women's pants have been named for different silhouettes, historically. Nowadays, pant names and their various fits have become interchangeable. These images are for reference in understanding the different fits.

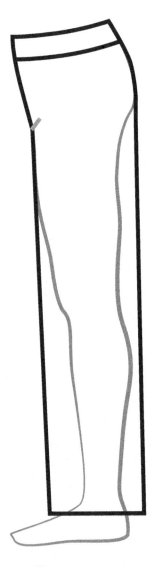

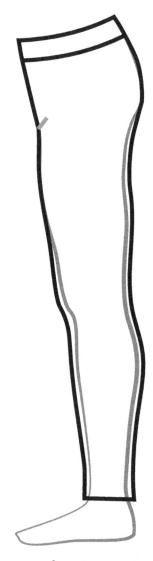

Trousers

The rise sits about 3/4"- 1 1/4" (1.9 - 3.2 cm) below the crotch point. The back lower bum area is **not** "cupped" by the fabric, and the thigh is not fitted.

Slacks

The rise sits about 1/2"-1" (1.3 - 2.5 cm) below the crotch point. The back lower bum area is slightly "cupped" by the fabric, and the thigh is slightly fitted.

Jeans

The rise sits about 1/4"-1/2" (0.6 - 1.3 cm) below the crotch point. The leg silhouette can vary. The back lower bum area is "cupped" by the fabric, and the thigh is generally fitted.

A Balanced Pants Pattern

Always Check the Balance of Pants Patterns

Before you begin working with a pants pattern, check if the pattern is 100% balanced. This is very important to achieve a nice fit. Here is a quick way to check if the patterns are balanced:

> **Good News:** If you are using a Gina Renee Designs' pattern you can skip this step, since GRD patterns are always balanced!

Checking the Balance of the Pattern - The best time to check the balance of the pattern is before you cut out anything. To check the balance, lay the front leg pattern piece on top of the back and complete the following steps. I like to work with the right front leg and back left leg so I can see the alignment better.

3. Align the top corners of the side seams on the horizontal guideline.

2. Draw a horizontal guideline through the back waist at the side seam, parallel to the hem. Draw a second parallel guideline through the crotch point on the front pattern piece.

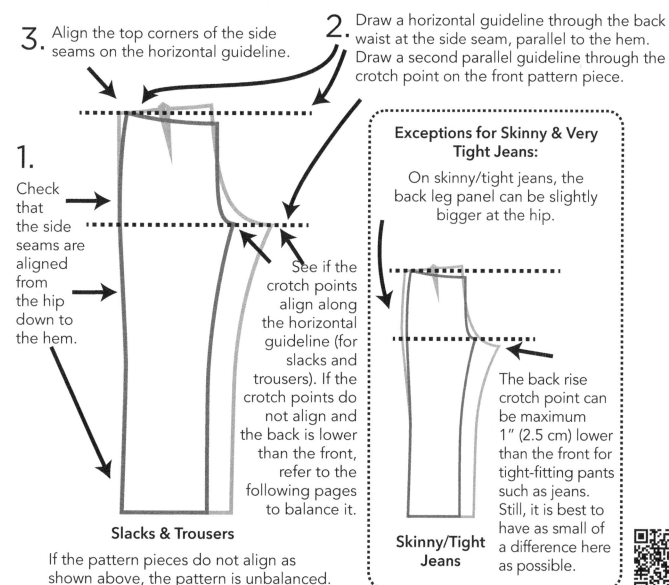

1. Check that the side seams are aligned from the hip down to the hem.

See if the crotch points align along the horizontal guideline (for slacks and trousers). If the crotch points do not align and the back is lower than the front, refer to the following pages to balance it.

Slacks & Trousers

If the pattern pieces do not align as shown above, the pattern is unbalanced.

Exceptions for Skinny & Very Tight Jeans:

On skinny/tight jeans, the back leg panel can be slightly bigger at the hip.

The back rise crotch point can be maximum 1" (2.5 cm) lower than the front for tight-fitting pants such as jeans. Still, it is best to have as small of a difference here as possible.

Skinny/Tight Jeans

Correcting an Unbalanced Pants Pattern

Symptoms: Twisted Inseams or Back Draglines

A) Identify the Issue - If you already made a fitting sample or garment, you can visually see if the pattern was balanced. The image below shows the most common symptoms of an unbalanced pants pattern. If the sample has these issues, double-check the balance of the pattern as found on the previous page. To balance the pattern, follow Step (B) on the next page.

Front

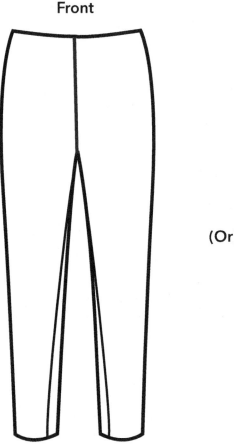

(Or)

Back

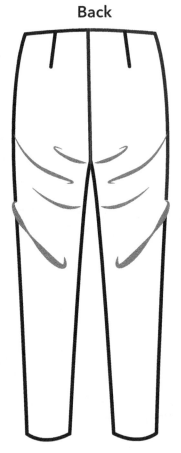

The inseam is twisting toward the front. The side seam is likely twisting to the back, but depending on the leg silhouette, it may be harder to see it on the side seam. I always reference the inseams because side seams are more often moved according to a designer's request. If the side seam was designed to be in the back, this is another topic. Evaluate the inseam position.

There are excessive diagonal draglines on the back.

> **Note:** These are visual symptoms of an unbalanced pattern. In addition, the garment may feel uncomfortable. The best way to check if the pattern is balanced is to follow the steps on the previous page.

Correcting an Unbalanced Pants Pattern

Symptoms: Twisted Inseams or Back Draglines *(continued)*

B) Correcting the Pattern - Follow the steps below to balance pants patterns.

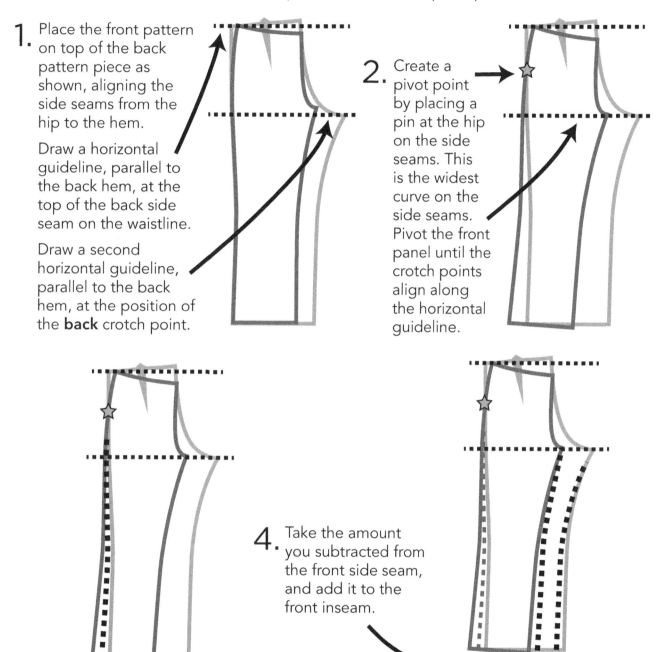

1. Place the front pattern on top of the back pattern piece as shown, aligning the side seams from the hip to the hem.

   Draw a horizontal guideline, parallel to the back hem, at the top of the back side seam on the waistline.

   Draw a second horizontal guideline, parallel to the back hem, at the position of the **back** crotch point.

2. Create a pivot point by placing a pin at the hip on the side seams. This is the widest curve on the side seams. Pivot the front panel until the crotch points align along the horizontal guideline.

4. Take the amount you subtracted from the front side seam, and add it to the front inseam.

Mark the halfway point between the front and back side seams to create the new side seam. This line will be the new front and back panel side seam. As the rule goes, it must be mirrored!

5. Take the amount you added to the back side seam, and subtract it from the back inseam.

(continued on next page)

Fitting Pants

Symptoms: Twisted Inseams or Back Draglines *(continued)*

B) Correcting the Pattern *(continued)*

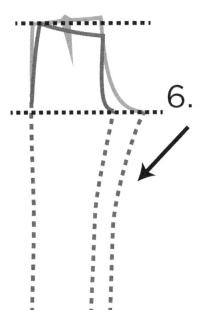

6. The newly-drawn lines will be the new leg panel lines. Disregard or erase the previous pattern leg lines.

7. After the front pattern is pivoted in the previous steps, it is common that the front side seam no longer reaches the horizontal guideline at the waist. The front and back panels should always be touching somewhere along the guideline. To fix this, add to the side seam length until it reaches the guideline. True the pattern, as shown on page 53, so the waistline is continuous.

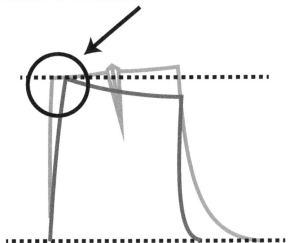

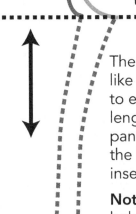

8. Update the front grainline to match the back grainline.

The final outcome will look like this. Measure the inseams to ensure they are the same length on the front and back panel. Adjust if needed at the hem to achieve the same inseam length.

Note: If the pattern is not balanced, this is an indication that there may be other issues with the pattern.

Why do I show a wearer's right front and a wearer's left back throughout this book? Answer: It is the easiest method to check the balance as you work on patterns. You can quickly lay the front on top of the back to check all the balancing points and lines.

Acceptable Front Wrinkles

Trousers, Slacks, and Jeans

The goal is to have minimal wrinkles in the front view on a pair of pants. Depending on body shapes and fabric selection, there may still be some wrinkles (draglines) in the front rise curve.

Front Views:

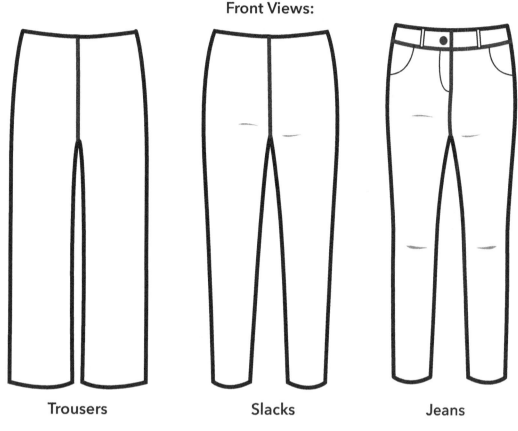

| Trousers | Slacks | Jeans |

For wide-leg pants, strive to have no wrinkles in the front rise. This means the fabric should be able to drape nicely all the way down to the hem.

For slacks and jeans, strive to have no draglines in the front rise. Some fabrics, however, may cause a few wrinkles. If there are wrinkles that you are not happy with, see the following pages to improve the pattern. However, some fits, fabrics, or body shapes cannot avoid all wrinkles (draglines).

Note: I prefer base patterns without front darts at the waist. This tutorial shows the front views without them. Some people prefer having darts. An explanation of darts can be found on pages 41-42.

Eliminating Front Rise Wrinkles

Front Whiskers at the Front Rise Curve

A) Identifying the Issue - Options 1, 2, & 3 - There are "whiskers," or excessive wrinkles, at the front rise on a pair of pants. The name "whiskers" is derived from the appearance of cat's whiskers. They are also referred to as wrinkles, draglines, or creases.

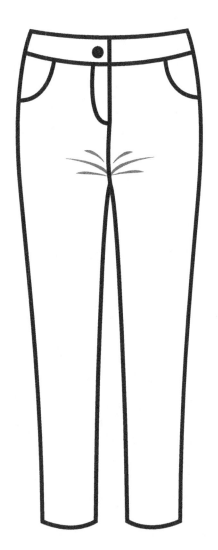

A) Identifying the Issue - Option 1 - In this option, the problem comes from a front rise that is too slanted. There are "whiskers," or excessive wrinkles, at the front rise on a pair of pants (as shown in the photo below). Unlike the other options, this option can be applied when the garment is bulging along the front rise (as shown in the sketch below).

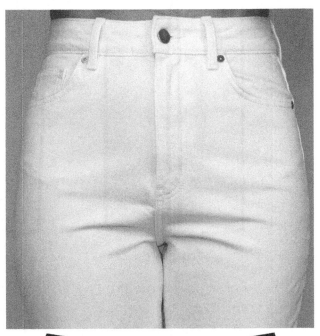

There are three suggested corrections for this issue on the following pages. If the pattern is not a Gina Renee sewing pattern, start with Option 1 because this is the most common issue.

Option 1: Adjust the front rise to be less slanted.

Option 2: Compare the thigh width to the pattern.

Option 3: Adjust the front rise curve.

Option 1 - Adjust the Front Rise To Be Less Slanted (*continued*)

B) Opening the Sample - Option 1 - Open the front fly on the pants, or cut open the fitting sample. If the creases automatically relax when you open the center front, this is the correction to follow.

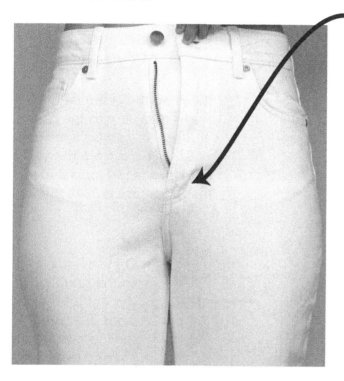

If you have already sewn a pair of pants, unzip the center front fly. Allow it to open until the wrinkles reduce or the bulging improves. Since the zipper length restricts the length you can open, you may not be able to totally eliminate the bulging in the lower part on the sample.

Bulging is a little different from the front rise wrinkles. If there is still bulging in the lower front rise area after this correction, move to Option 2. If after Option 2, there is still bulging, this can occur due to crotch positions that are too low. Raise both the front and back crotch points. If you can pin the bulging amount horizontally on the front rise, then half of that amount pinned is the amount you can raise the crotch points. As a quick pattern reference, page 226 shows how to adjust crotch points. However, instead of lowering them (as shown in that correction), you would RAISE the crotch points.

Measure the distance you opened the fitting sample.

If you have sewn a fitting sample, unpick the stitches at the center front.

Open the center front as much as needed to allow the wrinkles to relax at the front rise curve.

Eliminating Front Rise Wrinkles

Option 1 - Adjust the Front Rise To Be Less Slanted (continued)

C) Correcting the Pattern - Option 1 - Give to the front rise in order to straighten it. The amount added should be half of the measurement you took in the previous step.

4. The amount added to the front rise must be removed from the side seams. Take half of the measurement from the front and half from back side seams. For example, if you added 1/2" (1.2 cm) to the front rise, you would take off 1/4" (0.6 cm) from each the front and the back panels for a total of 1/2" (1.2 cm). End with the same waist measurement as you started.

3. Measure the distance between the vertical line to the new rise. The rise should be a maximum of 3/8" (1 cm) from the vertical parallel line. A good target measurement is 1/4" (6 mm).

1. Give to the front rise. Add half of the distance you opened the front rise at the center front. The corner where the rise meets the waistline should be a 90° angle for at least 1/2" (1.3 cm).

2. Draw a line parallel to the grainline at the end of the sharp front rise curve. The location where the sharp curve begins on the front rise is usually about 1/4 the way up the front rise seam from the crotch point.

Grainline

5. True the pattern as shown on page 53, making the waistline a continuous curve.

Note: If the style has no side seams and the front rise is too slanted, add side seams to achieve the correct shaping.

Eliminating Front Rise Wrinkles

Option 2 - Compare the Thigh Width to the Pattern (*continued from page 212*)

B) Checking the Sample - Option 2 - Cross-check the width of your thigh to the width of the rise curves on the pattern with the steps below.

1. Measure the width of your thigh, front to back. Use a flat ruler against the front of your thigh and along the side area. Reach down and feel that the ruler goes to the end of the back thigh.

2. Place the front and back pattern pieces together at the crotch points, aligning the inseams. Measure the space between the front and back pieces right before the sharp curve. This measurement should be the width of your thigh or more. If it is not, note the difference, and see the correction below. The sharp curve on the rise is generally 1/4 up from the inseam on the front rise and 1/3 up from the inseam on the back rise.

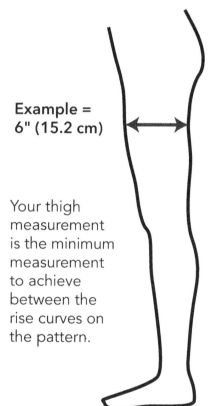

Example = 6" (15.2 cm)

Your thigh measurement is the minimum measurement to achieve between the rise curves on the pattern.

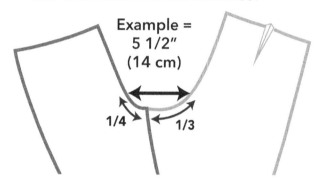

Example = 5 1/2" (14 cm)

1/4   1/3

If the distance of the pattern is already greater than your thigh width, see Option 3.

C) Correcting the Pattern - Option 2 - If the pattern measurement is less than your thigh measurement, increase the thigh at the inseam. Add half of the amount to the front inseam and half to the back inseam. If you are working with non-stretch fabrics, add additional ease.

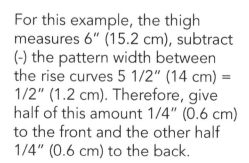

For this example, the thigh measures 6" (15.2 cm), subtract (-) the pattern width between the rise curves 5 1/2" (14 cm) = 1/2" (1.2 cm). Therefore, give half of this amount 1/4" (0.6 cm) to the front and the other half 1/4" (0.6 cm) to the back.

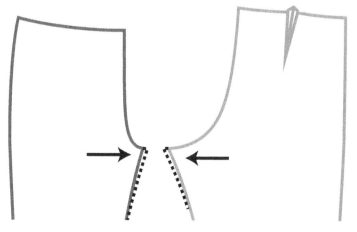

Fitting Pants

Eliminating Front Rise Wrinkles

Option 3 - Adjust the Front Rise Curve
(*continued from page 212*)

(*continued from page 212*)

If the previous correction was not needed or did not help, try this correction for eliminating the front whiskers.

B) Opening the Sample - Option 3
Remove the stitches along the front rise curve on the fitting sample. If this relaxes the whiskers, you have found the problem.

C) Correcting the Pattern - Option 3
Add to the front rise along the curve (i.e. fill in the curve). Add half of the measurement you opened the fitting sample. Half of the measurement is given because equal amounts are on the right and left sides.

Front View of Muslin/Toile

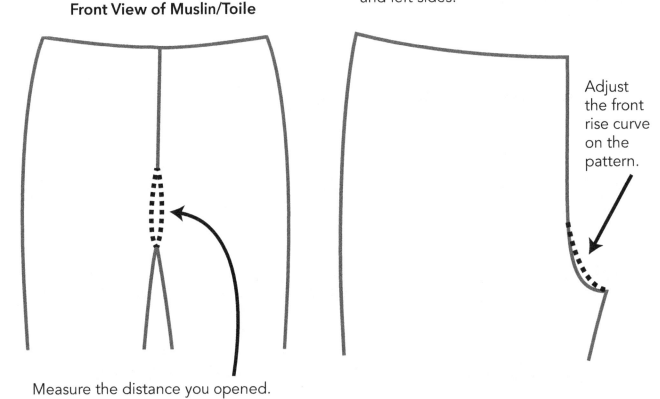

Adjust the front rise curve on the pattern.

Measure the distance you opened.

Excess at the Front Rise Curve

Reducing the Thigh Width on the Pattern

A) Identifying the Issue - There is excess fabric at the front rise curve. This creates vertical draglines near the front rise and at the thigh area. When the draglines look like the images below, compare the thigh width against the rise curve width (as found on page 215). The fitting issue can occur when the pattern distance between the front and back rise curves is much bigger than the thigh width.

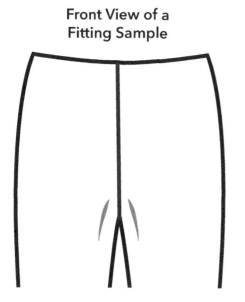

Front View of a Fitting Sample

Front View of Finished Pants

B) Pinning the Sample - Pin the excess fabric near the inseam on the fitting sample. You may pin the front and back together or separately. Try different options for pinning until you are pleased. Move around in the garment, and sit down to make sure there is enough ease.

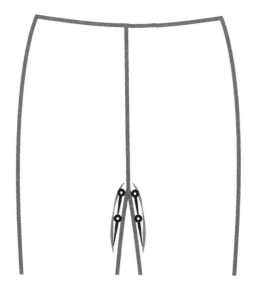

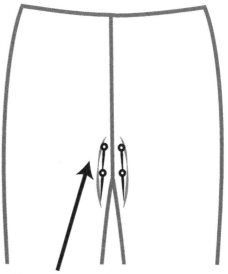

You may need to pin near the rise and the inseam.

Fitting Pants

Reducing the Thigh Width on the Pattern *(continued)*

C) Correcting the Pattern - Reduce the pattern at the thigh along the inseam. The amount to reduce is the amount you pinned the fitting sample.

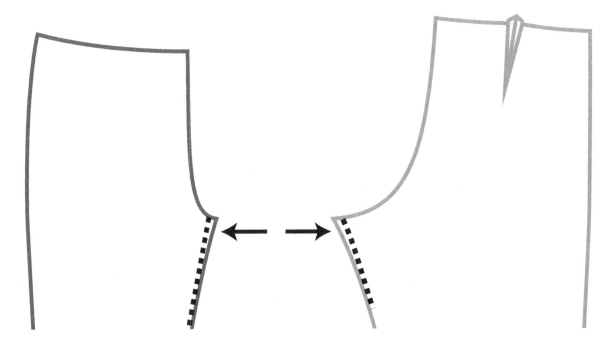

If you pinned only the front or the back inseams, adjust the pattern for only the panel you pinned. If you pinned both, then adjust each evenly.

If you pinned at the front rise area, move the front rise area inward the amount you pinned the fitting sample. Continue the reduction at the thigh inseam as pinned.

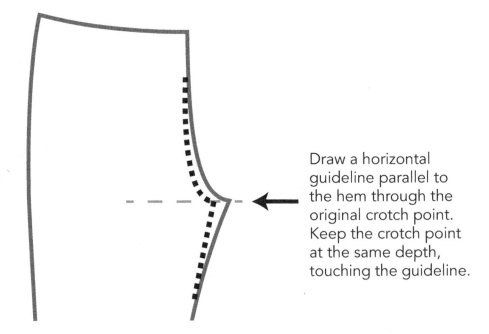

Draw a horizontal guideline parallel to the hem through the original crotch point. Keep the crotch point at the same depth, touching the guideline.

Camel Toe at the Front Rise Curve

Correcting a Tight Front Rise Curve

This correction is often needed in tight-fitting pants, especially when there are no side seams on the style. If there are no side seams, and the fitting issue still occurs after this correction, add side seams. Then, follow the correction on pages 212-214 to make the front rise less slanted.

A) Identifying the Issue - The front rise curve is too tight, and the shaping of the rise is cutting in toward the body. It may appear like there is excess fabric in the shaping. This can also be referred to as a "camel toe" at the front rise.

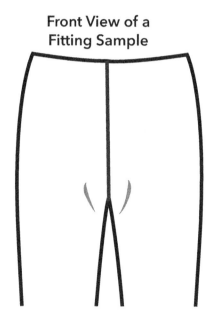

Front View of a Fitting Sample

Front View of Finished Pair of Pants

B) Pinning the Sample - Safety pin the excess fabric at the front rise curve. Pin the fabric until the draglines are gone. You may need to continue pinning at the crotch point of the front and back rises to eliminate all the draglines. This would lower the crotch point position.

Move around in the garment to test the comfort.

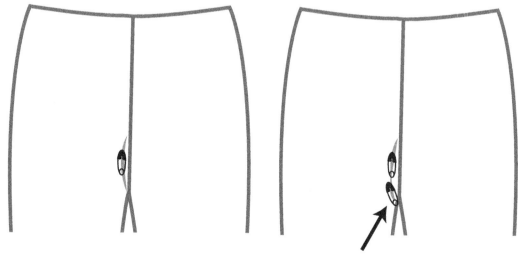

You may need to pin lower at the crotch point.

Fitting Pants

Camel Toe at the Front Rise Curve

Correcting a Tight Front Rise Curve (continued)

C) Correcting the Pattern - Adjust the front rise curve by scooping the pattern line the amount you pinned. If you pinned the crotch points, see the alternative correction below.

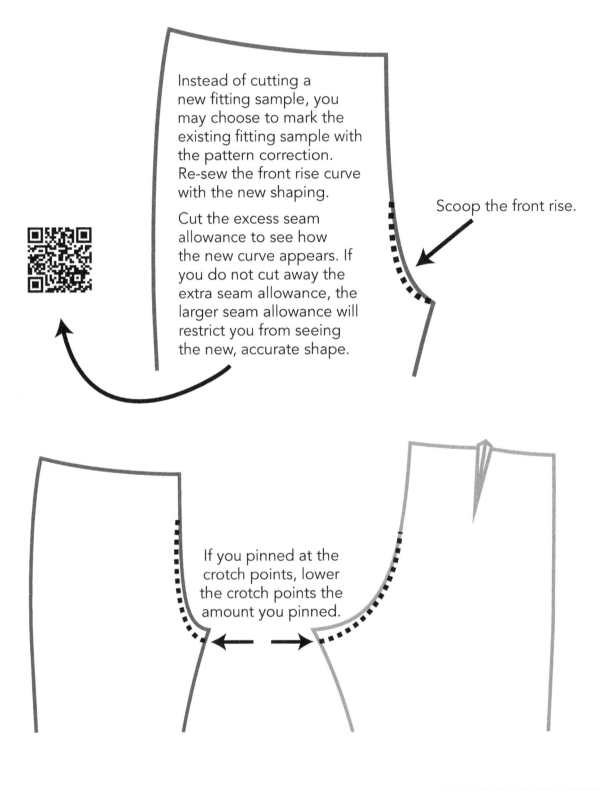

Instead of cutting a new fitting sample, you may choose to mark the existing fitting sample with the pattern correction. Re-sew the front rise curve with the new shaping.

Cut the excess seam allowance to see how the new curve appears. If you do not cut away the extra seam allowance, the larger seam allowance will restrict you from seeing the new, accurate shape.

Scoop the front rise.

If you pinned at the crotch points, lower the crotch points the amount you pinned.

Acceptable Back Draglines/Creases

Trousers, Slacks, and Jeans

Below are the back views of pants. Based on the different fits, there are different acceptable draglines. As the fit becomes tighter, the draglines appear more defined, like a crisp-looking crease close to the skin.

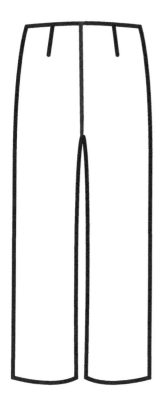

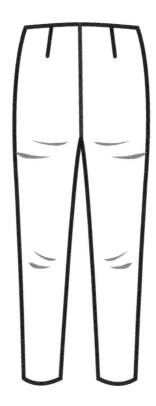

Trousers

On trousers, strive to have no draglines in the back because the fabric is not cupped under the bum area. This means the fabric should be able to drape nicely all the way down to the hem.

Slacks

On slacks, there will always be some draglines under the bum area and likely at the knees. This is acceptable. They allow you to lift your leg and offer more movement in the pants. However, the draglines should be horizontal, not slanted or diagonal. Horizontal draglines are generally acceptable in pants because they allow movement.

Jeans

On jeans, there will be some horizontal draglines. This is acceptable. They allow you to lift your leg and offer more movement in the pants. These draglines are the same as in slacks, but much more defined because they are tighter against the skin. They often do not show as much because they are snug. These draglines should never be diagonal or slanted, but only horizontal.

Fitting Pants

Acceptable Back Draglines/Creases

Horizontal Draglines Allow Movement

When are draglines not acceptable? The following pages show which types of draglines to try to eliminate. Some fabrics, body types, or fits will still have draglines that cannot be 100% eliminated.

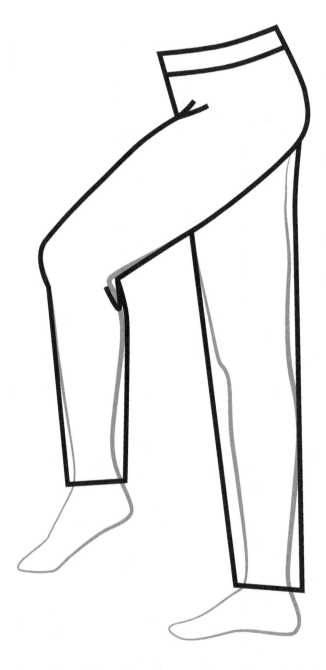

In general, the back draglines should not be diagonal or slanted when standing straight. A horizontal dragline or crease is an acceptable dragline as shown on the previous page. The excess fabric from the horizontal draglines allows the leg to lift.

Note: As you move, diagonal draglines will appear.

Eliminating Back Diagonal Draglines

A) Identifying the Issue - There are diagonal draglines on the back of the garment similar to the images below. Before making any corrections, make sure the pattern is balanced. After you have balanced the pattern, continue with this correction. The draglines below can still show up on a balanced pattern. It depends on fabrics and body shapes. Even if you do not have as many draglines as shown, you can still follow this correction.

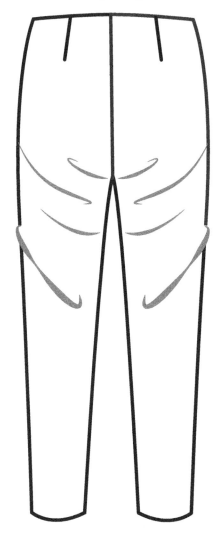

THOSE DREADED DRAGLINES!

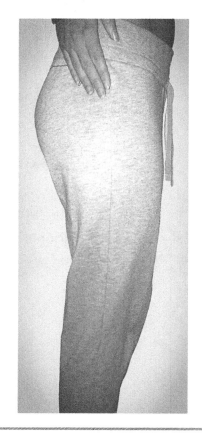

Fitting Pants

Eliminating Back Diagonal Draglines *(continued)*

B) Pinning the Sample - Begin pinning the center back near the waistline. Pin all the way around toward the sides until the draglines disappear. There will be a slight dragline in the back rise curve area, and the back rise will not feel comfortable. Safety pin the back rise curve to eliminate the dragline. This will make the back rise more shaped.

This correction follows The GRD Method™ in fitting. Diagonal draglines generally point down toward the area that should be raised and pinned up. The explanation of this topic is in the next chapter.

Sit in the pants to ensure you can still move well. If you cannot move well, you may need to lower the entire rise at the crotch points. This additional pattern correction is shown on page 226.

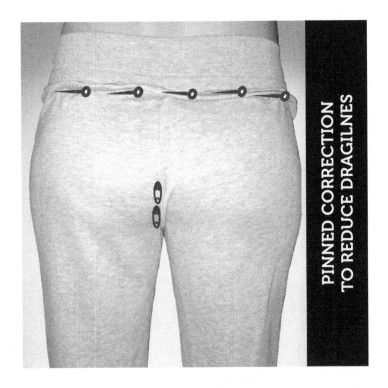
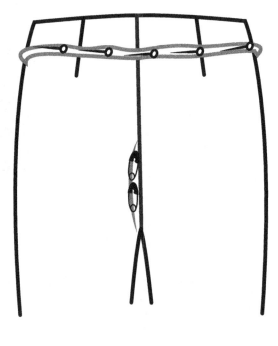

PINNED CORRECTION TO REDUCE DRAGILNES

The above images show the pinned correction.

Pin until the excessive diagonal lines are eliminated.
It may be required to pin on the front panels, too.

Those Dreaded Back Draglines on Pants

Eliminating Back Diagonal Draglines *(continued)*

C) Correcting the Pattern - "Scoop" the back rise, and "pick up" the back along the waistline the amount you pinned the sample. Do this by lowering the back waistline by the amount you pinned. Go to zero where you stopped pinning near or beyond the side seams.

If you are working with non-stretch fabrics, you may need to add to the side seam area where you scooped the back rise. This will help for movement if it was previously too tight. Add half of the amount taken from the back rise to the front side seam and half to the back side seam.

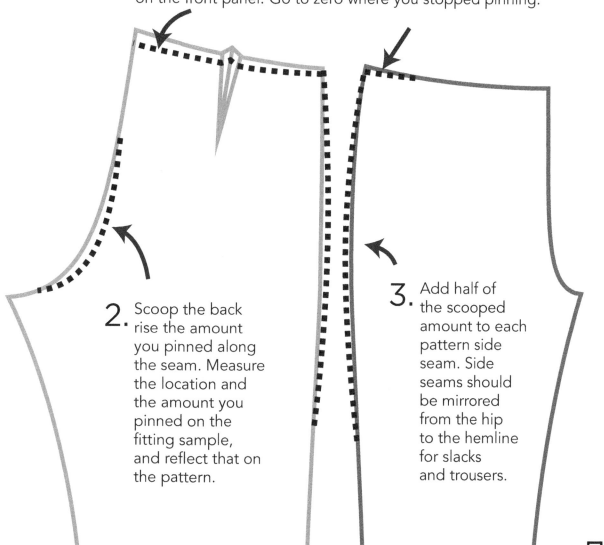

1. Lower the back waistline the amount you pinned the fitting sample. Depending on your pinning, you may not need to lower the waistline on the front panel. Go to zero where you stopped pinning.

2. Scoop the back rise the amount you pinned along the seam. Measure the location and the amount you pinned on the fitting sample, and reflect that on the pattern.

3. Add half of the scooped amount to each pattern side seam. Side seams should be mirrored from the hip to the hemline for slacks and trousers.

See the next page if you need to lower the entire rise at the crotch points.

(continued on next page)

Eliminating Back Diagonal Draglines *(continued)*

C) Correcting the Pattern *(continued)* - If the pants felt too high in the crotch area on the pinned fitting sample, lower the front and back rise depth evenly.

4. **Optional:** Lower the same amount in the front and the back to keep the balance.

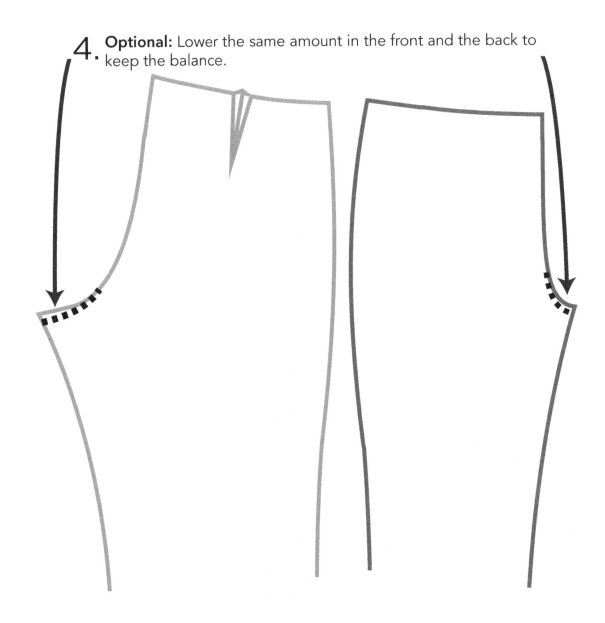

This step is an optional correction that is less common.
It is not needed every time.

Excessive and Deep Back Crease Lines

Adjusting for a Forward-tilting Pelvis

A) Identifying the Issue - There are back draglines under the backside, but they are not too angled or diagonal. This correction is commonly done for flatter backsides or forward-tilting pelvises.

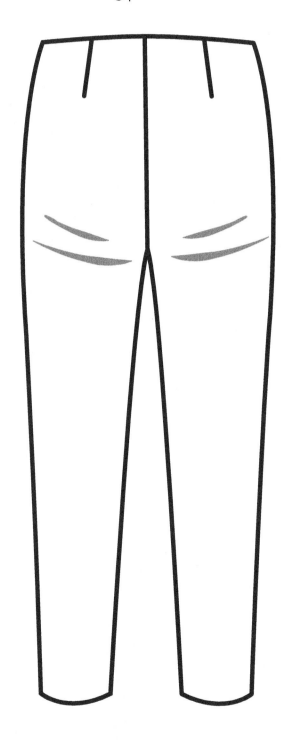

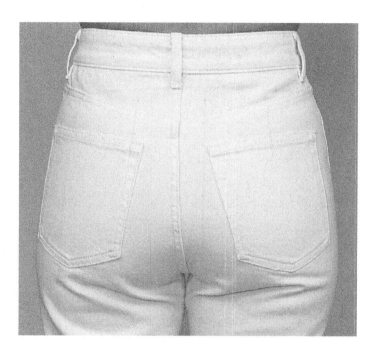

Adjusting for a Forward-tilting Pelvis *(continued)*

B) Pinning the Sample - Pin the back area under the backside. It is best to use safety pins. Try sitting down and moving around. If you can move easily, continue to the next step.

If you cannot move easily, reduce the amount you pinned and try sitting again. When you are happy with the results, go to the pattern correction.

If it is still not comfortable to sit, you will likely need to keep the back creases/draglines for your body or fabric type.

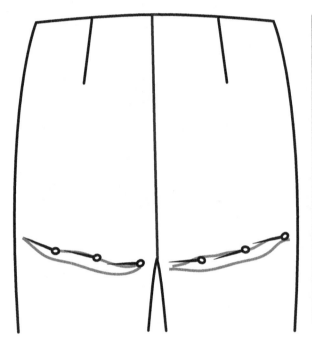 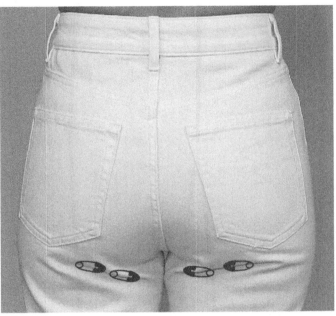

As you pin around the excess, you create what's known as a "fish-eye" shape.

Excessive and Deep Back Crease Lines

Adjusting for a Forward-tilting Pelvis *(continued)*

C) Correcting the Pattern - This is a Slash & Close correction. Follow the steps below to eliminate the back crease lines:

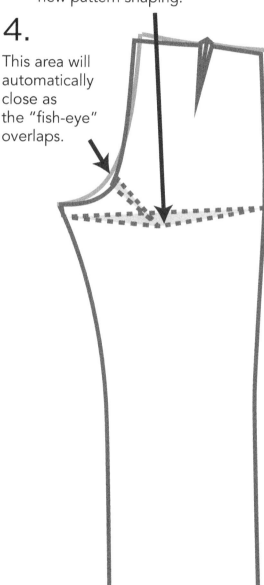

2.

Draw a straight line from the curve of the rise to the center of the "fish-eye." Cut along the line. Stop cutting when you are 1/16" (2 mm) away from the previous cut line.

3. Close the "fish-eye" the amount you pinned the fitting sample by overlapping the pattern pieces here. The darker grey outline shows how the pattern pivots when the "fish-eye" overlaps. This is the new pattern shaping.

4.

This area will automatically close as the "fish-eye" overlaps.

1.

Mark the "fish-eye" area you pinned as a straight line on the pattern. Cut along the line, stopping just before you come to the inseam and side seam.

5. True the rise seam at the overlap to make sure it is a continuous line. Make sure all other lines are continuous (true the seams).

Gaping at the Back Waist

Creating a More Contoured Waistline - Options 1 & 2

There are two options for pattern corrections. The first option is for slopers and styles without a waistband. The second option is for styles with a waistband. This correction may also be applied to skirts.

A) Identifying the Issue - The pants do not sit nicely against the back waist while standing or sitting. There is excess fabric at the back waist.

Side View   Back View

Option 1   Option 2

Gaping at the Back Waist

Creating a More Contoured Waistline
Options 1 & 2 *(continued)*

B) Pinning the Sample - Pin the back waist area until the waist sits nicely against the body. If there is a dart, pin in the location of the dart. If there is no dart, pin in the area where the gaping occurs.

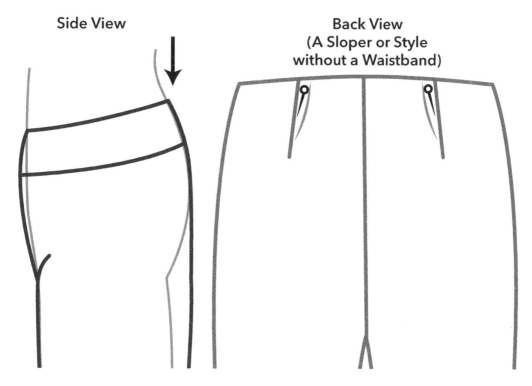

Side View

Back View
(A Sloper or Style
without a Waistband)

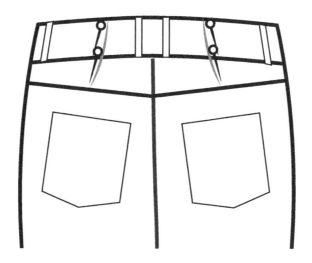

Back View
(Style Pattern)

Option 1

Option 2

Gaping at the Back Waist

Option 1 - On a Sloper or Pattern without a Waistband (continued)

C) Correcting the Pattern - Option 1 - Follow the steps below to eliminate the back waist gaping on a sloper or style without a waistband.

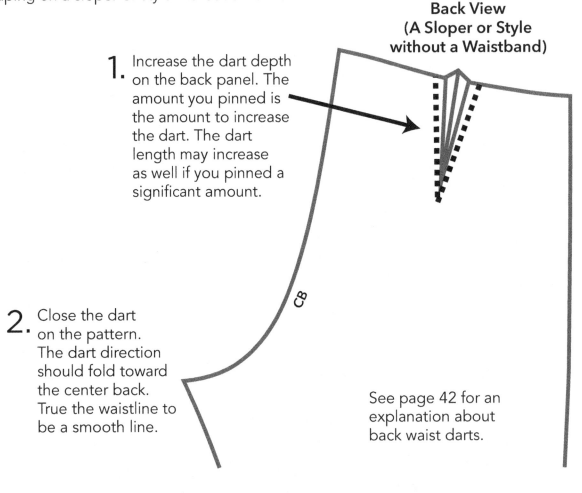

**Back View
(A Sloper or Style
without a Waistband)**

1. Increase the dart depth on the back panel. The amount you pinned is the amount to increase the dart. The dart length may increase as well if you pinned a significant amount.

2. Close the dart on the pattern. The dart direction should fold toward the center back. True the waistline to be a smooth line.

CB

See page 42 for an explanation about back waist darts.

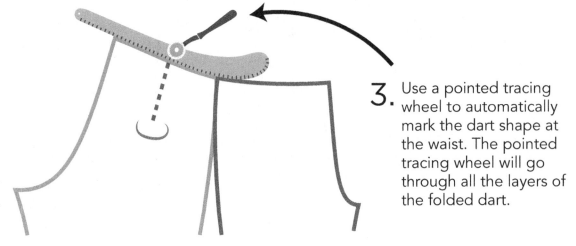

3. Use a pointed tracing wheel to automatically mark the dart shape at the waist. The pointed tracing wheel will go through all the layers of the folded dart.

Gaping at the Back Waist

Option 2 - On a Style Pattern with a Waistband
(*continued from page 230-231*)

C) Correcting the Pattern - Option 2 - This is a Slash & Close correction. Follow the steps below to eliminate the back waist gaping on a style pattern with a waistband.

Waistband Adjustments

1. Draw a straight line down the waistband where you pinned the fitting sample. Cut along the line.

2. Slash & Close (overlap the paper pattern) the amount you pinned at the top edge of the waist and the bottom waistband. In some cases, you may go to zero (no overlap) at the bottom of the waistband. If this is the case, the correction is complete after Step 3.

3. True the waistline where the pieces overlapped, making it a continuous curve.

Yoke Adjustments

4. Draw a straight line down the yoke where you pinned the fitting sample. Cut along the line.

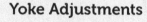

7. If you overlapped the bottom of the yoke, reduce the leg panel as needed at side seam and center back rise to match the yoke.

5. Slash & Close (overlap the paper pattern) the amount you pinned at the top edge of the yoke. If the fitting sample was not pinned at the bottom of the yoke, go to zero. If it was pinned at the bottom of the yoke, follow Step 7.

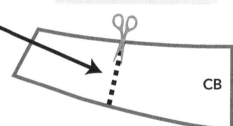

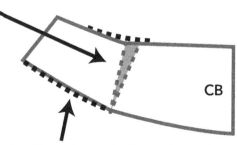

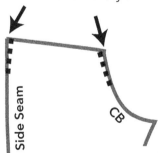

6. True the waistline where the pieces overlapped, making it a continuous curve.

Making a Pocket Opening Bigger

On Curved Pocket Openings

A) Identifying the Issue - The pocket opening is too tight and too difficult to get your hand into. This is most commonly an issue on tight-fitting pants and skinny jeans. This correction is only for curved pocket openings. Generally, on straight pocket openings, this issue does not occur.

You may have a horizontal dragline, indicating the pocket is tight.

B) Checking the Sample - Does the pocket opening feel too tight for your hand? If the hips are too tight, open up the side seams so the hip area can increase. If you can comfortably put your hands into the pockets once the side seams open, make the hip larger at the side seams (as shown on pages 196-197). Otherwise, skip straight to Step (C) to fix only the pocket opening on the pattern.

C) Correcting the Pattern - Adjust only the pocket opening and any other pieces which have a curved pocket opening seam on the pattern.

1.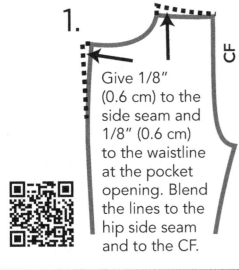
Give 1/8" (0.6 cm) to the side seam and 1/8" (0.6 cm) to the waistline at the pocket opening. Blend the lines to the hip side seam and to the CF.

2. If there are facings, pocket bags, or linings that correspond to the pocket opening seam, do the same correction.

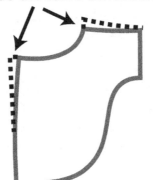

3. Keep the inner pocket facing that connects to the leg panel as is with no changes. By leaving this piece the original size, it allows a gap for the hand. The hand will slide into the pocket since there is a gap between the facing and the larger pocket opening.

Gaping Pocket Openings

On Straight Pocket Openings

A) Identifying the Issue - The pocket is gaping open and does not sit well against the body. This is very common with straight, more vertical pocket openings. The legs bend at the hip joint so the constant movement of the leg causes the gaping.

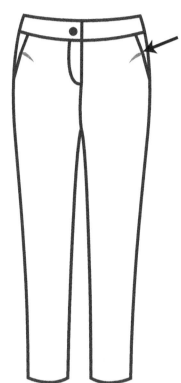

The pocket opening does not sit flush against the body. It gapes open.

The more vertical the pocket is in this region, the more gaping there will be. If the pocket is more horizontal, the fit improves. This is why curved pockets fit nicer on jeans because they tend to be more horizontal and less vertical.

B) Pinning the Sample - Pin the sample where the gaping occurs. Measure the amount you pinned.

C) Correcting the Pattern - Adjust only the pocket opening and any other pieces which have the pocket opening seam on the pattern.

1.
Take off the amount you pinned along the waistline at the pocket opening. The maximum you should reduce is 1/4" (0.6 cm).

2.
I like to add a very slight curve to my straight pockets, to hug the body better.

3.
If there are facings, pocket bags, or linings that correspond to the pocket opening seam, do the same correction.

4.
Keep the inner pocket facing that connects to the leg panel as is with no changes.

Making the Calf Larger on the Pattern - Options 1 & 2

A) Identifying the Issue - The calf area is too tight or there are draglines at the back calf area.

Back View

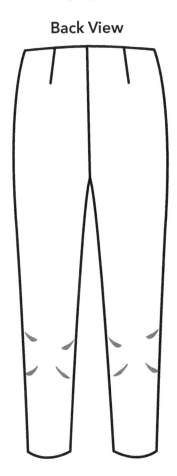

B) Cutting the Sample - Cut open the calf area along the inseams and side seams. Measure the amount you opened.

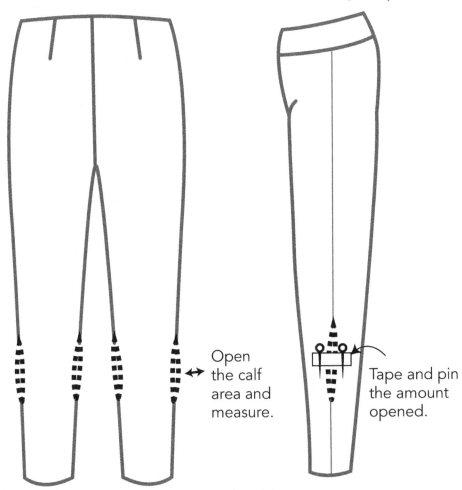

Open the calf area and measure.

Tape and pin the amount opened.

In both of the following correction options, give half of the measurement to the front panel and the other half to the back panel on the pattern correction. For example, if you open up the leg 1/2" (1.3 cm) at the inseam, you would give 1/4" (0.6 cm) to the front leg and 1/4" (0.6 cm) to the back leg on the inseam.

Calf Adjustment

Making the Calf Larger on the Pattern - Option 1 *(continued)*

C) Correcting the Pattern - Option 1 - Give to the leg panels the amounts you opened the fitting sample. Measure the sample for the location of where to increase. Continue all the way to the hem for a nice, continuous line.

Note: There are other correction methods of slashing and opening the leg, but the result is similar. I find this method to be the easiest.

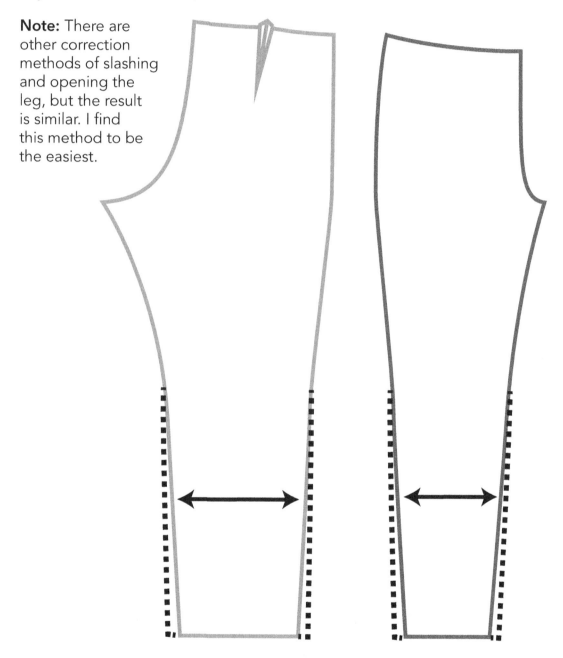

If you do not want the bottom opening to be bigger, you will need to make an irregular shape at the inseams and side seams (see the next page for Option 2).

Making the Calf Larger on the Pattern - Option 2
(*continued from page 236*)

C) Correcting the Pattern - Option 2 - You need to master the rules before you break them! You may prefer to keep the bottom opening as it was originally. You can break the rule of having a straighter line down the inseam and side seam. If you only want the calf area to be larger, you can "cheat" a little and give to the calf area. Then go back to zero at the hem for skinny jeans or slim pants.

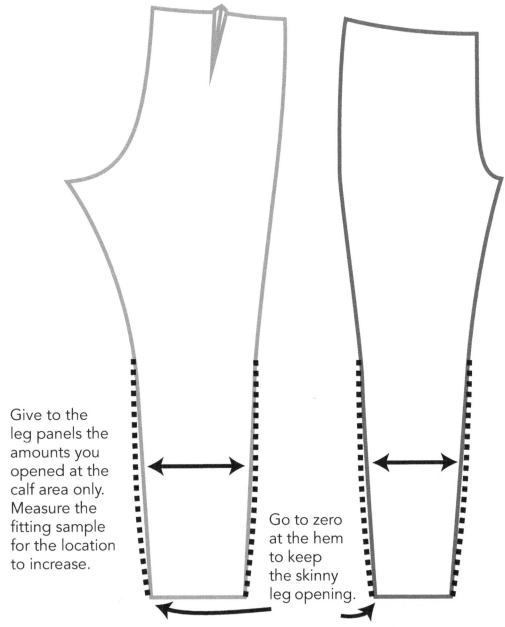

Give to the leg panels the amounts you opened at the calf area only. Measure the fitting sample for the location to increase.

Go to zero at the hem to keep the skinny leg opening.

If you are thinking, "These curved lines are a little strange," well, you are right. When there is a tight-fitting garment, the curved seams align to the shapes of the body. This is acceptable.

Eliminating the Winged-Leg Look on Shorts

Making the Hem Parallel to the Floor

A) Identifying the Issue - The legs of the garment "wing" out, and the hemlines are not parallel to the floor. This issue most commonly shows up in shorts. It is harder to catch in pants.

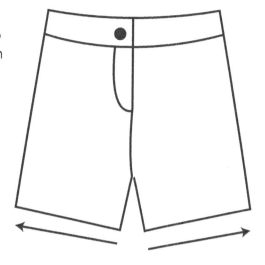

B) Cutting the Sample - Cut along the waist, and let the garment relax open. If there is a waistband, cut just below it; otherwise, cut about 1" (2.5 cm) below the top edge of the waist. When the hem becomes more horizontal and you are happy with the result, tape the slashed area open. Measure the amount opened.

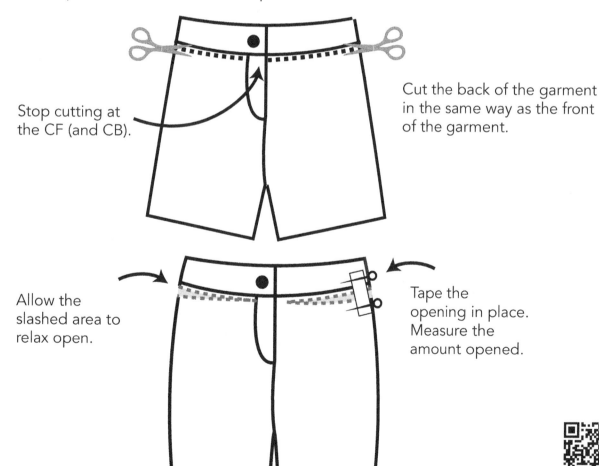

Stop cutting at the CF (and CB).

Cut the back of the garment in the same way as the front of the garment.

Allow the slashed area to relax open.

Tape the opening in place. Measure the amount opened.

Fitting Pants

Eliminating the Winged-Leg Look on Shorts

Making the Hem Parallel to the Floor *(continued)*

C) Correcting the Pattern - Measure the amount you opened on the sample, and add it to the height of the side seam at the waist.

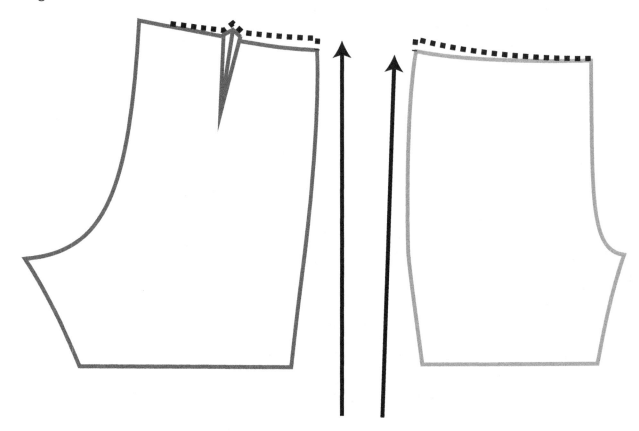

Even though you have cut below the waistline on the sample, amend the sloper pattern at the top waist edge.

Fold the dart closed, and true the waistline seams with the side seams aligned.

If you are amending the pattern on the style level, you can keep the waistband as it is and amend the leg panels only.

THE GRD METHOD™ IN FITTING

Diagonal Draglines
Demystified

Draglines, also known as wrinkles, in the garment signify a shape misalignment between the person and the pattern. In this chapter, I share my biggest discovery when it comes to diagonal draglines.

When you utilize this method, you will see the fitting issue immediately and know how to solve it. As with all pattern corrections, it takes practice, but it is a huge eye-opener once you see how easy it is.

A lot of the content in this chapter is from my online patternmaking course. The same concepts apply to any styles you are correcting, whether the style has darts, princess seams, or other design lines. Think of this chapter as an overall concept of how to fix diagonal draglines.

This is something I wish someone would have explained to me years ago, but I figured it out on my own. In the past, I heard the statement, "Diagonal draglines always point to the problem." But to me, this was never clear enough. Many times, in my opinion, it does not point to the problem. The problem usually lies in the shaping of the pattern seams above the draglines. The direction of the diagonal draglines signifies which way to correct the shapes.

If the fitting issue is horizontal or vertical draglines, I touch on this subject on pages 67-70 in "First Steps in Assessing the Fit."

I cannot wait to share my secret fitting method with you in this chapter!

Making a Moulage and Sloper with The GRD Method™

What is The GRD Method™?

I have developed this fitting method of identifying the causes of diagonal draglines over the many years I have worked in the garment industry since 2003. I call it The GRD Method™ in fitting. This is a method which I have found to be extremely helpful in my career of fitting thousands of garments for many clothing brands. It is something I wish someone would have taught me when I first began my fitting and sewing journey. I am happy to share my fitting method with you in this chapter.

The GRD Method™ is a new patternmaking and fitting method that I teach in my online course, "Making a Moulage - The GRD Method™." This course teaches you how to draft a moulage based on your measurements. You will learn how to add ease to create a customized sloper.

How is The GRD Method™ online course different from other courses?

- It populates custom dart depths based on your measurements - NO industry standards.
- It utilizes your custom shoulder slope - NO industry standards.
- The math is done for you, leading to fewer chances of making mistakes.
- It is a step-by-step process with videos and tutorials.
- I give you personalized assistance and feedback during your fitting process, to help keep you on track with your corrections.

Do not waste time using other methods which use industry standards for dart depths and shoulder slopes. These are what contribute to 80% of fitting issues in the armhole and bust areas. The entire point of drafting a pattern from your measurements is to avoid fitting corrections due to the use of industry standard slopers by commercial and indie pattern companies. When you draft from your own measurements and use these measurements for all the calculations, you achieve a more customized fit from the beginning of the customization process. It gives you a solid foundation to design the clothes you dream of.

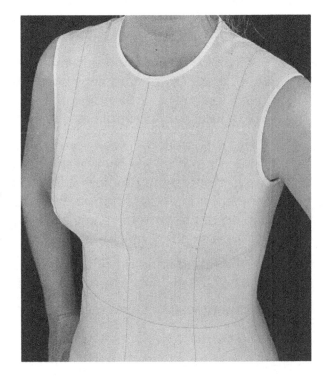

Take The GRD Method™ Online Course.

Join the waitlist for "Making a Moulage – The GRD Method™" by scanning the QR code below.

The GRD Method™ Demystifies Draglines

Let's dive into draglines! A dragline can also be called a wrinkle or deep crease in the fabric. An explanation of draglines can be found on page 18. The GRD Method™ in fitting applies to diagonal draglines coming from the same direction. It does not apply to diagonal draglines coming from multiple directions as shown on page 269.

This is The GRD Method™ in fitting, which I have developed when it comes to diagonal draglines:

> "Diagonal draglines generally point down toward the area that should be raised and pinned up. Alternatively, diagonal draglines point up toward the area that should be cut open and lowered."
>
> **- Gina Renee (The GRD Method™)**

You may eliminate diagonal draglines using either option: (1) Raising an area by pinning or (2) Cutting it open to lower an area. Below and on the next page is the same example shown with each option.

Let's look at the first part of The GRD Method™, "Diagonal draglines generally point down toward the area that should be raised and pinned up." This means, at the bottom of the dragline, the area above it should be "picked up" and pinned. Locate the bottom point of the dragline(s), and raise the area by pinning above it.

In this example, the waist seam was pinned above the bottom point of the dragline. Pinning allowed the area to be raised. This eliminated the draglines.

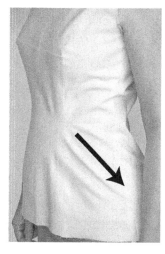 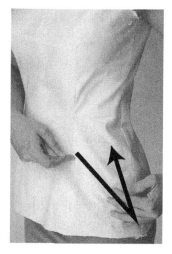 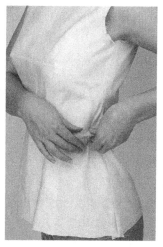 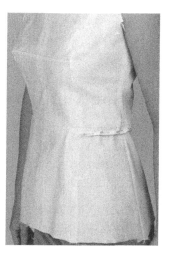

The draglines point down toward the side seam.	Begin by "picking up" the area above the bottom points of the draglines.	Pin the area above the bottom points of the draglines. Pinning it raises the area.	The draglines are now eliminated.

(continued on next page)

The GRD Method™ Demystifies Draglines

"Diagonal draglines generally point down toward the area that should be raised and pinned up. Alternatively, diagonal draglines point up toward the area that should be cut open and lowered."

- Gina Renee (The GRD Method™)

Let's look at the second part of the statement, "Alternatively, diagonal draglines point up toward the area that should be cut open and lowered." This means, at the top of the dragline, the area above it should be cut (released) and lowered. Locate the top of the dragline, and cut above it.

In the same example as previously shown, the waist seam was cut open above the top point of the dragline. Cutting allowed the area to lower and relax. This eliminated the draglines.

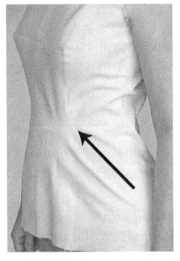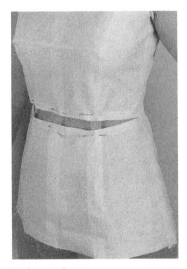

With this method, you can achieve new shapes for the pattern pieces. When there are diagonal draglines, it is a sign that the shape of the pattern is incorrect.

You can view the diagonal dragline either way, pointing down or up, and achieve the same new pattern shape.

If you would like to watch a video with a more in-depth explanation, sign up for the free patternmaking mini-course series through the QR code below. You will not want to miss out. This course only runs once or twice per year.

Why are there so many darts on a moulage?

The bodice examples in this chapter are taken from my online course, "Making a Moulage – The GRD Method™." You will notice that the pattern pieces have many darts to allow for the most freedom of design and best fit possible. However, you can apply the same methodology to patterns without all the darts.

As you create a moulage that is customized to your body measurements, you will notice that the moulage has five darts in the front and two darts in the back. To perfect the fitting of this moulage, you will sew a garment with princess seams by closing the darts on the moulage pattern. You will note and pin all the corrections on this princess-seamed garment, but the corrections will be made to the original five-dart moulage. That is why you will notice that the fitting images show a garment with princess seams, and the pattern pieces show a garment with darts.

This chapter gives a sneak peek into the fitting module of the online course. When you put this method into practice, it will help you tremendously in your fittings!

Recognizing Diagonal Draglines

Assessing the Garment

While The GRD Method™ in fitting diagonal draglines might sound simple enough, it takes practice recognizing the issues on the fitting sample. Always analyze the fit for draglines when the person is standing straight and relaxed. Below are some examples, viewing the draglines as **pointing down** toward the area that should be **raised and pinned up**.

The draglines point down toward the armhole seams.

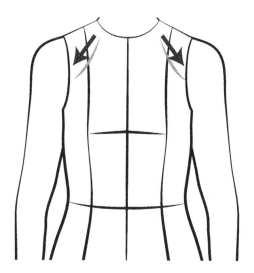

The draglines point down toward the side seams.

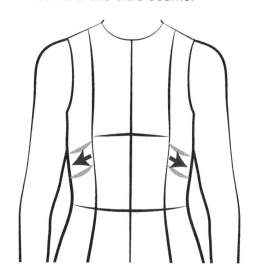

The draglines point down toward the center front/center back seam.

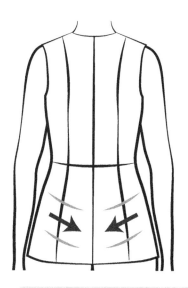

The draglines point down toward the side seams.

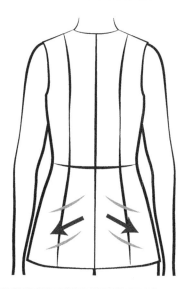

> Draglines appear on garments as soon as the body moves, and this is acceptable. However, if there are diagonal draglines while standing straight and relaxed, they should be corrected.

Recognizing Diagonal Draglines

Assessing the Garment (*continued*)

You may view diagonal draglines in either direction - pointing down or up. The directional point only signifies options of how to correct the problem. The correction will result in the same new lines and shape either way you interpret the dragline direction. You can choose how you view it, so there is no wrong way.

Below are the same examples as the previous page. However, this time, the draglines are viewed as **pointing up** toward the area that should be **cut open and lowered.**

The draglines point up toward the neckline.

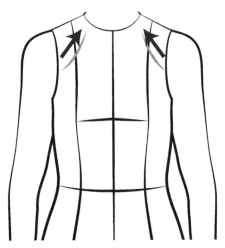

The draglines point up toward the princess seams.

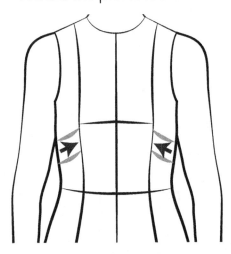

The draglines point up toward the side seams.

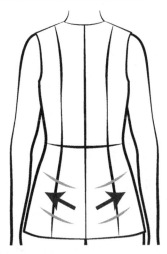

The draglines point up toward the center front/center back seam.

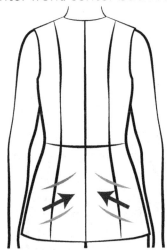

"Diagonal draglines generally point down toward the area that should be raised and pinned up. Alternatively, diagonal draglines point up toward the area that should be cut open and lowered."

- Gina Renee (The GRD Method™)

Recognizing Diagonal Draglines

How do you know if the dragline is going up or down?

You may look at diagonal draglines as either pointing down or up. The directional point only signifies the two options of how to correct the problem:

The bottom point of the dragline = the area above it should be "picked up" and **pinned**, raising the area.

The top point of the dragline = the area above it should be **cut** (released) and lowered.

It is your choice how to correct the pattern. The result of either correction gives **the same new pattern shape.** The shape of the pattern piece must change for the garment to fit the shape of the body.

It is easier to pin the garment (pick it up) than it is to cut it (release it). Therefore, try the pinning method first, **viewing it as the dragline pointing down:**

- **Begin pinning** the area above the **bottom point** of the dragline.
- **Stop pinning** above the **top point** of the dragline.
- Pin along the nearest seam above the dragline when possible.

It may not be possible to pin every diagonal dragline issue.

It may be required to cut and lower the area, **viewing the dragline as pointing up:**

- **Begin cutting** to release the fabric above the **top point** of the dragline.
- **Stop cutting** above the **bottom point** of the dragline.
- Cut along the nearest seam above the dragline when possible.

Sometimes there are no seams above the dragline(s), but the correction can still be made by pinning or cutting. This would then result in a Slash & Close or Slash & Spread correction. You may also correct it by adding design lines or yoke seams.

After you practice both methods, it will become apparent to tell which option will be easier for each correction.

The only difference between correcting a dragline one way or the other is that the garment length may change:

- When the garment is pinned, the fabric is removed. This shortens the area.
- When the garment is cut open, the pattern correction requires more fabric. This additional fabric adds length to the area.
- The change may affect the position of the bust, waist, hips, and armhole.

Quiz Question: How should I look at the dragline - as pointing down or up?

Answer: Either way will yield the same new shape!

Quiz Question: Which option should I try first, pinning or cutting?

Answer: It is easier to begin by pinning the garment (viewed as the draglines pointing down). When pinning is not possible, select the option of cutting (viewed as the draglines pointing up).

Diagonal Draglines Demystified

Option 1 - Draglines Pointing Down

On the next five pages, I will show you both ways of looking at The GRD Method™ in fitting on the same example:

> **Option 1 -** As pointing **down**, indicating you should **pin** above the bottom point of the dragline.

> **Option 2 -** As pointing **up**, indicating you should **cut** above the top point of the dragline.

You will then see the comparison of both patterns on top of each other with the result of both methods having the same new pattern shape.

A) Identifying the Issue - Option 1 - The draglines go diagonally from the high point shoulders (HPS) to the armholes. This may show on either the front panel, the back panel, or both.

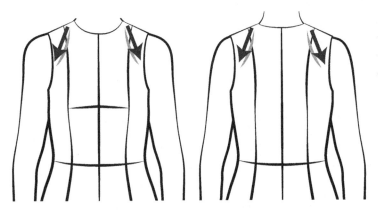

It is easier to pin the garment (pick it up) than it is to cut it (release it). Therefore, try the pinning method first, **viewed as the dragline pointing down.**

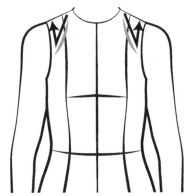

B) Pinning the Sample - Option 1 - The draglines point down toward the armhole from the HPS and neckline.

Begin pinning the area above the **bottom point** of the dragline. This is at the LPS along the shoulder seam. This raises the area at the LPS.

Stop pinning above the **top point** of the dragline. This is at the HPS along the shoulder seam.

If there are draglines in the front and back, pin both panels. If there are draglines on only one side, pin that side.

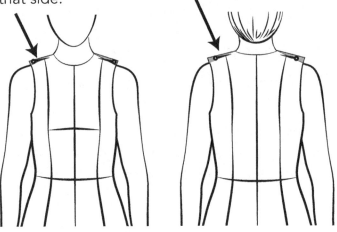

Notice how the armhole feels after the garment is pinned. Check the location of the bust position. If the armhole and the bust position appear too high, you may want to correct it the other way, viewing the dragline as pointing up.

Diagonal Draglines from the HPS the Armhole

Option 1 - Draglines Pointing Down *(continued)*

C) Correcting the Pattern - Option 1 - Mark the new shoulder slope on the pattern the amount you pinned. If you only pinned the front or back, correct only the panel you pinned.

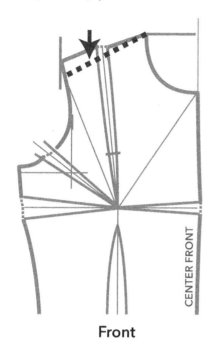

Front

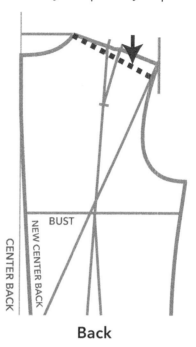

Back

Close the shoulder darts and true the shoulder slope, making it a continuous line.

> **Remember:** "Diagonal draglines generally point down toward the area that should be raised and pinned up."
>
> **- Gina Renee (The GRD Method™)**

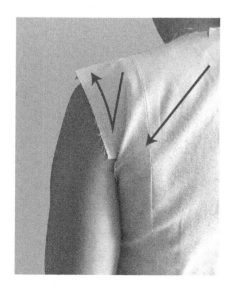

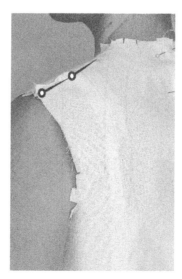

In this photo example, only the back panel had to be pinned at the shoulder seam. In addition, the back armhole was too high. The back armhole was "scooped" and lowered.

If the armhole is too high, but the bust position is still good after pinning the fitting sample, the armhole position should be lowered, as shown on page 134.

Option 2 - Draglines Pointing Up

Let's look at this the second way. **Option 2** - as pointing **up,** indicating you should **cut** above the top point of the dragline. In general, I recommend following the previous correction first since it is easier to pin than it is to open a garment.

A) Identifying the Issue - Option 2

The draglines go diagonally from the armholes to the high point shoulder (HPS). This may show on either the front panel, back panel, or both.

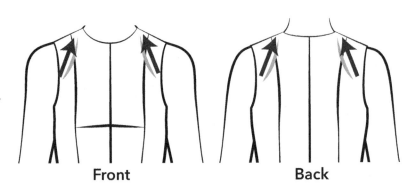

Front   Back

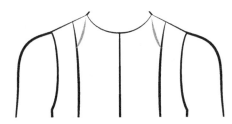

Specifically, use this method if the draglines are only on the center front or center back panel.

B) Taping and Pinning the Sample - Option 2 - The draglines point up toward the neckline and high point shoulder (HPS).

Begin cutting to release the fabric above the **top point** of the dragline. This is along the shoulder seam at the HPS. This lowers the area at the HPS.

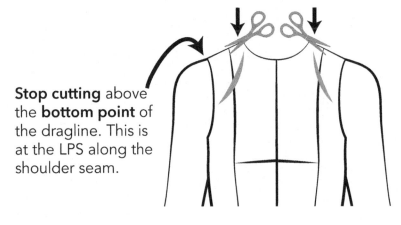

Stop cutting above the **bottom point** of the dragline. This is at the LPS along the shoulder seam.

Diagonal Draglines from the HPS the Armhole

Option 2 - Draglines Pointing Up *(continued)*

B) Taping and Pinning the Sample - Option 2 - *(continued)* - To determine the amount to add to the panel(s), look in the mirror and determine where the shoulder seam should be. Draw that line on the tape. Take off the sample and measure the shoulder line to determine how much to add to the front panel, back panel, or both.

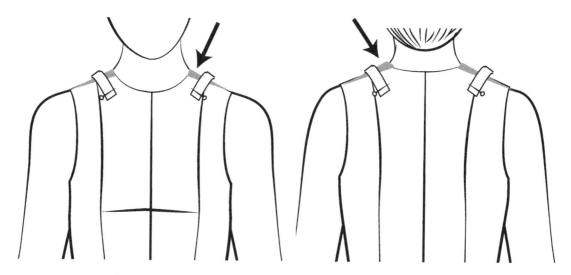

C) Correcting the Pattern - Option 2 - Mark the new shoulder seam on the pattern the same amount opened on the fitting sample. Add to the panels based on the shoulder seam you drew on the fitting sample.

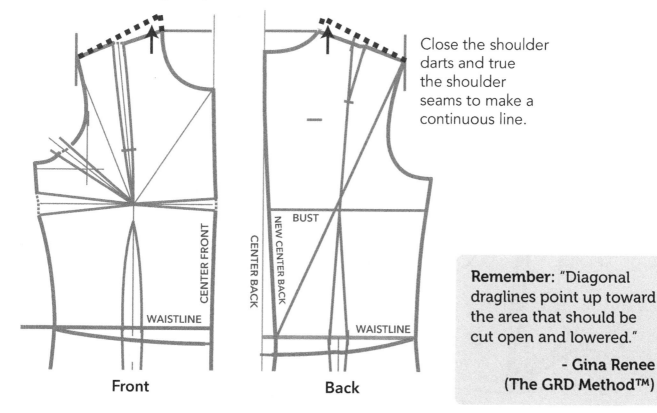

Close the shoulder darts and true the shoulder seams to make a continuous line.

> **Remember:** "Diagonal draglines point up toward the area that should be cut open and lowered."
>
> **- Gina Renee (The GRD Method™)**

Comparing Corrections from Options 1 & 2

Let's compare the two patterns for the previous corrections on pages 251 and 253.

   1) Interpreted as draglines **pointing down** toward the area to be **pinned up** (page 251), and

   2) Interpreted as draglines **pointing up** toward the area to be **cut and lowered** (page 253).

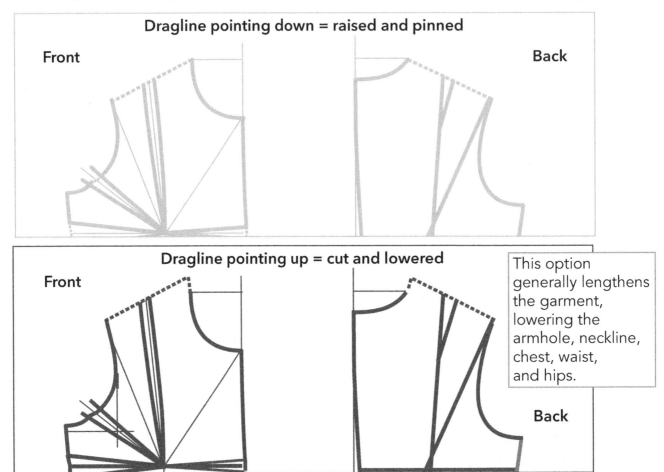

Dragline pointing down = raised and pinned

Front   Back

Dragline pointing up = cut and lowered

Front

This option generally lengthens the garment, lowering the armhole, neckline, chest, waist, and hips.

Back

Below are both options on top of each other. The shape of the shoulder slope was the issue, and the resulting shoulder slopes are the same in the two corrections. However, the "cut and lowered" correction lowers some areas, as shown here and increases the length of the garment slightly.

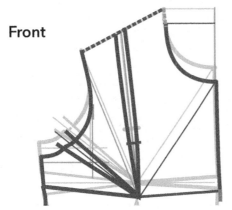

Front

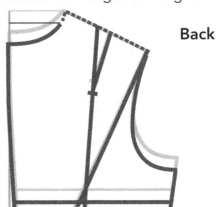

Back

Diagonal Draglines from the Apex to the Side Seam

Draglines Pointing Down - Options 1 & 2

There are two pattern correction options. One is for a pattern with a side dart, and the other is with a princess seam. The fitting sample shows a princess-seamed garment, but you may apply the same method to a style with a side dart.

A) Identifying the Issue - There are draglines pointing down toward the side seams from the apex.

Since the draglines **point down** toward the side seams, the area above the bottom point needs to be **raised and pinned up.**

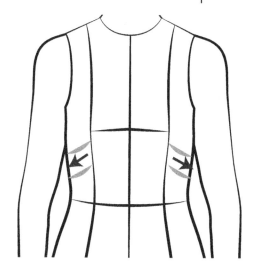
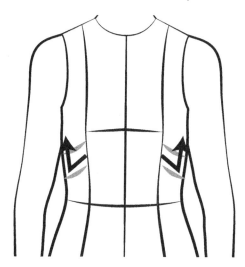

B) Pinning the Sample - **Pin** the area above the **bottom point** of the dragline. This is on the side panel in the area where a side dart would be.

Stop pinning above the **top point** of the dragline. This is at the apex on the side panel.

Pin a greater amount at the side seam, narrowing to nothing at the apex.

Pin around the back horizontally the same amount you pinned at the front side seams.

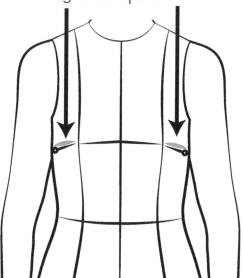

> **Remember:**
> "Diagonal draglines generally point down toward the area that should be raised and pinned up."
> - Gina Renee
> (The GRD Method™)

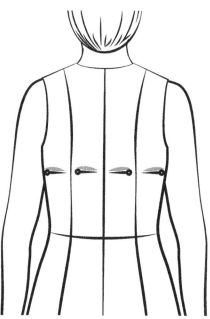

Diagonal Draglines from the Apex to the Side Seam

Draglines Pointing Down - Option 1 - Side Darts (continued)

This is how the correction would look on a moulage or sloper pattern. This method can also be applied to patterns with side darts. The next page shows the correction for a pattern with princess seams.

C) Correcting the Pattern - Option 1 Side Darts - Increase the dart depth the amount you pinned. True the side seam with the new dart closed.

Fold the back pattern piece so the lines meet. The amount folded should be the same as the increased dart depth.

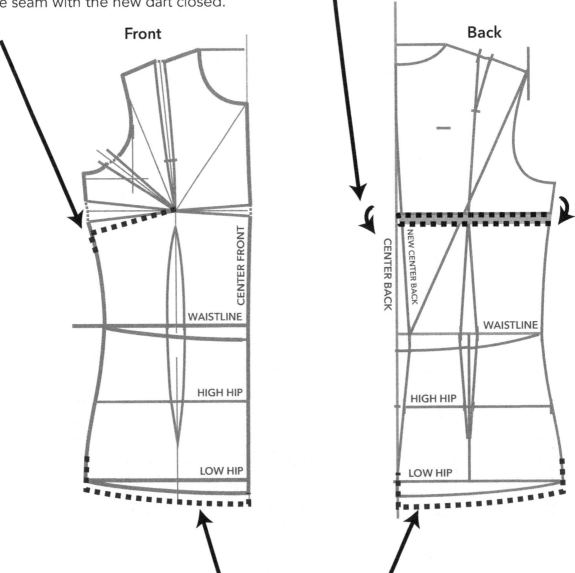

Optional: Lower the hemline the same amount you increased the dart depth.

Draglines Pointing Down - Option 2
Princess Seams (*continued from page 255*)

C) Correcting the Pattern - Option 2 - Princess Seams - Slash & Close (fold out the amount that is pinned on the sample. Stop at the apex, and close the amount in the side seam area only.

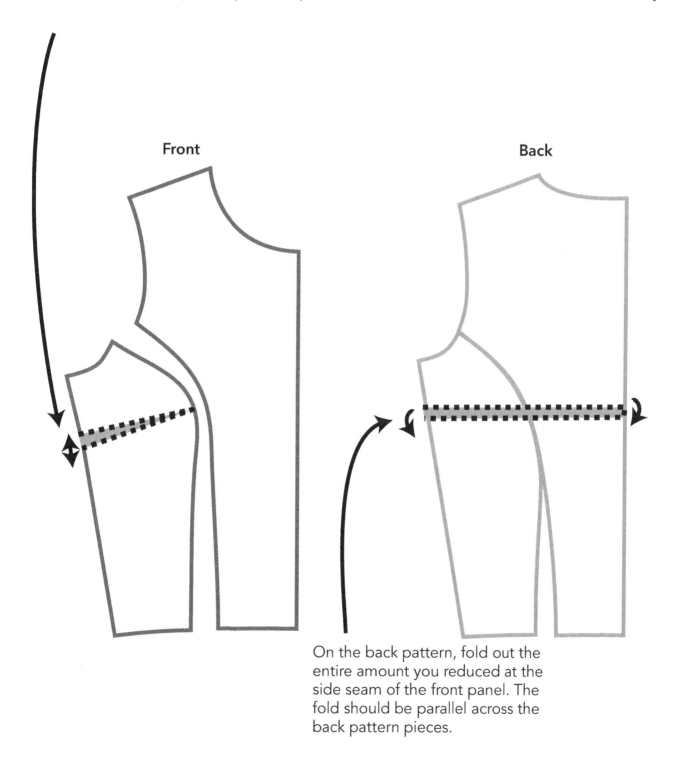

Front

Back

On the back pattern, fold out the entire amount you reduced at the side seam of the front panel. The fold should be parallel across the back pattern pieces.

Draglines from the Princess Seam to the Side Seam

Draglines Pointing Up - Options 1 & 2

As always, the diagonal dragline can be corrected either way:

1) As **pointing down**, indicating you should **pin** above the bottom of the dragline, or

2) As **pointing up,** indicating you should **cut** above the top of dragline.

For the fitting issue below, the cutting method is easier.

There are two pattern correction options. One is for a pattern with a side dart, and the other is with a princess seam. The fitting sample shows a princess-seamed garment, but you may apply the same cutting method to a style with a side dart.

A) Identifying the Issue - There are draglines pointing up toward the side seams from the princess seams.

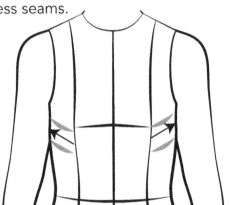

The draglines **point up**, indicating you should **cut** above the top of dragline. Cutting allows the area to lower. This is on the side panel in the position of the side dart.

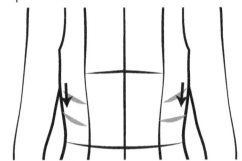

B) Cutting the Sample - Cut the sample on the side panel from the apex to the side seam. The cut should be where a side seam dart would normally be.

3. Allow the imaginary side bust dart to relax open until the draglines are eliminated. Tape and pin the area open. Measure the amount you opened.

1.

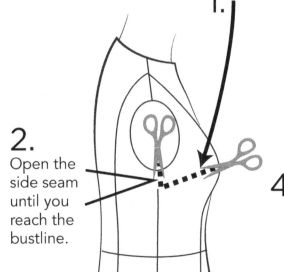

2. Open the side seam until you reach the bustline.

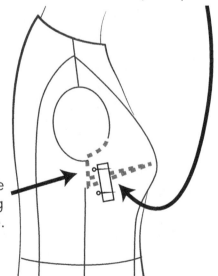

4. Pin the side seam along the cut line.

Draglines Pointing Up - Option 1 - Side Darts (continued)

This is how the correction would look on a moulage or sloper pattern. This method can also be applied to patterns with side darts. The next page shows the correction for a pattern with princess seams.

C) Correcting the Pattern - Option 1 - Side Darts - Reduce the dart depth on the side seam. Raise the waistline and hemline the same amount you reduced the dart depth. The back side seam length now fits to the front side seam length.

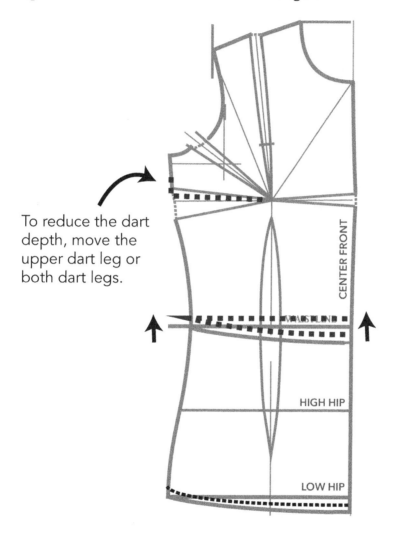

To reduce the dart depth, move the upper dart leg or both dart legs.

CENTER FRONT

WAISTLINE

HIGH HIP

LOW HIP

Tip: Princess seams are created by folding the side dart closed. The sloper had a side dart, but it was closed to create a princess seam. Always correct the original sloper pattern with the side dart.

Draglines Pointing Up - Option 2
Princess Seams (*continued from page 258*)

C) Correcting the Pattern - Option 2 - Princess Seams - Cut the pattern in the same area as you cut the fitting sample.

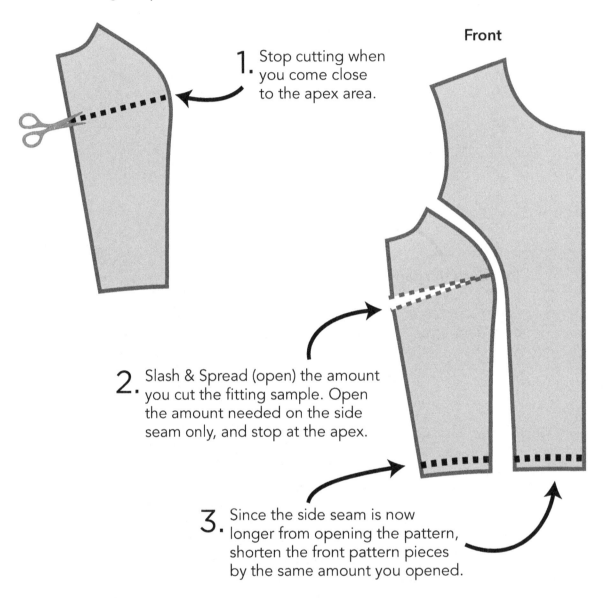

Front

1. Stop cutting when you come close to the apex area.

2. Slash & Spread (open) the amount you cut the fitting sample. Open the amount needed on the side seam only, and stop at the apex.

3. Since the side seam is now longer from opening the pattern, shorten the front pattern pieces by the same amount you opened.

"Diagonal draglines generally point down toward the area that should be raised and pinned up. Alternatively, diagonal draglines point up toward the area that should be cut open and lowered."

- Gina Renee (The GRD Method™)

Diagonal Draglines from Side Seams to the CF or CB

Draglines Pointing Down

> **Remember:** Draglines appear on garments as soon as the body moves, and this is acceptable. However, if there are diagonal draglines while standing straight and relaxed, they should be corrected.

This correction is the same for the front or back bodice.

A) Identifying the Issue - There are diagonal draglines below the waist pointing down toward the center front or center back.

Since the draglines **point down** toward the center front or back, the waistline needs to be **raised and pinned up.**

B) Pinning the Sample - Pin along the waist until the draglines disappear. Measure the amount you pinned.

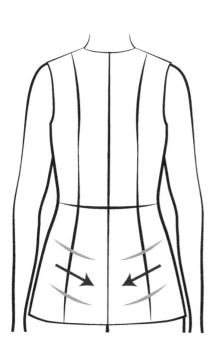

Pin the lower body at the center front or center back only. Stop pinning above the top points of the draglines, near the side seams.

This correction can be done along any horizontal seam on the body. For example, draglines at the yoke seam or empire waistline could be fixed with the same correction.

Draglines Pointing Down (continued)

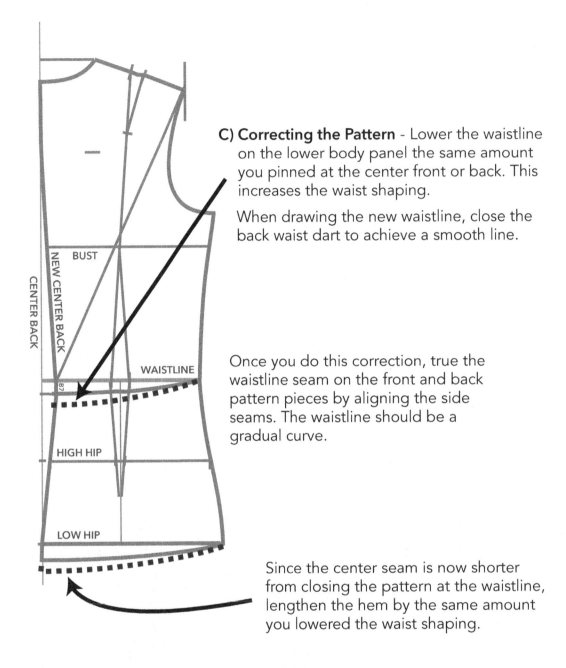

C) Correcting the Pattern - Lower the waistline on the lower body panel the same amount you pinned at the center front or back. This increases the waist shaping.

When drawing the new waistline, close the back waist dart to achieve a smooth line.

Once you do this correction, true the waistline seam on the front and back pattern pieces by aligning the side seams. The waistline should be a gradual curve.

Since the center seam is now shorter from closing the pattern at the waistline, lengthen the hem by the same amount you lowered the waist shaping.

These corrections are the same for the front and back pattern pieces.

Draglines Pointing Down - Option 1

This correction looks similar to the previous fitting issue. However, the draglines are going the opposite way. This correction may be done on the front or back of your garment.

A) Identify the Issue

There are diagonal draglines below the waist. This fitting issue will show both options of looking at the diagonal draglines. Option 1 is shown on this page and Option 2 is shown on the following page.

Option 1 - The draglines point **down** from the center front or back to the side seams.

Option 1 - The draglines point **down** toward the area that needs to **raise.** Therefore, **pin** the waistline seam above the **bottom point** of the dragline.

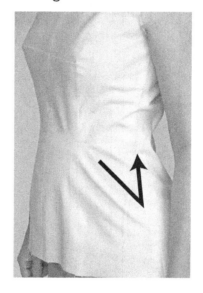

B) Pinning the Sample - Option 1 - Draglines Point Down - The draglines point **down** toward the area that needs to **raise.** Therefore, **pin** the waistline seam above the **bottom point** of the dragline. Stop pinning where the dragline ends.

If there are draglines on both sides, pin both. Measure the amount you pinned.

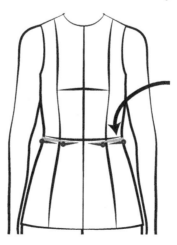

Measure the amount you pinned.

Diagonal Draglines Demystified

Diagonal Draglines from Side Seams to the CF or CB

Draglines Pointing Up - Option 2

A) Identify the Issue - There are diagonal draglines below the waist. This shows the same issue as the previous page but as Option 2.

Option 2
The draglines point **up** from the side seams to the center front or back.

Option 2
The draglines point **up** toward the area that needs to be **cut open** and **lowered.** Therefore, **cut** the waistline seam above the **top point** of the dragline.

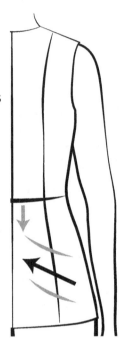

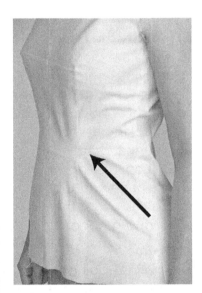

B) Pinning the Sample - Option 2 - Draglines Pointing Up - The draglines point **up** toward the area that needs to be **cut open** and **lowered.** Therefore, cut the waistline seam above the **top point** of the dragline. Stop cutting above the bottom point of the dragline, leaving the side seams intact.

Allow the waist at the center front or back to drop down until the draglines disappear. Tape and pin the new waistline opening in place.

Measure the amount you opened.

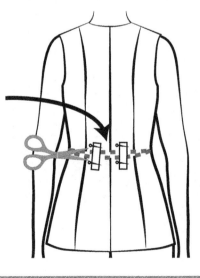

Diagonal Draglines from Side Seams to the CF or CB

Draglines Pointing Up or Down - Options 1 & 2 *(continued)*

C) Correcting the Pattern - Both Options - This correction is needed to adjust the waist shaping. Reduce the amount of waist shaping at the center front or back. To do this, raise the waist shaping line at the CB or CF the amount you pinned at the side seam, or cut open at the CB or CF. The lower line along the waist is referred to as the waist shaping line. The waist shaping line is used in a moulage and sloper pattern to give the correct curvature for the body. The lower waist shaping line is the lower section of the fitting sample where you pinned or cut open.

When designing with a sloper, you will often utilize this waist shaping line to achieve a beautifully-fitted garment.

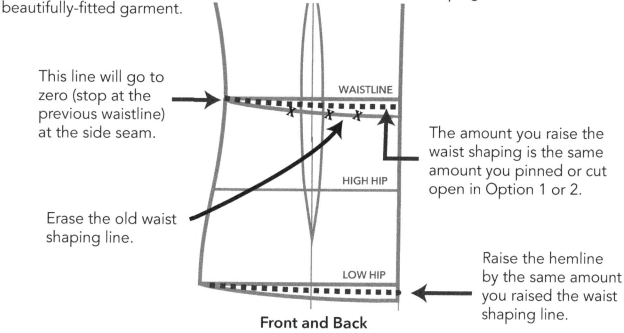

This line will go to zero (stop at the previous waistline) at the side seam.

WAISTLINE

The amount you raise the waist shaping is the same amount you pinned or cut open in Option 1 or 2.

HIGH HIP

Erase the old waist shaping line.

LOW HIP

Raise the hemline by the same amount you raised the waist shaping line.

Front and Back

This correction could totally eliminate the waist shaping. This is acceptable. Not every person needs waist shaping on their garment. If the waist shaping line needs to be moved up to the original waistline, the waist shaping line is removed.

Once the corrections are done, true the waistline seam on the front and back pattern by aligning the side seams. Make the waistline a gradual curve.

Note: Even though in Option 1, you pinned the garment at the side seam area, you will still adjust the pattern at the CF/CB waistline seam. If you adjust the waistline seam at the side seam, the result will be the same new waist shaping curve. To keep a cleaner moulage or sloper, update the pattern as shown here. If you update a style pattern, you may adjust the waistline at the same side seam area you pinned.

> "Diagonal draglines generally point down toward the area that should be raised and pinned up. Alternatively, diagonal draglines point up toward the area that should be cut open and lowered."
>
> - Gina Renee (The GRD Method™)

Identifying Diagonal Draglines on Sleeves

Additional Dragline Examples from Earlier in the Book

You have already seen this correction on page 149.

If you look closely at the correction, you can see that it follows The GRD Method™ in fitting diagonal draglines.

The diagonal draglines point **up** toward the area which needs to be **cut open** and **lowered**. In this situation, the cap height needs to be opened.

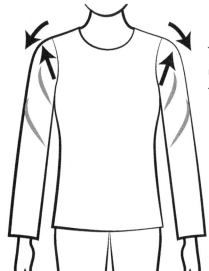

The diagonal draglines at the underarm area are a sign that the cap height is too short.

By cutting open the sample at the sleeve cap along the armhole, you are releasing the area that was stressed. It allows the sleeve cap to lower. This correction adds to the cap height. Consider that the more you add to the cap height, the less "lift" your arm has.

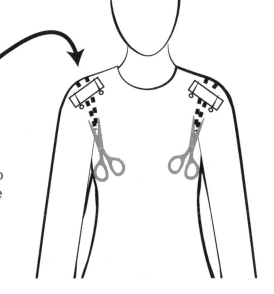

"Diagonal draglines generally point down toward the area that should be raised and pinned up. Alternatively, diagonal draglines point up toward the area that should be cut open and lowered."

- Gina Renee (The GRD Method™)

See page 149 for the pattern correction options.

Additional Dragline Examples from Earlier in the Book

You have already seen this correction on pages 182-183.

If you look closely at the Option 1 correction, you can see that it follows The GRD Method™ in fitting diagonal draglines.

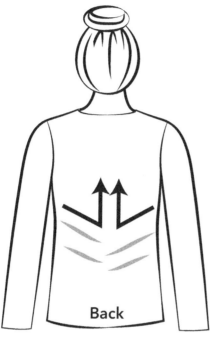

Back

The back diagonal draglines point **down** toward the area that should be **raised** and **pinned.**

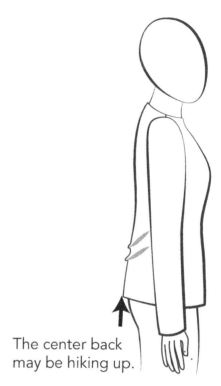

The center back may be hiking up.

Raise the shoulder blade area, and pin it to create a yoke. This "picks up" the garment, eliminating the lower draglines. Stop pinning above the top points of the draglines, near the armholes.

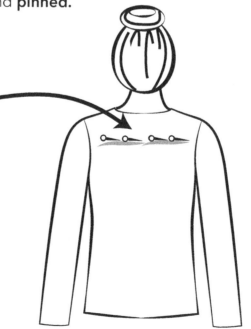

See page 183 for the pattern correction options.

Diagonal Draglines Demystified

Identifying Diagonal Draglines on Pants

Additional Dragline Examples from Earlier in the Book

You have already seen this correction on pages 223-225.

If you look closely at the correction, you can see that it follows The GRD Method™ in fitting diagonal draglines.

The back diagonal draglines point **down** toward the area that should be **raised** and **pinned.**

Raise the back waist area mainly at the center back, and pin it. This "picks up" the garment, eliminating the diagonal draglines. Stop pinning above the top points of the draglines, near or beyond the side seams.

You will often need to scoop (curve) the back rise more when doing this correction.

Back

> "Diagonal draglines generally point down toward the area that should be raised and pinned up. Alternatively, diagonal draglines point up toward the area that should be cut open and lowered."
>
> - Gina Renee (The GRD Method™)

See pages 223-225 for the pattern correction options.

Draglines Coming from Multiple Directions

Draglines Pointing toward One Area

In this example you saw earlier in the book on pages 202-203, there are draglines coming from multiple directions pointing toward one area. When this occurs, it is often due to additional shaping that is required in the pattern to allow for the fullness or shape of the body.

When there are multiple draglines coming from many directions, you generally need to add darts or increase existing darts to accommodate for the body shapes. Fitting issues such as this would not follow the simplicity of The GRD Method™ in fitting since the draglines come from many locations. However, if you break it down between the lower draglines and upper draglines, it still follows the method but in a more complex manner.

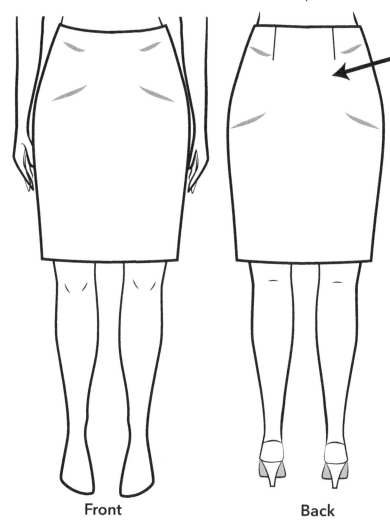

The skirt has draglines toward the abdomen or backside. The draglines are coming from multiple directions, and pointing toward the fullness of the body shapes.

Front　　　　**Back**

Alternatively, when draglines are pointing toward one area and coming from multiple locations, check the seam truing, ensuring all the seams match.

See page 203 for the pattern correction options.

FINAL
THOUGHTS